Engine of modernity

Manchester University Press

Series editors: Anna Barton, Andrew Smith

Editorial board: David Amigoni, Isobel Armstrong, Philip Holden, Jerome McGann, Joanne Wilkes, Julia M. Wright

Interventions: Rethinking the Nineteenth Century seeks to make a significant intervention into the critical narratives that dominate conventional and established understandings of nineteenth-century literature. Informed by the latest developments in criticism and theory the series provides a focus for how texts from the long nineteenth century, and more recent adaptations of them, revitalise our knowledge of and engagement with the period. It explores the radical possibilities offered by new methods, unexplored contexts and neglected authors and texts to re-map the literary-cultural landscape of the period and rigorously re-imagine its geographical and historical parameters. The series includes monographs, edited collections, and scholarly sourcebooks.

Already published

Spain in the nineteenth century: New essays on experiences of culture and society
Andrew Ginger and Geraldine Lawless

Creating character: Theories of nature and nurture in Victorian sensation fiction
Helena Ifill

Margaret Harkness: Writing social engagement 1880–1921   Flore Janssen and Lisa C. Robertson (eds)

Richard Marsh, popular fiction and literary culture, 1890–1915: Re-reading the fin de siècle
Victoria Margree, Daniel Orrells and Minna Vuohelainen (eds)

Charlotte Brontë: Legacies and afterlives   Amber K. Regis and Deborah Wynne (eds)

The Great Exhibition, 1851: A sourcebook   Jonathon Shears (ed.)

Interventions: Rethinking the nineteenth century   Andrew Smith and Anna Barton (eds)

Counterfactual Romanticism   Damian Walford Davies (ed.)

Engine of modernity
The omnibus and urban culture in nineteenth-century Paris

Masha Belenky

Manchester University Press

Copyright © Masha Belenky 2019

The right of Masha Belenky to be identified as the author of this work has been asserted by her in accordance with the Copyright, Designs and Patents Act 1988.

An electronic version of this book is also available under a Creative Commons (CC-BYNC-ND) licence which permits non-commercial use, distribution and reproduction provided the author and Manchester University Press are fully cited and no modifications or adaptations are made. Details of the licence can be viewed at: https://creativecommons.org/licenses/by-nc-nd/3.0/uk/

Published by Manchester University Press
Oxford Road, Manchester M13 9PL
www.manchesteruniversitypress.co.uk

British Library Cataloguing-in-Publication Data
A catalogue record for this book is available from the British Library

ISBN 978 1 5261 3859 0 hardback
ISBN 978 1 5261 6021 8 paperback
ISBN 978 1 5261 3860 6 open access

First published 2019

Paperback published 2021

The publisher has no responsibility for the persistence or accuracy of URLs for any external or third-party internet websites referred to in this book, and does not guarantee that any content on such websites is, or will remain, accurate or appropriate.

Typeset by
Sunrise Setting Ltd, Brixham

Contents

List of plates vi
List of figures vii
Acknowledgements x

Introduction 1

Part I: Omnibus literature in context

1 Modernity in motion: omnibus literature and popular culture in nineteenth-century Paris 35
2 Transitory tales: reading the omnibus repertoire 61

Part II: Class, gender and locomotion: social dynamics on the omnibus

3 Circulation and visibility: staging class aboard the omnibus 101
4 Moral geographies: women and public transport 133

Epilogue: final stop 165
Bibliography 169
Index 177

Plates

1 Omnibus de la Companie des 'Dames Blanches'. 1828. Bibliothèque historique de la ville de Paris/Roger-Viollet
2 *Jeu des Omnibus et Dames Blanches*. 1828. Board game. Bibliothèque nationale de France
3 Camille Pissarro, *Boulevard des Italiens, soleil du matin*. 1897 Oil on canvas. Chester Dale Collection, National Gallery of Art, Washington, DC
4 Victor Ratier, 'Un banc d'Omnibus. Trois, six, et trois… huit, encore une place! serrez-vous, Messieurs et Dames!'. 1829. Bibliothèque nationale de France/Roger-Viollet
5 J. J. Grandville, 'Comment, ces gens-là vont monter aussi? – Omnibus!! Madame!', *Les Métamorphoses du jour*. 1828–29. Bibliothèques de Nancy
6 Victor Ratier, 'Echantillons de mœurs Parisiennes. Un banc d'Omnibus de la Madelaine à la porte St Martin. Pour deux… Fait historique, dessiné d'après nature. Maris honnêtes garde à vous!'. 1829. Musée Carnavalet/Roger-Viollet
7 Maurice Delondre, *En omnibus*. 1880. Oil on canvas. Musée Carnavalet/Roger-Viollet
8 Mary Cassatt, *En omnibus*. 1890–91. Colour print. National Gallery of Art, Washington, DC

Figures

I.1	'Enterrement du dernier omnibus'. Agence Rol, 11 January 1913. Bibliothèque nationale de France	2
I.2	'Ordonnance sur l'établissement des voitures publiques dites omnibus'. 1828. Bibliothèque historique de la ville de Paris	14
I.3	Charles-Valentin Alkan, 'Les Omnibus', variation for piano in C major. 1828. Frontispiece. Author's copy	16
I.4	Tableau synoptique de la circulation des omnibus à correspondances de Paris. 1840. Collection RATP	17
I.5	Plan de la ville de Paris représentant les nouvelles voitures publiques à 30 centimes la course. 1829. Bibliothèque historique de la ville de Paris	17
I.6	Honoré Daumier, 'Le mauvais côté des nouveaux omnibus'. *Le Charivari*, 4 September 1856. Courtesy of the Robert D. Farber University Archives & Special Collections Department, Brandeis University	19
I.7	Honoré Daumier, 'Quinze centimes un bain complet… parole, c'est pas payé!…'. *Le Charivari*, 30 August 1856. Courtesy of the Robert D. Farber University Archives & Special Collections Department, Brandeis University	20
I.8	Honoré Daumier, 'Commençant à trouver que l'impériale des omnibus n'est pas une invention aussi agréable qu'il se l'était d'abord imaginé'. *Le Charivari*, 10 February 1858. Corcoran Collection, National Gallery of Art, Washington, DC	21
I.9	Cham, 'Les nouveaux omnibus du boulevard pendant l'hiver'. 1840	22
I.10	'L'enterrement de "la dernière" omnibus'. *Excelsior*, 12 January 1913. Bibliothèque nationale de France	23
I.11	'Feu l'Omnibus enterré joyeusement'. *La Presse*, 12 January 1913	24
I.12	Charles Vernier. 'Entrée dans un omnibus, rue Notre-Dame de Lorette'. *La Crinolonomanie*. 1856. Bibliothèque nationale de France	27

1.1 M. Sahib, 'L'intérieur d'un omnibus'. 1874. Bibliothèque historique de la ville de Paris — 39
1.2 'Les cochers de fiacres aux prises avec ceux des omnibus'. c. 1830. Musée Carnavalet/Roger-Viollet — 41
1.3 Jean Georges Frey, 'Les Dames Blanches et le fiacre: Y-s-auront le tems d'engraisser nos chevaux!!!!!'. 1828. Musée Carnavalet/Roger-Viollet — 42
2.1 Honoré Daumier, '–N'est-il pas vrai, brave turco, que vous préférez les Françaises aux Africaines? –Chut!... ma bonne... tu vois bien que tu vas le faire rougir!'. *Le Charivari*, 31 August 1859. Courtesy of the Robert D. Farber University Archives & Special Collections Department, Brandeis University — 74
2.2 M. de Penne, 'Le public des omnibus dans les bureaux de correspondence'. *L'Illustration*, 31 July 1868 — 77
2.3 Honoré Daumier, *En omnibus*. 1864. Daumier-Register — 78
2.4 Honoré Daumier, 'Une rencontre désagréable'. *La Comédie humaine*, 1843. Courtesy of the Robert D. Farber University Archives & Special Collections Department, Brandeis University — 88
2.5 'Un mariage en omnibus'. 1882. Cover, sheet-music score. Author's photo — 90
2.6 'Mon voisin d'omnibus'. 1888. Cover, sheet-music score. Author's photo — 91
3.1 A. Darjou, 'Actualités. – Oui Messieurs c'est quarte sous l'impériale; pour trois sous vous n'avez plus que le droit de suivre en courant'. n.d. Bibliothèque historique de la ville de Paris — 103
3.2 Honoré Daumier, 'Désolé, citoyenne, mais on ne reçoit pas de chien. –Aristocrate, va!'. 1848. Courtesy of the Robert D. Farber University Archives & Special Collections Department, Brandeis University — 114
3.3 Gobert, 'Intérieur d'un équipage de la petite propriété'. 1829. Bibliothèque historique de la ville de Paris — 123
3.4 Honoré Daumier, 'Madeleine-Bastille. Un zeste, un rien... et l'omnibus se trouve complet'. 1862. Courtesy of the Robert D. Farber University Archives & Special Collections Department, Brandeis University — 124
3.5 Honoré Daumier, 'Intérieur d'un omnibus. Entre un homme ivre et un charcutier'. 1839. Courtesy of the Robert D. Farber University Archives & Special Collections Department, Brandeis University — 125

Figures

4.1	Emile Dartès, *Contes en omnibus*. Illustration, 'Madeleine–Bastille'. 1894. Author's photo	145
4.2	Emile Dartès, *Contes en omnibus*. Illustration, 'Madeleine–Bastille'. 1894. Author's photo	146
4.3	'Madame Crinoliska faisant son entrée dans un omnibus'. *Paris Grotesque*, 1859. Musée Carnavalet/Roger-Viollet	150
4.4	'Une poule mouillée'. 1865. Based on a painting by Morlon. Collection RATP	153

Acknowledgements

This book is about new forms of sociability that emerged in the nineteenth century. It is in large measure to intellectual sociability that it owes its existence. Many colleagues and friends generously contributed to shaping the ideas at the core of this project.

I am grateful to my home institution, the George Washington University and especially to the Columbian College of Arts and Sciences for providing generous funding that made the research and writing of this book possible. I am particularly thankful to deans Eric Arnesen, Yongwu Rong and Ben Vinson III, for their unflagging support for this project over the years. A GW-NHC summer residential fellowship at the National Humanities Center, a magical place that offered much needed physical and mental space for thinking and writing, allowed me to complete the manuscript.

Much of the research for this book was conducted in the graceful reading room of the Bibliothèque historique de la ville de Paris, and I would like to express my deep appreciation of this magnificent space steeped in history, and of its staff and librarians, especially Séverine Montigny and Bérangère de l'Epine for their invaluable help in tracking down obscure omnibus materials, and Yves Chagniot for his help in the reading room. I also want to thank the staff of Bibliothèque de l'Arsenal, Bibliothèque Fournay and Bibliothèque nationale de France, as well as Gerard Leyris and Vinh Nguyen at the Cabinet des arts graphiques of the Musée Carnavalet, Delphine Meyssard at the Médiateque RATP and, last but not least, the staff of Bibliothèque de la Maison de Balzac, where a much needed copy of *Le Charivari* was found at the eleventh hour.

I am thankful to The Den, the Politics and Prose coffee shop, where many a page of this book was written, for providing a warm and hospitable place to work.

I am grateful for invitations to present my work at various symposia: feedback from colleagues sometimes inspired me to explore new directions. In particular, I thank Sarah Kennel for inviting me to give a talk at a symposium on Charles Marville at the National Gallery of Art, and to Carsten Meiner for his gracious invitation to participate in a symposium on Literary History and Topology at the University of Copenhagen.

Acknowledgements

My sincere gratitude is due to Andrew Smith and Anna Barton, the series editors for *Interventions: Rethinking the Nineteenth Century* at Manchester University Press, and to Matthew Frost, for their enthusiasm for this project and for shepherding the book through the evaluation process with incomparable grace. I am grateful to Jennifer Solheim, whose expert editing made this book so much more readable.

Many friends and colleagues generously read portions of the manuscript, shared their own work and insights with me and encouraged me along the way. I thank Leah Chang for first suggesting that I could write an entire book on the omnibus and for her insightful comments on early versions of the manuscript. Many thanks to the members of the Washington DC Modern French reading group, who created a warm and encouraging scholarly community and provided valuable feedback on portions of this book: Elise Lipkovitz, Katrin Schultheiss, Kathryn Kleppinger, Chelsea Stieber and Erin Twohig.

My warmest thanks are due to fellow *dix-neuviémistes* on both sides of the Atlantic and especially to the participants in the annual Nineteenth-Century French Studies Colloquium, who over the years offered valuable insights and ideas which helped make this book better: Aimee Boutin, Heidi Brevik-Zender, Andrea Goulet, Mary Hunter, Cheryl Krueger, Cathy Nesci, Bill Paulson, Pratima Prasad, Willa Silverman, Kasia Stempniak, Peggy Waller, Alex Wettlaufer, Nick White and many others. Many friends and colleagues shared their omnibus finds with me over the years, and for that I am especially grateful to Elisabeth Emery, Michael Garval and Chapman Wing.

I am very thankful to Janet Beizer for her support over the years and for generous comments on the manuscript. I also offer thanks to Jessica Tanner for her insightful and supportive comments on Chapter 4. Lisa Leff is a dear friend who offered perceptive advice, invaluable feedback on the manuscript and moral support along the way. I thank Lynn Westwater for her friendship, for sharing 'library writing dates' with me and for her thoughtful comments on parts of the manuscript. Anne O'Neil-Henry shared her deep knowledge of nineteenth-century popular culture with me, and I am so grateful to her for her perceptive readings of numerous drafts of this book, as well as her collaboration and friendship.

'Writing Four' writing group provided much needed structure and motivation at a crucial moment. I could not have written this book without the critical acumen and moral support of its members, whose own brilliant work continues to be an inspiration. I thank Marni Kessler for her insightful comments and suggestions, for teaching me so much about nineteenth-century visual culture and for nudging me to sharpen my prose. Lise Schreier's astute criticisms helped make this book better. Susan Hiner, a dear friend for the past two decades, read numerous drafts of the book, offered wise council and warm encouragement and has been there for me in countless ways.

Two unforgettable research trips in the company of Rachel Mesch serve as bookends to this project: the first one in 2010, as I was beginning to dive into omnibus literature, and the second one in 2018, as I was putting finishing touches on the manuscript. I am infinitely grateful to her for sharing Paris library adventures with me, for reading countless versions of the manuscript, talking me through many a writing crisis and helping me sharpen my thinking about the material and ideas in this book. Above all, I am grateful for many years of friendship.

I also wish to thank friends and colleagues in Washington, DC, New York, Paris and elsewhere who nourished and sustained me in so many ways: Vered and Nathan Guttman, Margaret Talbot and Arthur Allen, Masha and Robert Levy, Gwyn Isaac and Christian Widmer, Nadya and Tim Bartol, Holly Dugan, Meg Bortin, Carolyn Betensky, Susanna Lee, the Leff family, Gayle Wald, Marina van Zuylen, Johanna Bockman and Andrew Zimmerman.

I offer my warmest thanks to my wonderful family for their unwavering love and support that made the writing of this book possible and even pleasurable: Norma and Stanley Skolnik, Yelena Raben and Bill Hurst, Masha Makovoz and Vadim, Liz and Isaak Goldin and Ira Makovoz. My parents, Nina Raben and Mark Belenky, have been my most stalwart supporters and fans, amazing interlocutors on topics academic and otherwise, incomparable travel companions and a source of unending admiration. My children, Tosha and Sonia, patiently listened to endless omnibus tales, cheerfully accompanied me on research trips and offered good humour, love and a healthy dose of sanity in an otherwise hectic academic life. I offer my deepest thanks to Jonathan Skolnik for his love, his insightful comments on the manuscript, for sharing the vicissitudes of academia with me, for picking up slack on the home front and for making me laugh.

I could not have written this book without the steadfast encouragement of Priscilla Ferguson, who passed away as I was writing these acknowledgements. A brilliant scholar, generous teacher, wise and kind mentor and dear friend, her groundbreaking work on the literature of Paris paved the way for this study, which I hope is in some small measure an homage, however modest, to her innumerable contribution to French studies. Her mark is on every page of this book.

Earlier portions of some chapters derived in part from the following articles: 'From transit to transitoire: omnibus and modernity', which appeared in *Nineteenth-Century French Studies*, 35:2 (2007) and 'Transitory tales: writing the omnibus in nineteenth-century Paris', *Dix-Neuf*, 16:3 (2012). I am grateful to the editors for permission to use this material.

Unless otherwise indicated, all translations from French are my own.

Introduction

> Shakespeare said, 'All the world is a *stage*:' we say, 'All the world is an *omnibus*.'
> George W. M. Reynolds, *The Mysteries of London*

In 2013, experimental poet Jacques Roubaud published *Ode à la ligne 29 des autobus parisiens*, a volume of whimsical poems that takes us on a journey through Paris aboard a bus crossing the city eastward from the Gare Saint-Lazare to the Porte de Montempoivre.[1] Inspired by the poet's own experience of urban locomotion and his long-standing fondness for Parisian cityscapes, the volume is organised in six cantos and thirty-five stanzas corresponding to the thirty-five stops along this particular bus line. Roubaud treats us to a panoply of imaginative strategies in order to convey the sensorial and social richness of the bus-riding experience. From inventive spelling and visual rhymes to ingenious uses of typography (the poems are printed in green, red and blue ink), a broad variety of topics and a dizzying choice of volume covers (six!), *Ode à la ligne 29* playfully connects literary innovation with urban modernity, in all their kaleidoscopic multiplicity.

The city bus is an apt metaphor for urban diversity, a sum total of human experiences contained both within the cramped space of the vehicle and between the book's covers. But the tradition of engaging public transportation as a way to invoke a cultural moment, to grapple with a multitude of central themes of the time, and to experiment with literary form did not begin with Roubaud's *Ode*. In fact, cultural fascination with public transport emerged at the same time as the first vehicle of mass transit – the omnibus – was launched in Paris in 1828 (Plate 1). A horse-drawn public conveyance, the original omnibus accommodated up to fourteen passengers and travelled along assigned routes. The name *omnibus*, from the dative plural of 'all' in Latin and signifying 'for everybody', was particularly well suited to a vehicle open to any passenger regardless of class, gender or rank. The only requirement was the ability to pay a modest fare of 30 centimes.

Engine of modernity

Figure I.1 'Enterrement du dernier omnibus'. 11 January 1913.

From the day the first omnibus rolled on to the Paris streets in April 1828 until it was decommissioned with great fanfare in January 1913 (Figure I.1), different forms of popular culture seized upon the omnibus as a subject of interest. Scores of texts and images – including newspaper articles, literary city guides, short stories, *physiologies* and other works of urban observation, vaudevilles, poems, a popular board game (Plate 2), caricatures, postcards, songs and even a piano variation – featured omnibus travel. What accounted for this cultural obsession, and what does it tell us about nineteenth-century French society and its preoccupations? *Engine of modernity* sets out to answer these questions by considering ways in which the omnibus was imagined and deployed in popular literature and visual culture to express key themes of modernity in nineteenth-century Paris.[2]

As the first vehicle of mass transit in Paris, the omnibus radically changed everyday life and transformed the relationship of city dwellers to urban space. But for many nineteenth-century French writers, the omnibus was much more than a mode of transportation; indeed, it served as a powerful storytelling device through which they represented the city in transition, explored evolving social dynamics of class and gender, and reflected upon literary practices. It wasn't only that there was a flood of literature in the mid-nineteenth century about the omnibus: many works adopted what was structurally original about this new feature of urban life as an organising principle, combining narrative innovation with social commentary. In his pioneering work on the railway,

Introduction

historian Wolfgang Schivelbusch convincingly demonstrates that transport technologies profoundly altered perceptions of distance, time and space.[3] What makes the nineteenth-century Parisian omnibus distinct is that it also helped shape the cultural production of the period, as writers harnessed the vehicle's salient qualities, such as mixing diverse elements and bringing together varied perspectives within the same space, and put them to literary ends.[4] In the documents I consider here, the omnibus quite literally represented a fluid cultural moment; omnibus literature, like the real-life public transit experience, offered snapshots of everyday life, capturing its provisional, transitory and fragmented nature. In short, it is through the omnibus that many nineteenth-century authors grappled with emerging urban modernity.

Modernity at a horse's trot

It may seem paradoxical to refer to the omnibus as an 'engine of modernity', because, after all, this horse-drawn vehicle was not a radical technological innovation, unlike the steam locomotive, introduced in France in the 1840s. Although, as historian Peter Soppelsa demonstrates, the horse was construed as a form of modern technology during the nineteenth century, the omnibus in this respect did not differ significantly from other horse-drawn vehicles that populated city streets at the time.[5] And yet its arrival on the streets of Paris – and in the pages of popular literature – served as the motor for a fundamental cultural shift in how people perceived the city, society and the literature that sought to represent them. The omnibus became inseparable from concepts associated with 'the modern', such as motion, spectacle and flux, all of which were key to understanding not only the rapidly changing Parisian landscape but also an increasingly complex French society. As we shall see, the omnibus ushered in modernity on several levels: it changed material conditions of urban life, created radically new modes of sociability and inspired innovations in literary form.

To be sure, 'modernity' is a complex and multivalent concept that eludes a straightforward definition. Modernity refers to moments of rupture and change, both as historical and aesthetic categories. In Baudelaire's famous formulation, modernity also resides in the tension between what is permanent and what is transitory: 'La modernité, c'est le transitoire, le fugitif, le contingent, la moitié de l'art, dont l'autre moitié est l'éternel et l'immuable'[6] (Modernity is the transient, the fleeting, the contingent; it is one half of art, the other being the eternal and the immovable). Until recently, the notion of historical modernity in relation to nineteenth-century Paris was associated with Haussmannisation, the massive reconstruction of public urban spaces and of the city's infrastructure in the 1850s and 1860s, as well as the advent of capitalism, technological innovations, modern forms of commerce and the concomitant changes in social relations and culture. Yet recent scholarship has convincingly argued for dating nascent Parisian modernity to the years of the July Monarchy.[7] For example, H. Hazel Hahn suggests that cultural transformations associated with modernity emerged during the first half of the nineteenth century: 'Much of what would comprise the modernity of the Second Empire, such as café culture, preceded the transformative urban changes and needs to be placed in the broader context of the evolution of both the urban fabric and the urban imaginary.'[8] The omnibus and the cultural production it inspired exemplify this early manifestation of modernity.

Another useful concept in thinking about representations of the omnibus in literature and visual culture is what Sharon Marcus calls 'cultural modernity'. Marcus provides a useful distinction between 'cultural modernity' and a more historically determined 'chronological modernity'. Cultural modernity encompasses two central characteristics: first, it is an attitude, an awareness of the self as modern, and a celebration of innovation; second, it is characterised by privileging social spaces of spectacle. Cultural modernity does not depend solely on the physical transformation and modernisation of urban spaces. Rather, it involves the perception and representation of a phenomenon as new, a self-conscious understanding of one's moment as radically departing from what preceded it.[9] The documents I examine in this book reveal a remarkable awareness of the omnibus as the embodiment of the new.[10]

To begin with, the omnibus represented a major advance in urban locomotion, one that allowed Parisians of any social class to traverse the capital in comfort and at a speed the majority of them had never experienced. The omnibus not only facilitated getting to and from work, but it also promoted commercial and entertainment activities, such as shopping and going to the theatre.[11] Although, as I mentioned above, the omnibus itself was not a technological innovation, its presence on the Paris streets was among the considerations that drove urban planning. The increased traffic and congestion caused by these large conveyances informed urban planners of the need for broader streets in a modern metropolis, a problem addressed by urban renovation works under Napoleon III during the second half of the nineteenth century. In this way, the omnibus was a motor of dramatic urban change.

Beyond its impact on the physical aspect of the city, the omnibus fostered new social practices in the urban environment. Sociologist Georg Simmel attributed changes in the ways city dwellers related to one another to the introduction of public transport:

> Interpersonal relationships in big cities are distinguished by a marked preponderance of the activity of the eye over the activity of the ear. The main reason for this is the public means of transportation. Before the development of buses,

railroads, and trams in the nineteenth century, people had never been in situations where they had to look at one another for long minutes or even hours without speaking to one another.[12]

The configuration of vehicles of mass transportation imposed distinctive physical and visual closeness upon passengers. A space of gender and class mixing, as men and women of different classes shared the narrowly confined space for the duration of a trip, the omnibus generated unprecedented forms of sociability among urban dwellers. And so the omnibus became an ideal social laboratory for urban observers interested in contemporary ways of life. If the latter part of the century was dominated by the 'boulevard culture' of theatres and cafés (as Vanessa Schwartz convincingly demonstrates), as well as the department store that came to epitomise class mixing associated with modernity, it was the omnibus that arguably played this role during the middle decades of the nineteenth century.[13]

Yet this imposed physical proximity of men and women from different social classes was met with ambivalence and a degree of anxiety among contemporary commentators. Textual and visual representations of the omnibus range from celebrations of the vehicle's class and sex inclusiveness, hailing it as a harbinger of progress, to indictments of the vehicle as a dangerous threat to the existing social order. The omnibus became both a daily practice and a visual symbol that brought city dwellers together at the same time as it underscored that which separated them.

But what made the omnibus truly unique was the innovations in literary forms it inspired. The omnibus was a storytelling device through which the urban writers I study conveyed the intricate texture of Parisian society on the cusp of modernity. If the omnibus was a fitting metaphor for a cultural moment marked by radically changing social and cultural practices, it was also an ideal vehicle for a nascent popular literature – the very literature that aimed to represent Paris and its inhabitants – to convey new ideas about the city and the complex composition of a changing French society. Urban writers found the omnibus such an appealing a topic because they recognised its powerful figurative and self-reflexive potential. For them, it became both embodiment and symbol of cultural modernity, a signal of the advent of the new. To writers concerned with deciphering and understanding city spaces and city dwellers, the omnibus offered unrivalled possibilities for urban observation, social commentary and storytelling. The omnibus was a setting through which to make sense of new forms of sociability and to grapple with cultural anxieties associated with different aspects of change: opportunities for social mobility, class mixing, the increased presence of women in public spaces and the promises and perils of the democratisation of public life. Perhaps even more importantly, many writers adapted the vehicle's intrinsic characteristics for literary use.

A number of innovative features particular to the omnibus as a mode of transport appealed to contemporary writers. The diversity of passengers gathered within the enclosed space of the vehicle reflected an ever changing multiplicity of backgrounds and perspectives that characterised the modern city. Many works about the omnibus took up this idea of mixing diverse elements as an organising principle, for they often combined different genres within the same volume. For example, Charles Soullier's 1863 *Les Omnibus de Paris* offers a detailed and deeply erudite history of the omnibus, a poem exalting the vehicle's virtues alongside a daily omnibus schedule, and a list of stops. Other texts were authored by multiple writers, each bringing a distinctive style and perspective. The 1854 *Paris-en-omnibus*, for example, co-written by journalists and popular writers Taxile Delord, Arnould Frémy and Edmond Texier, contains a great variety of tones, registers, styles and genres, from satirical sketches to factual historical accounts, philosophical musings and slapstick vignettes. Another feature of the vehicle deployed in omnibus literature was episodic narrative. In works such as Emile Dartès's 1894 *Contes en omnibus*, a volume of short stories that centre on a passenger or a group of passengers, the beginning and the end of each tale are delineated by the length of the character's ride. Here the very nature of an omnibus ride supplies a narrative structure.[14]

While other forms of urban public transit were introduced throughout the nineteenth century – the tram, the bâteau-omnibus and, at the turn of the century, the metro – none had as strong an impact on the cultural imagination of the era as the omnibus. As we shall see in the chapters that follow, it not only provided popular literature with a narrative vehicle through which to present a wide range of social issues, but it also drove the popular literature itself. This literature emerged just as the city of Paris was undergoing dramatic changes.

A city in transition

Although the systematic reconstruction and modernisation of Paris spearheaded by Napoleon III did not get underway until the early 1850s, changes that would ultimately transform the French capital from a medieval city into a modern metropolis began much earlier in the century. Historians agree that Haussmann's reconstruction project did not represent a radical break from the work that was accomplished during the first half of the nineteenth century; rather, it built on developments and ideas of urban planners going back to the First Empire.[15] As readers familiar with Balzac know, the Paris of the 1830s and 1840s was already a city on the cusp of modernity, characterised by increasing traffic, speed, congestion, crowds, fragmentation of urban experience and a sense of flux. Reflecting on the multifaceted and increasingly mobile and disjointed character of the city in his quintessentially

Introduction

Parisian novel of 1833, *Ferragus*, Balzac famously described Paris as a 'monstrueuse merveille, étonnant assemblage de mouvements, de machines, de pensées, la ville aux cent mille romans'[16] (a monstrous marvel, a stunning assemblage of movements, machines, and ideas, a city of a hundred thousand novels). Here Balzac captures some of the key terms that defined modern Paris, a city of paradoxes ('monstrueuse merveille'), characterised by movement and the presence of the menacing yet exhilarating machine, a city as a producer of narrative.

A dramatic upturn in the number of vehicles and people contributed to the impression that life in Paris was speeding up. The population of Paris doubled during the first half of the nineteenth century, and this influx was accompanied by an acceleration of industrial and commercial activities. The introduction of the omnibus in 1828 was part of the early modernisation taking hold in Paris. The concepts of speed and change, both real and perceived, were key to the city's transformation. As Priscilla Ferguson notes, 'The modernity commonly ascribed to nineteenth-century Paris is rooted in this sense of movement, the perpetually unfinished, always provisional nature of the present and the imminence of change.'[17] This modernisation was happening not only on the streets of Paris, bustling with people and vehicles, but also in the minds of contemporary writers. In his 1834 essay 'Les voitures publiques', in *Nouveau tableau de Paris au XIXe siècle*, Louis Huart offers a telling commentary on the accelerating speed of modern life:

> Il semble que de nos jours on vive plus vite que du temps passé; l'activité fiévreuse qui anime le Parisien ne lui permet plus de supporter la marche paisible de ces moyens de transport qui convenaient aux siècles précédents, siècles tout froids, tout compassés, qui s'accommodaient parfaitement de cette monotone lenteur; aussi tout le monde aujourd'hui va-t-il en voiture.[18]
>
> (It appears that nowadays we live faster than in the past. A feverish activity that animates Parisians prevents them from accepting the peaceful pace of modes of transport that suited previous centuries, which, cold and prim, adapted to the monotony of slow speed. And so, today everyone moves about in a carriage.)

For Huart, the intensification of the pace of urban life stems directly from the growing number of vehicles that criss-crossed the streets of Paris:

> Lorsque je vois le nombre de voitures qui circulent incessamment dans les rues de Paris, je m'étonne toujours d'une chose, – c'est de trouver encore des piétons sur les trottoirs. Fiacres, cabriolets, diligences, tilburys, calèches, landaus, omnibus, voitures à six chevaux, tout cela se rencontre, se croise, se heurte, s'accroche, se décroche, se renverse nuit et jour dans les rues de cette ville, surnommée depuis long-temps le *paradis des femmes*, et qui mérite encore, à bien plus juste titre, son autre surnom d'*enfer des chevaux*.[19]

(When I see the number of carriages circulating incessantly in the streets of Paris, there is only one thing that surprises me – it's that we still find pedestrians at all. Hackney cabs, cabriolets, stage-coaches, tilburys, barouches, landaus, omnibuses, carriage with six horses – all these vehicles run into each other, cross paths, collide, pick up, drop off, and knock over day and night in the streets of this city that has long been called 'paradise for women' and that also deserves its other nickname, 'hell for the horses'.)[20]

Huart's very phrasing, a chaotic piling up of vehicle names and verbs of motion in rapid succession, mimics the frenetic texture and rhythm of modern urban environment, and textually reproduces the image of hopelessly congested streets dominated by constant movement and chaos. By stylistically replicating the features of the modern city, Huart's text itself becomes a site of modernity.

Similarly, in her weekly column in *La Presse* from June 1837, Delphine de Girardin lamented that the abundance of vehicles and the speed with which the city moves have destroyed the pleasures of walking, and pointed her finger at the omnibus as the emblem of this unwelcome change:

La promenade est impossible; il y a peine de mort pour le flâneur; *l'Omnibus* et la *Dame blanche* ont envahi la cité; ils la traversent dans tous les sens; on ne marche plus, on court; chaque habitant de la ville insensée semble avoir derrière lui l'Euménide vengeresse qui le poursuit. Qu'est-il devenu, cet être aimé des dieux, chéri du poète, béni du pauvre, cet inconnu que chacun veut séduire, cet indifférent qui vous apporte l'espérance malgré lui, cet être indéfini que l'on appelle le PASSANT?[21]

(Strolling became impossible: a *flâneur* risks his life; the *Omnibus* and the *Dame blanche* have invaded the city; they criss-cross it in all directions. One no longer walks – one runs instead. Every crazed city dweller appears to have a vengeful Eumenides chasing after him. What ever became of him, that being so beloved by gods, cherished by poets, blessed by beggars, that stranger that everyone wants to seduce, that indifferent person who gives you hope despite himself, that hard-to define creature called the PASSERBY?)

Speed and change continued to be powerful motifs in urban literature well into the second part of the nineteenth century, and the omnibus was often cast as an agent of these new developments.[22] In the early years of Haussmann's reconstruction project, authors of literary guidebooks both marvelled at and lamented the way the city was changing beyond recognition before their very eyes. In his preface to Edouard Fournier's 1854 *Paris Démoli*, for example, Théophile Gautier writes that new urban practices cannot develop and flourish without changing the physical aspect of the city: 'Le Paris moderne serait impossible dans le Paris d'autrefois. Où passaient la mule de l'homme de robe et le cheval de l'homme d'épée entre deux murailles qui se touchaient presque, faites donc circuler l'omnibus, ce Léviathan de la carrosserie, et ces voitures si nombreuses s'entre-croisant avec la rapidité de l'éclair!' (The modern Paris could not exist within the walls of old Paris. In streets where in the olden days a priest's mule or a gentleman's horse squeezed between walls so narrow they almost touched, now let circulate the omnibus, this Leviathan of carriages, and other vehicles passing each other with lightning speed.) Speed, the hallmark of the changing city, demanded a new spatial organisation to accommodate what Gautier calls 'son activité effrénée et son mouvement perpétuel'[23] (frenetic activity and perpetual movement). Furthermore, the omnibus and other vehicles are themselves depicted as agents of change, as it is their presence in the streets that propels the modernisation of the city. The use of 'Leviathan' to describe the omnibus conveys the ambivalent way in which Gautier and many of his contemporaries perceived this vehicle and the modernity it represented: at once monstrous, formidable and awe-inspiring. Unlike Baudelaire, who famously bemoaned the destruction of the old Paris in 'Le cygne' and other poems ('Paris change! mais rien dans ma mélancolie/ N'a bougé!/ palais neufs, échafaudages, blocs,/ Vieux faubourgs, tout pour moi devient allégorie' (Paris changes! But nothing in my melancholy has moved! New palaces, scaffoldings, old neighbourhoods, everything is becoming allegory for me[24])), Gautier embraces the dramatic transformation of the city and the acceleration of the pace of life while acknowledging its disorienting and troubling effects on urban dwellers.

In another contemporaneous publication, also co-edited by Gautier, we see not only an awareness of the frenetic pace of change but also a desire to capitalise on the city's constant transformation for both literary and commercial gain. In a semi-ironic introduction to the lavish *Paris et les Parisiens au XIXe siècle*, published in 1856, during the first phase of Haussmannisation, Gautier explains that a new guidebook – his guidebook – is absolutely indispensable given the constantly changing aspect of Paris, a topic that never ceases to renew itself:

> En effet Paris est la mine inépuisable, le sujet toujours neuf, le thème sur lequel l'antiquaire, le philosophe et le poète peuvent broder à l'infini; c'est un modèle aux aspects multiples et que chaque peintre saisit à sa manière; et puis que de Paris différents dans Paris ! . . . Quelle diversité ondoyante ! quelle physionomie mobile ! A chaque heure il faut faire son portrait : celui d'hier ne ressemble déjà plus.[25]

> (Indeed, Paris is an inexhaustible mine, a subject always new, a topic that the antiquarian, the philosopher and the poet can embellish endlessly. It is a model with different facets, one that every painter depicts in his own way. And what's more, so many different Parises within Paris! . . . What fluctuating assortment! What changeable appearance! Paint it every hour: its portrait from yesterday no longer resembles at all what it is today.)

Gautier even provocatively suggests that after a short four-to-five-year absence, a Parisian would not recognise his own city: 'il trouvera le nouveau Louvre fermant cette vaste place du Carrousel encombrée naguère de baraques et d'échoppes; il cherchera des îles de maisons anéanties, des rues dont il ne reste pas même la trace'[26] (he will find the new Louvre marking the edge of the vast Place du Carroussel, formerly cluttered with shacks and shops; he will search for houses that were wiped out, streets that disappeared without a trace). Gautier's introduction reflects both a desire to arrest the constantly changing reality through and in writing and an acknowledgement that this goal is unattainable.[27] Paris has changed so irrevocably that even native Parisians would be hopelessly lost without the help of this timely new guidebook:

> Ainsi vous comprenez que *Paris et les Parisiens* arrivent vraiment à l'heure; il faut un guide même à l'indigène pour se reconnaître dans sa ville. N'allez pas, de grâce, consulter quelque livre vieux d'un an, il vous tromperait; vous y liriez des choses aussi arriérées que si c'était un bouquin piqué de vers et ranci dans sa couverture de parchemin jaune; il en est de la physionomie des villes comme de la physionomie des hommes.[28]

> (Thus you realise that *Paris et les Parisiens* is a timely book. Even a native needs a guidebook to find his way in the city. And for heaven's sake, don't consult some old volume that's a year old – it will deceive you. There you will find things that are just as outdated as what you see in an ancient tome with a rancid yellow parchment cover consumed by worms. Faces of cities are just like faces of men.)

While Paris literature written during the years of Haussmannisation responds to a particularly acute sense of change, literature of the two previous decades already showed a keen awareness of the city in the process of transformation. And, in fact, this leitmotif of the impossibility of fixing urban change on the page remains a constant until the end of the nineteenth century. In the Preface to his 1900 *La Locomotion à travers le temps*, the prolific writer, journalist, cultural critic and bibliophile Octave Uzanne laments the fleeting nature of 'progress' (and, by extension, of 'the modern') that characterises transportation (but also fashion and book technology, his other interests) and that the notion of 'the contemporary' is impossible to pin down on paper:

> Hélas! Sur un sujet d'aussi rapide évolution progressive que celui-ci, il est impossible d'écrire le mot *fin* ou d'envisager une *conclusion* satisfaisante. Le progrès du jour à peine enregistré est déjà vieux le lendemain. Nous ne saurions nous flatter d'avoir fait dans nos derniers chapitres de l'histoire contemporaine. Lorsqu'on traite de la vitesse, on devient rétrospectif et aussitôt distancié par le fait même qu'on s'arrête.[29]

Introduction

(Alas! When writing on a topic that evolves as rapidly as this one, it is impossible to write the words *The end* or to envision a satisfactory *conclusion*. The progress of today, barely recorded, becomes obsolete the next day. We won't pretend that what we have written in these chapters is contemporary history. When you are writing about speed, you become retrospective and distanced from your topic by the very fact that you stopped writing.)

Like his predecessors of earlier decades, Uzanne considers public transport in general, and the omnibus in particular, as the epitome of transformation, even as this mode of transport itself becomes outmoded.

Such changes to the physical aspect of the city occurred in tandem with political turmoil and dramatic transformations of the fabric of society. Over the course of the nineteenth century, France experienced six different regimes (including two monarchies, two empires and two republics) and was rocked by two revolutions, a coup d'état and a violent uprising. These political cataclysms were accompanied by a move from a traditional economy to a capitalist industrial one, as well as by profound shifts in social structures and hierarchies (initially upended by the French Revolution). Money, rather than lineage, emerged as the major determinant of one's status, and the bourgeoisie established its economic, political and cultural power. The new topography of Paris reflected these shifting social structures, as different neighbourhoods became firmly associated with particular social groups (for instance, the area of the Chaussée d'Antin was inhabited by the newly enriched banking and industrial bourgeoisie and represented modernity, while the Faubourg Saint-Germain belonged to the ancien régime aristocratic elite and symbolised distinction).[30]

And yet the boundaries between these sections of Paris were consistently challenged and blurred as circulation increased throughout the city, just as the boundaries between different social groups were becoming increasingly fluid and unstable. The omnibus stands as the embodiment of these urban, cultural and social developments because it pushed the limits of topographic and social divisions on several levels. While its interior became a site of class mixing (and ultimately a space of social equalising), the vehicle itself traversed diverse social worlds as it made its way through different sections of the city, subverting, in a sense, topographic segregation by class. Indeed, one of the first omnibus lines, the Madeleine–Bastille, exemplified the social diversity that the omnibus came to represent, as it joined together two parts of the city that seemed worlds apart: the neighbourhood of Bastille was working-class, while the area of Madeleine was associated with wealth and power. Just as the Madeleine–Bastille line was emblematic of the tensions and contradictions that defined Paris throughout the nineteenth century, the entire history of the omnibus service is inextricably bound up with the city's history.

Omnibus: a history

Until the seventeenth century, the only vehicles circulating in Paris were private carriages. Emblazoned with their owners' coats of arms, carriages were a major status symbol whose function was not only to ferry their aristocratic passengers but also to publicly and spectacularly display their wealth and social position.[31] By the beginning of the seventeenth century, a number of public vehicles for hire, such as *chaises à porteurs* (sedan chairs), existed in Paris for those who were unable to afford the luxury of a private carriage but wished to travel in the city other than on foot.[32] Beginning in the eighteenth century, small carriages, such as *fiacres* (horse-drawn taxicabs), *cabriolet* and *coucou* (light, two-wheeled vehicles pulled by one horse), could be hired for a day or for a few hours.[33] *Fiacres* persisted until the end of the nineteenth century, when they were replaced by motorised taxicabs.

The ancestor of the nineteenth-century omnibus that most resembled it was a short-lived *carrosse à cinq sols*, the first mode of urban public transportation in Paris, devised and developed by Blaise Pascal in collaboration with the Duc de Roannez. Pascal and Roannez were given a monopoly by King Louis XIV to start an urban transit service in Paris. Significantly, the original royal decree did not impose any limitations on the social class of people who could take advantage of the *carrosses à cinq sols*. The service was launched on 18 March 1662 and originally deployed twelve carriages. They travelled along fixed routes, followed a schedule, accommodated up to eight passengers and two employees and were pulled by four horses. The cost of a ride, according to Joan Dejean, was twenty-four times less than the cost of renting a vehicle for hire. Like their nineteenth-century successor, the *carrosses à cinq sols* were open to both men and women.[34]

The new service was enormously successful with all Parisians, and soon five different lines were criss-crossing Paris, including a circle line along the perimeter of the city. The drivers wore red and blue, the colours of the city, and each vehicle was marked by a number of *fleur-de-lis* corresponding to the number of the line. This urban transit service was heavily advertised on posters plastered throughout the city: the omnibus circulated not only literally on the roads but also visually in print.

Although the service was originally intended for people of all classes, it quickly became apparent that wealthy and privileged passengers did not feel comfortable being in close proximity to passengers of a lower class. Dejean describes how privileged Parisians would board the vehicle, pay for all the seats and direct the driver not to accept any other passengers, thus reserving the entire *carrosse* to themselves. Under pressure from upper-class Parisians, the Parliament issued a new regulation excluding lower-class passengers: 'les soldats, pages, laquais et autres gens de livrée, même les manœuvres et gens de bras, ne pourroient entrer lesdits carrosses'[35] (soldiers, pages, domestic servants, as well as manual labourers would not be allowed on board of said carriages). The reaction was swift and violent, as members of the excluded groups attacked the carriages the very day the new edict was issued. A new regulation severely punishing such attacks put an end to violence, but the *carrosses à cinq sols* never regained their initial popularity and went out of circulation in the 1690s.[36] Parisians would have to wait until 1828 to see a truly public transit service come into existence. Nineteenth-century commentators often alluded to the restrictive nature of the *carrosse à cinq sols* to praise the social inclusiveness of the omnibus service.

The omnibus came to Paris at a time of immense population change, especially among the working and lower-middle classes. The number of Parisians increased from 550,000 in 1800 to 700,000 in 1830 and reached one million in 1846, the city acquiring between 16,000 and 25,000 new residents every year between 1840 and 1850.[37] Since many workers lived on the periphery but worked in the fashionable centre of the city, a vehicle capable of transporting large numbers of people and travelling along fixed routes was urgently needed. Moreover, as readers of Balzac's *Le père Goriot* will recall, Parisian streets were covered with an extraordinary amount of mud and sewage, and getting around without a vehicle was exceedingly unpleasant. Three hundred requests were submitted to the Paris *préfecture* in 1828 alone by companies wishing to start an urban coach business, which shows the pressing need for such a service. However, all requests were initially rejected because the authorities feared (with good reason) that a large vehicle of this kind might aggravate rather than solve the already severe traffic problem by creating even more congestion on the overcrowded narrow streets of pre-Haussmann Paris.[38]

Eventually, however, the need for public transportation led the authorities to approve the first omnibus service, launched by Stanislas Baudry, a former colonel in Napoleon's army and a successful businessman. Baudry had first opened an urban coach service in Nantes in 1826, initially to transport residents from the city centre to a bathhouse he operated on the outskirts. He noticed that although not many residents frequented the bathhouse, the urban coach service was widely successful. A shrewd entrepreneur, Baudry grasped the commercial potential of urban public transportation. Having achieved success with his coach service in Nantes, he decided to try for a bigger, more lucrative market in Paris. After a new police prefect authorised Baudry to create an urban coach company in the capital, he launched L'Entreprise générale d'omnibus, and the first *voiture omnibus* appeared on the streets of Paris in April 1828 (Figure I.2). The omnibus owed its unusual name to the inscription on the milliner's shop in front of which the urban coach station was located. The shop belonged to a Monsieur Omnès, whose motto was 'Omnès omnibus' (Omnès hats for

Engine of modernity

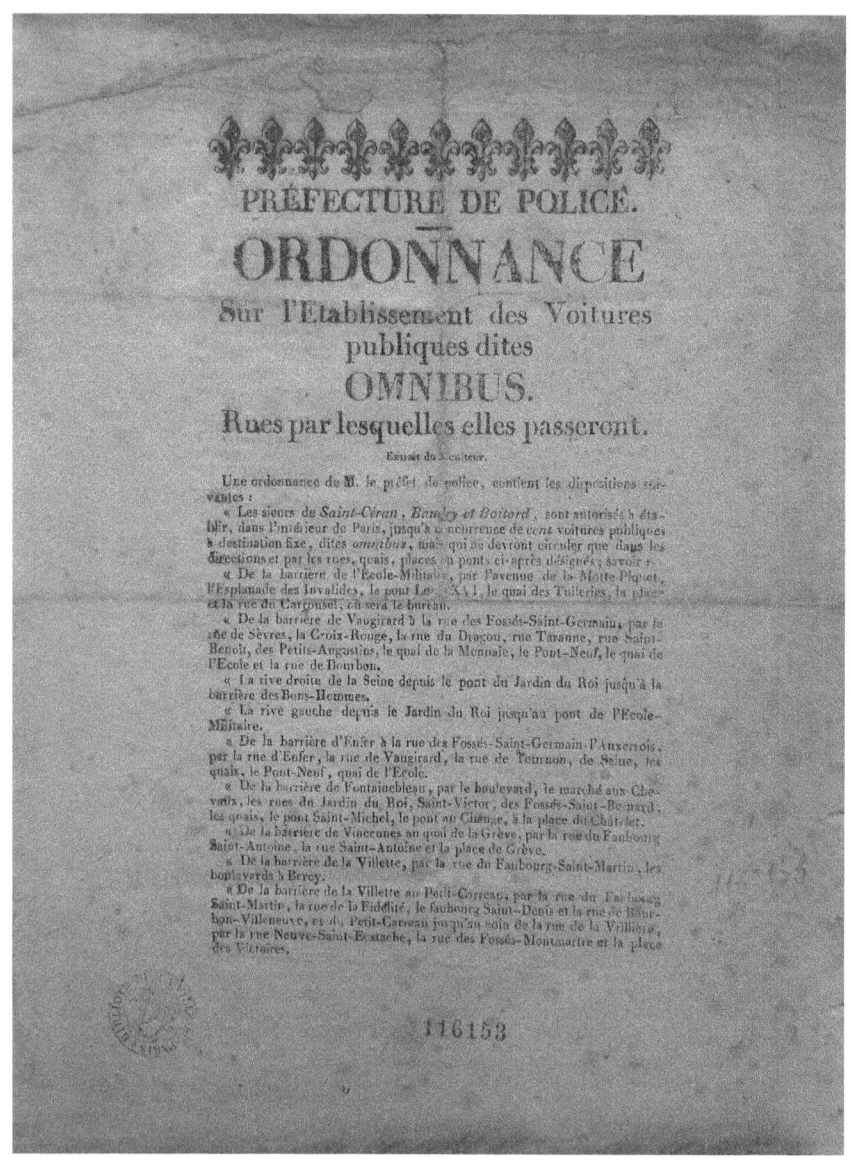

Figure I.2 'Ordonnance sur l'établissement des voitures publiques dites omnibus'. 1828.

everybody). Baudry found the name 'omnibus' – 'for everybody' – particularly appropriate for his vehicle, which he intended for passengers of all social classes.

In an 1867 article on 'Les voitures publiques' published in *La Revue des Deux Mondes*, Maxime Du Camp describes the first omnibuses as 'lourdes voitures dont la forme extérieure rappelait celle des gondoles'[39] (heavy vehicles whose exterior shape recalled that of gondolas). Baudry's vehicle accommodated fourteen passengers and was initially pulled by three horses. It travelled along fixed routes and had no pre-assigned stops. The driver announced the omnibus arrival by sounding a trumpet with the help of a pedal, and passengers signalled their intent to board by flagging down the vehicle. In addition to the sound of the trumpet, the omnibus wheels, covered with metal bands, also made considerable noise when rolling on badly paved streets.[40] It was the low cost of the omnibus relative to vehicles for hire that made it particularly attractive: the original fare was 25 centimes (going up to 30 centimes shortly thereafter), which was much cheaper than the fares for private carriages: 1 franc 25 for a *cabriolet* or 1 franc 50 for a *carrosse* ride.[41]

Initially, however, the omnibus service was only a moderate commercial success: although it was extremely popular with Parisians, and the demand was great, using three horses proved to be unprofitable. Baudry and his associates redesigned the omnibus to make it narrower and longer with two more seats inside, and the new vehicle was pulled by two horses instead of three, making it less unwieldy and more cost-effective.

Several other omnibus companies soon opened, boasting catchy names such as 'Dames Blanches' (the terminal was in front of the theatre playing a popular opera of the same name), 'Les Algériennes' (in reference to the military campaign in Algeria about to begin), 'Les Sylphides', 'Les Gazelles', 'Les Ecossaises' and 'Les Tricycles'.[42] There was also 'Les Carolines', named in honour of Princess Caroline, Duchess de Berry, who had made a 10,000-franc wager with the king that she would ride in a new vehicle. She not only won the bet but also contributed to the popularity of the new conveyance.[43] The attractive names, a marketing strategy evoking the feminine, the ephemeral, the mysterious and the exotic, obviously clashed with the reality of the gigantic, unwieldy and somewhat monstrous vehicle itself. They point toward an enduring association of the omnibus with female sexuality, and as we shall see in subsequent chapters, in popular literature and visual culture across the nineteenth century the omnibus was often construed as a site of erotic adventures and women's transgression. We may wonder whether it was the impressive new conveyance itself or the seductive names that in 1828 inspired a sixteen-year-old fledgling composer and piano virtuoso Charles-Valentin Alkan to write a variation for piano called 'Les Omnibus', dedicated to the 'Dames Blanches'[44] (Figure I.3).

By the end of 1829, ten new companies ran 264 omnibuses in Paris, each transporting a total of 300 passengers a day. By 1838, the number of omnibuses had increased to 409. A system of free transfers (*correspondances*) between different lines, introduced in 1834 by L'Entreprise générale d'omnibus, was an important

Figure I.3 Charles-Valentin Alkan, 'Les Omnibus', variation for piano in C major. 1828. Frontispiece.

improvement, and from 1840 passengers could transfer between lines run by different companies, as we can see in contemporary maps (Figures I.4 and I.5).[45]

Another innovation, aimed at increasing omnibus capacity, was the establishment of the *impériale*,[46] or the upper deck, in 1853. The *impériale* had fourteen seats at 15 centimes (i.e. half the regular price) and was initially open only to men. Women were excluded because it was deemed unbecoming, if

Introduction

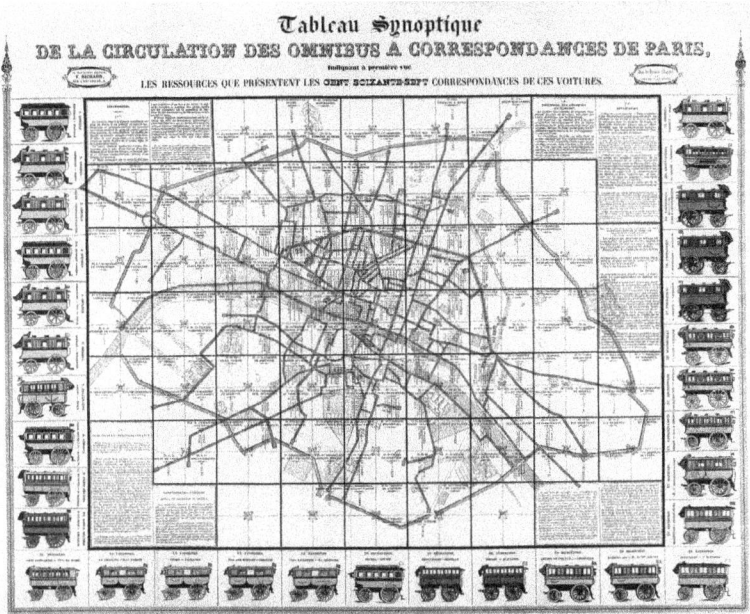

Figure I.4 Tableau synoptique de la circulation des omnibus à correspondances de Paris. 1840.

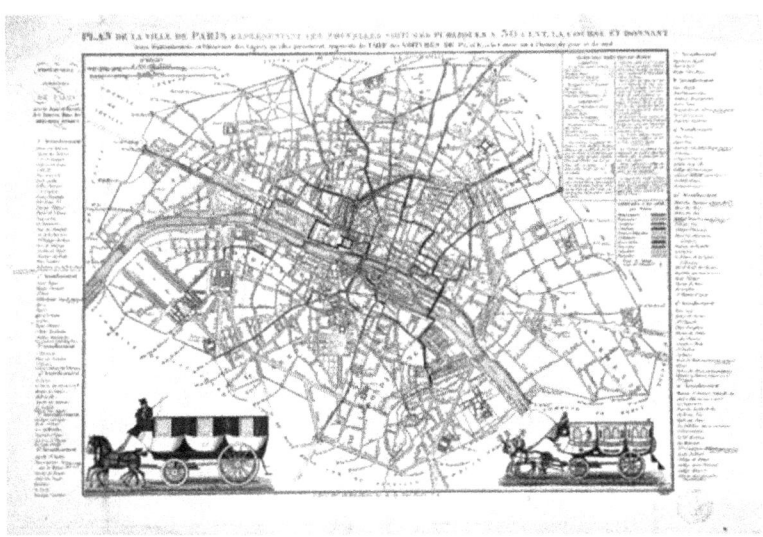

Figure I.5 Plan de la ville de Paris représentant les nouvelles voitures publiques à 30 centimes la course. 1829.

not impossible, for them to climb the precarious ladder leading to the upper deck, and because their skirts were particularly voluminous at the time.[47] Moreover, the exclusion was due to the perception that women were more fragile than men and would not be able to withstand the hardships that often befell the *impériale* passengers.

Indeed, the inconveniences of riding on the upper deck, exposed to the elements, became a favoured satirical subject for artists such as Honoré Daumier and others. In one caricature, Daumier depicts a man attempting to climb on the *impériale* by stepping on another passenger's head (Figure I.6). Several images portray the misery of an *impériale* ride in torrential rain (Figures I.7 and I.8). In Figure I.7, the caption plays on the word 'complet' ('full') ('Quinze centime un bain complet ... Parole, c'est pas payé!' (A full bath for 15 centimes ... a real bargain)). In a similar vein, a caricature by Cham shows a man carrying on his shoulder an *impériale* passenger who is frozen stiff (Figure I.9). But, despite these shortcomings, the new addition allowed a larger swathe of the population access to the omnibus. The *impériale* was considerably more affordable, and it alleviated some of the crowding aboard the vehicle.

Yet the original omnibus service was marred by serious problems and inefficiencies. The main issue was that the numerous companies wished to run their lines in the centre of the city, where they could attract the largest number of passengers, creating unnecessary competition and congestion, while the less urbanised areas on the city periphery were neglected.[48] According to Papayanis, for example, only two of the first ten lines run by L'Entreprise générale d'omnibus served the Left Bank, while other lines concentrated around the commercial and political centres of the Right Bank.[49]

This imbalance was remedied only in 1855 when, on Haussmann's orders, all of the omnibus companies were consolidated into one privately run transportation monopoly, La Compagnie générale des omnibus (CGO). In addition to streamlining the service, the consolidation, part of Napoleon III's move toward centralisation and uniformity, was prompted by several interrelated factors. The construction of broad boulevards as part of the rebuilding and modernisation of Paris facilitated circulation of large vehicles, and the continuous population growth in Paris, as well as the upcoming universal exposition of 1855, which would bring scores of visitors into the city, necessitated an updated transportation system.

The CGO obtained the exclusive right to operate urban transportation in Paris for the next three decades and brought numerous improvements to the public transit service. The monopoly was especially useful to the public in that multiple lines were established outside the city centre. When Paris expanded dramatically in 1860 by annexing neighbouring villages such as Auteuil, Passy, les Batignolles, Montmartre and others, the CGO obtained the exclusive concession to operate in these newly incorporated areas, thus ensuring a more

Figure I.6 Honoré Daumier, 'Le mauvais côté des nouveaux omnibus'. *Le Charivari*, 4 September 1856.

equitable distribution of the transportation services. By 1861, the company ran twenty-one omnibus lines throughout the city and possessed 500 vehicles and 6,700 horses (the latter number grew to 17,500 a few years later, the largest private cavalry in the world).[50] According to David Harvey, the number of omnibus passengers more than tripled between 1855 (the date of the merger) and 1860, when it reached 110 million per year (Plate 3).[51]

The CGO dominated the Parisian transportation market well into the second half of the nineteenth century. During the Second Empire, the only other

Engine of modernity

Figure I.7 Honoré Daumier, 'Quinze centimes un bain complet… parole, c'est pas payé! …'. *Le Charivari*, 30 August 1856.

mass transportation available to Parisians was the boat. In the 1870s, the tramway service launched in 1854 was further developed alongside omnibuses. New omnibus models were also introduced: in 1878, a large forty-passenger vehicle was inaugurated, and in 1888–89, a thirty-passenger omnibus was added to the fleet.[52] The *impériale* became more accessible thanks to a better-designed spiral staircase (*un escalier hélicoïdal*), and women were allowed entry from the late 1880s. By this time, large crinoline skirts had gone out of fashion, and it became both physically more manageable and socially more acceptable for a woman to ride on the upper deck. Yet despite these innovations, during the last two decades of the nineteenth century the omnibus service began to show signs of wear, and its deficiencies became more visible, as we can glean from the press from the 1880s to the 1900s. Problems included inadequate service, overcrowding, long waits, an ageing fleet and poor treatment of horses. The CGO rejected repeated requests from the city administration to modernise the service, and frequent labour disputes resulted in strikes by CGO personnel.[53]

The horse-drawn omnibuses (*les omnibus hyppomobiles*) lasted into the second decade of the twentieth century, coexisting for several years with newer

Figure I.8 Honoré Daumier, 'Commençant à trouver que l'impériale des omnibus n'est pas une invention aussi agréable qu'il se l'était d'abord imaginé'. *Le Charivari*, 10 February 1858.

means of transportation, such as the automobile, the metro (opened in Paris in 1900) and motorised buses (*omnibus automobiles*), launched in 1905.[54] When the last horse-drawn omnibus was finally decommissioned in January 1913, it was accompanied on its final journey with great pomp by huge crowds wishing to bid farewell to what had been a fixture of the Parisian landscape for nearly ninety years. Major newspapers carried the story on their front pages (Figures I.1, I.10 and I.11). The procession, described in several newspaper accounts as 'funérailles' (a funeral), featured an omnibus from the La Villette–Saint-Sulpice line, one of the last lines to run horse-drawn vehicles. Nearly 100,000 Parisians came to pay their last respects to the omnibus, along with a cortège of automobiles. The vehicle, filled to capacity and surrounded on all sides by people of different ages and social classes, was decorated with flower wreaths and memorial messages, such as a poster with a horse's head and the word 'merci' written on it, and a note that said 'Sic transit gloria equi.'[55] The event was bittersweet, as the headline in *La Presse* indicates: 'Feu l'Omnibus enterré joyeusement'[56] (The late Omnibus buried joyfully). If the first omnibuses were depicted as flighty females, at the end of its distinguished career the vehicle was personified as a loyal employee who has fulfilled his duty to society, as one newspaper account suggests: 'L'omnibus meurt en loyal serviteur

Engine of modernity

Figure I.9 Cham, 'Les nouveaux omnibus du boulevard pendant l'hiver'. 1840.

après une carrière bien remplie. Nous lui devons un souvenir très ému'[57] (The omnibus dies a loyal servant, following a fulfilling career. We remember him/ it fondly).

With echoes of another famous funeral, that of Victor Hugo in 1885, the omnibus travelled on its final journey surrounded by grateful crowds propelled by excitement, affection and nostalgia for the vanishing world it represented. While by 1913 the omnibus was outmoded and inefficient as a mode of transport, the enthusiasm and sheer size of the crowds accompanying it to its final resting place testified to its privileged place in the cultural *imaginaire*. In a particularly fitting postscript, most of the retired omnibus fleet was used for scrap metal during the First World War. The final passing of the vehicle, which embodied so many of the nineteenth century's key concerns, thus became linked to the pivotal event that marked the end of the long nineteenth century.[58]

A route map to the book

The omnibus stories I present in this book are drawn from a broad range of works of popular culture created during the years of the vehicle's operation (1828–1913). The material I consider includes numerous works of popular

Figure I.10 'L'enterrement de "la dernière" omnibus'. *Excelsior*, 12 January 1913.

Figure I.11 'Feu l'Omnibus enterré joyeusement'. Front page of the iconic newspaper *La Presse*, reporting on the 'funeral' of the omnibus, 12 January 1913.

urban literature (some well known and others that my research has uncovered), articles from the nineteenth-century press, fiction by both canonical and lesser-known writers and representations of the omnibus in popular visual culture. My aim is to unearth the cultural valence of the omnibus contained in this rich and wide-ranging archive. From chapters in celebrated literary guidebooks such as

Introduction

Paris, ou le livre des cent-et-un and *Les Français peints par eux-mêmes* to the less familiar *Physiologie de l'omnibus* or *Paris-en-omnibus*, from Emile Zola's canonical novel *La Curée* to novellas by the then immensely popular but now forgotten Paul de Kock, and from caricatures by renowned artist Daumier to lithographs by anonymous artists, omnibus literature and visual representations offer a unique perspective on cultural perceptions of the everyday. They also provide a distinctive view into the social dynamics and tensions generated by new forms of sociability among men and women of different classes, as well as changing urban practices.[59] In considering these sources, I do not privilege canonical over popular literature or fiction over non-fiction. Rather, I examine these works on a continuum that offers a deeper understanding of the cultural imaginary of the time.[60]

Engine of modernity consists of two parts. Part I, 'Omnibus literature in context', theorises the sub-genre of what I am calling 'omnibus literature' and explores specific textual strategies associated with it. Part II, 'Class, gender and locomotion: social dynamics on the omnibus', is organised thematically and focuses on two central concerns in the omnibus corpus: representations of class and gender. Part II throws into relief the deeply ambivalent attitudes about the omnibus during the long nineteenth century and, by extension, about the modernity this mode of transport represented in French culture.

Chapter 1, 'Modernity in motion: omnibus literature and popular culture in nineteenth-century Paris', introduces the omnibus literature and places it in the broader context of popular literary and print culture of the 1830s, 1840s and 1850s. Omnibus literature comprises works that not only take on public transportation as either subject or setting but also are characterised by shared formal features such as episodic narrative, collaborative authorship and multi-genre texts. In order to establish omnibus literature as a sub-genre, I draw on the concepts Margaret Cohen developed in her analysis of panoramic literature.[61] Features such as multiple authorship, micronarratives and heterogeneity were part and parcel of these types of literature as a whole. However, I argue that in the case of the omnibus literature, these features stem directly from its subject, one that generated innovative modes of writing. Thus, Chapter 1 establishes specific ways in which the omnibus provided a literary model for works of popular literature such as Edouard Gourdon's *Physiologie de l'omnibus* (1842), Louis Huart's 'Les voitures publiques' from *Nouveau Tableau de Paris au XIXe siècle* (1834), *Paris-en-omnibus* (1856) and the vaudeville play *Un omnibus ou la revue en voiture* (1828), among others. The narrative form of omnibus literature mirrors the vehicle's capacity to capture the multiplicity of urban experiences.

Chapter 2, 'Transitory tales: reading the omnibus repertoire', examines specific textual strategies and patterns of representation found in the omnibus literature. The corpus that I examine is an eclectic group of texts that includes works of panoramic literature, conduct manuals, city guides, literary guidebooks and popular songs. Despite their generic differences, these texts share thematic patterns and features that were developed and recycled across a broad range of works of popular literature spanning the nineteenth century. This chapter also introduces several recurring social types associated with omnibus literature, such as 'the omnibus flâneur' (an omniscient first-person narrator-passenger) and characters associated with omnibus labour, such as the conductor and the driver, all of whom figure in numerous works of popular literature. By analysing these features of omnibus literature, the chapter brings to the fore some of the central themes of nineteenth-century urban modernity: alienation, legibility of urban space, social mobility, anxiety about new technologies and new modes of labour.

Part II focuses upon ways in which cultural documents used the figure of the omnibus to navigate complex social dynamics of class and gender. Close readings of a variety of examples from popular literature and visual culture reveal that the omnibus was a multidimensional and often ambivalent symbol of modernity, one whose meaning was not permanently fixed but, rather, shifted and evolved. If some works celebrated the omnibus as an embodiment of progress, others deployed it to express anxieties about social change, such as class mobility and the increased visibility of women in public spaces. Part II also highlights how cultural representations of the omnibus constructed its different mythologies, which often departed from the lived experiences of contemporaries.

In Chapter 3, 'Circulation and visibility: staging class aboard the omnibus', I consider the omnibus as a central urban site where class relations and class identity were articulated, debated and contested. It is no coincidence that in a key scene in Victor Hugo's *Les Misérables*, a barricade is constructed using an overturned omnibus. This powerful image, capturing the symbolic power of the omnibus as an embodiment of revolutionary spirit, appears in a number of nineteenth-century texts. Contemporary writers noted that the name *omnibus* was particularly well suited to a mode of public transport that was by law open to everyone regardless of class, rank or social standing. In theory, the omnibus incarnated democratic promise, class equality and French Republican values. Yet a careful analysis of contemporary documents shows that the omnibus was a much more ambivalent class signifier than heretofore believed. While some works hailed it as a symbol of progress and democratic potential – a space in which social distinctions were erased and all passengers were treated equally – others bemoaned that the omnibus fell short as a vehicle of equality. Finally, some documents reveal a profound anxiety about class mixing aboard the omnibus, which for many symbolised the upending of existing social hierarchies. The omnibus was thus a locus for engaging with both class aspirations and class anxieties. Some urban observers perceived social mobility as a promise; others saw it as a dangerous challenge to the social order.

Chapter 4, 'Moral geographies: women and public transport', focuses on representations of female passengers and the ways that popular literature and

Introduction

visual culture grappled with gendered perceptions of public spaces. The omnibus was among the few public sites where men and women could legitimately share close quarters without violating rules of propriety. Yet in many documents the omnibus was portrayed as a site of female sexual transgression. Its narrow interior encapsulated the tensions and ambiguities surrounding women who were out and about in the city. We can see this concern about women's presence on public transport in an 1856 satirical lithograph by Charles Vernier depicting a man awkwardly making his way to his seat through a sea of gigantic crinoline skirts that have invaded the omnibus interior. In addition to poking fun at women's fashion, the image suggests the women's lack of respectability and their low social standing by linking them to Notre-Dame de Lorette, an area of Paris associated with prostitution (Figure I.12).

From young bourgeois maidens flirting with their seatmates to kitchen cooks holding baskets with suggestively spilling produce, from prostitutes soliciting clients to adulteresses giving assignations to lovers, and from pregnant women delivering babies to wet nurses exposing their voluminous bosoms, representations of female passengers highlight, beyond their frequent comic effect, a profound unease about the collapse of boundaries between public and private spheres, and about women's newly found visibility and freedom of

Figure I.12 Charles Vernier. 'Entrée dans un omnibus, rue Notre-Dame de Lorette'. *La Crinolonomanie*. 1856.

urban locomotion. In this chapter, I offer an analysis of a mythology that linked female omnibus passengers with transgressive sexual behaviour in texts by well-known authors such as Emile Zola and Guy de Maupassant as well as lesser-known writers such as Gourdon and Delord, in addition to works of visual culture.

Finally, in the Epilogue, I consider how two later nineteenth-century texts – Zola's department store novel *Au Bonheur des dames* (1883) and Fortuné du Boisgobey's murder-mystery *Le Crime de l'omnibus* (1881) – illustrate the power of the omnibus as a symbol of ambivalence toward modernity, even during a time when the vehicle itself was becoming obsolete. In these novels, the omnibus stands for anxieties surrounding multiple facets of modernity, such as rapidly expanding capitalism, the intrusion of the machine in everyday life and urban alienation. These texts demonstrate that literature and other cultural forms continued to use the omnibus as a prism through which to examine pressing concerns of the time – long after the vehicle itself ceased to be a novelty. A text by Octave Uzanne from 1900 provides a counterpoint to these novels' vision.

In the chapters that follow, I chart ways in which the omnibus operated as an 'engine of modernity' in nineteenth-century Paris. As a material reality, the vehicle contributed to the transformation of city spaces and the development of new urban practices. As a concept, it encapsulated numerous aspects of the modern urban experience: fragmentation, circulation, spectacle, urban alienation and flux, among others. As a literary form, the omnibus both reflected and shaped innovation in writing during the middle decades of the nineteenth century, a period that saw the emergence of mass-market literature and the popular press. The omnibus was not only an engine of transport, of urbanisation and of commerce: it was also one of cultural change and social anxiety. Like a refracting mirror, the omnibus provided nineteenth-century popular culture with new ways to represent and to navigate the world.

Notes

1 Jacques Roubaud, *Ode à la ligne 29 des autobus parisiens* (Paris: Attila, 2013).
2 I use the term 'popular literature and culture' here not in the French sense ('littérature populaire', i.e. referring to the social origin of the cultural documents' producers) but rather to mean what might be called middlebrow literature and visual culture addressed to and consumed by a broad range and number of consumers.
3 Wolfgang Schivelbusch, *The Railway Journey: The Industrialization of Time and Space in the Nineteenth Century* (Berkeley, CA: University of California Press, 1986).
4 In an excellent recent study, Anne Green similarly argues that the changing material world, including new forms of transport, shaped the literature of the time. My book expands on this idea with a focus on a different corpus and timeframe. See Anne Green, *Changing France: Literature and Material Culture in the Second Empire* (London: Anthem Press, 2011).

Introduction

5 Peter Soppelsa, 'The instrumentalisation of horses in nineteenth-century Paris', in Rob Boddice (ed.), *Anthropocentrism: Humans, Animals, Environments* (Leiden and Boston: Brill, 2011). Soppelsa discusses what he calls the instrumentalisation of horses – 'transformation of horses into tools' (p. 246) – in the context of the nineteenth-century Parisian urban economy, in which the horse became a crucial 'powering machine' (p. 245).
6 Charles Baudelaire, 'Le peintre de la vie moderne', in *Œuvres complètes* (Paris: Gallimard, 1938), p. 335.
7 On rethinking the concept of modernity in relation to nineteenth-century France, see the following studies: David Harvey, *Paris, Capital of Modernity* (New York: Routledge, 2005); Mary Gluck, *Popular Bohemia: Modernism and Urban Culture in Nineteenth-Century Paris* (Cambridge, MA: Harvard University Press, 2005); H. Hazel Hahn, *Scenes of Parisian Modernity: Culture and Consumption in the Nineteenth Century* (New York: Palgrave, 2009); Karen Bowie (ed.), *La Modernité avant Haussmann: formes de l'espace urbain à Paris, 1801–1853* (Paris: Editions Recherches, 2000). Much of this work builds upon, expands or contests Walter Benjamin's pioneering work on nineteenth-century Paris, modernity and the rise of consumer culture.
8 Hahn, *Scenes of Parisian Modernity*, p. 62.
9 Sharon Marcus, 'Transparence de l'appartement parisien entre 1820 et 1848', in Bowie (ed.), *Modernité avant Haussmann*, pp. 397–8.
10 It is worth noting that the word 'omnibus' (designating the vehicle) was also a nineteenth-century neologism, so the idea of 'the new' was inscribed in the name itself.
11 On the connections between public entertainment and public transport in the 1830s, see Jennifer Terni, 'A genre for early mass culture: French vaudeville and the city, 1830–1848', *Theater Journal*, 58:2 (2006), 241–8.
12 Georg Simmel, 'The metropolis and mental life', in Gary Bridge and Sophie Watson (eds), *The Blackwell City Reader* (Malden: Blackwell, 2002), pp. 11–19.
13 Vanessa Schwartz, *Spectacular Realities: Early Mass Culture in Fin-de-siècle Paris* (Berkeley, CA: University of California Press, 1998), p. 19.
14 I will analyse these texts and their features in greater detail in Chapter 1.
15 See in particular Nicholas Papayanis, *Paris before Haussmann* (Baltimore, MD and London: Johns Hopkins University Press, 2004) and David H. Pinkney, *Decisive Years in France 1840–1847* (Princeton, NJ: Princeton University Press, 1986). See also Hahn, *Scenes of Parisian Modernity*.
16 Honoré de Balzac, *Ferragus*, in *Histoire des treize* (Paris: Garnier-Flammarion, 1988), p. 79.
17 Priscilla Parkhurst Ferguson, *Paris as Revolution: Writing the Nineteenth-Century City* (Berkeley, CA: University of California Press, 1994), p. 35.
18 Louis Huart, 'Les voitures publiques', in *Nouveau tableau de Paris au XIXe siècle*, vol. 4 (Paris: Madame Charles-Béchet, 1834–35), p. 164.
19 Huart, 'Les voitures publiques', pp. 161–2.
20 A reference to a French proverb: 'Paris est l'enfer des chevaux, le purgatoire des hommes et le paradis des femmes' (Paris is hell for the horses, purgatory for men and paradise for women).

21 Delphine de Girardin, *Chroniques parisiennes*, Jean-Louis Vissière (ed.) (Paris: Des femmes, 1986), pp. 110–11. Caps are in the original.
22 For an insightful reflection on the concept of speed in the nineteenth century and ways in which it shaped fiction, see David Bell, *Real Time: Accelerating Narrative from Balzac to Zola* (Chicago, IL: University of Illinois Press, 2004).
23 Théophile Gautier, 'Préface', in Edouard Fournier, *Paris Démoli* (Paris: E. Dentu, 1883), p. v. Gautier's preface was added to the second edition published in 1855, a year after the initial publication in 1854.
24 Baudelaire, 'Le cygne', in *Œuvres complètes*, pp. 98–100.
25 Théophile Gautier, Alexandre Dumas, Paul de Musset *et al.*, *Paris et les Parisiens au XIXe siècle* (Morizot: Paris, 1856), p. ii.
26 Gautier *et al.*, *Paris et les Parisiens au XIXe siècle*, p. ii.
27 Behind these statements, there is also undoubtedly a desire to benefit financially from this trend. A city and a society in flux were certainly profitable for writers who wished to capture and explain contemporary life and to do so over and over again.
28 Gautier *et al.*, *Paris et les Parisiens au XIXe siècle*, p. ii.
29 Octave Uzanne, *La Locomotion à travers le temps, les mœurs et l'espace. Résumé pittoresque et anecdotique de l'histoire générale des moyens de transports terrestres et aériens* (Paris: Librairies Paul Ollendorf, 1900), p. x.
30 Anne Martin-Fugier provides an excellent explanation of the symbolic meaning of each of the four *quartiers* associated with different strata of high society (*le monde*): la Chaussée d'Antin, Faubourg Saint-Honoré, Faubourg Saint-Germain and le Marais. See *La Vie élégante, ou, la formation de Tout-Paris 1815–1848* (Paris: Fayard, 1990), pp. 100–12.
31 For a lively history of early transportation in Paris, see Joan Dejean, *How Paris Became Paris: The Invention of the Modern City* (New York and London: Bloomsbury, 2014), especially chapter 6, 'City of speed and light: city services that transformed urban life', pp. 122–43.
32 In this section, I draw upon both nineteenth-century histories of public transport in Paris and contemporary scholarship. The following works have been particularly useful in drafting this overview of the history of the Parisian omnibus: Eugène d'Auriac, *Histoire anecdotique de l'industrie française* (Paris: E. Dentu, 1861); Maxime Du Camp, 'Les voitures publiques dans les rues de Paris', in *Revue des deux mondes* (15 May 1867); René Bellu, *Les Autobus parisiens, des origines à nos jours* (Paris: Delville, 1979); Marc Gaillard, *Du Madeleine-Bastille à Météor: histoire des transports parisiens* (Amiens: Martelle, 1991); Marc Gaillard, *Histoire des transports parisiens: de Blaise Pascal à nos jours* (Le Coteau: Horvath, 1987); Roger-Henri Guerrand, *Mœurs citadines. Histoire de la culture urbaine, XIXe–XXe siècles* (Paris: Edima, 1992); Nicholas Papayanis, *Horse-Drawn Cabs and Omnibuses in Paris: The Idea of Circulation and the Business of Public Transit* (Baton Rouge, LA: Louisiana State University Press, 1996); Henri Zuber, Sheila Hallsted-Baumert and Claude Berton (eds), *Guide des sources de l'histoire des transports publics urbains à Paris et en Ile-de-France XIXe–XXe siècle* (Paris: Publications de la Sorbonne, 1998).
33 Gaillard, *Du Madeleine-Bastille à Météor*, p. 12.
34 Dejean, *How Paris Became Paris*, p. 127.

Introduction

35 Quoted in d'Auriac, *Histoire anecdotique de l'industrie française*, p. 250.
36 There seems to be no specific evidence as to when the *carrosses à cinq sols* ceased to exist. Dejean reports that the Duc de Roannez sold his stake in the company in 1691, but according to nineteenth-century historians, it appears that the service went out of fashion sometime after 1677. This is also the date cited by Gaillard. See Gaillard, *Du Madeleine-Bastille à Météor*, p. 10.
37 Patrice Higonnet, *Paris: Capital of the World* (Cambridge, MA: Harvard University Press, 2002), p. 77.
38 Papayanis, *Horse-Drawn Cabs*, p. 58.
39 Du Camp, 'Les voitures publiques', 342.
40 Bellu, *Les Autobus parisiens*, p. 11. This inconvenience led to the creation of the tramway service in 1854. The tramway, shaped like an omnibus and also horse-drawn, ran on rails. However, the tramway service did not gain in popularity until the 1870s.
41 *Almanach des Omnibus, des Dames blanches et autres voitures nouvellement établies...* (Paris: Lenormant fils, 1829) provides further details about the pricing: for *cabriolets*, for example, the cost per trip between 6 a.m. and 12 a.m. was 1 franc 25; at other times, the first hour was 1 franc 75, and the second hour and following 1 franc 50.
42 Guerrand, *Mœurs citadines,* p. 120; Gaillard, *Histoire des transports parisiens*, p. 18.
43 Robert Hénard, 'Les Omnibus', in *Magasin Pittoresque* (January 1898), 348.
44 I thank Hugh MacDonald for bringing Alkan's work to my attention. Charles-Valentin Alkan, 'Les Omnibus', variation for piano in C major (Paris: M. Schlesinger, 1828). Alkan (1813–88) was a child prodigy who became one of the greatest virtuoso pianists of the 1830s and 1840s. During this period, Alkan belonged to the same artistic circles as Franz Liszt, Frederic Chopin, George Sand and Victor Hugo. Despite his early fame, he withdrew from public life after 1850 and spent the rest of his life in relative obscurity. www.bach-cantatas.com/Lib/Alkan-Charles.htm, accessed 9 June 2017.
45 Papayanis, *Horse-Drawn Cabs,* pp. 65–7; Gaillard, *Histoire des transports parisiens*, p. 18.
46 In the seventeenth century, the word *impériale* designated the top of a carriage, perhaps because the ornate roof evoked the imperial crown. In the nineteenth century, the word designated by analogy the upper deck of a public vehicle.
47 The introduction of the *impériale* in 1856 coincided almost exactly with the fashion craze for very large hoop skirts. Such skirts made riding in a public conveyance extremely cumbersome, and they certainly made it impossible for women wearing crinolines to negotiate the narrow winding ladder leading to the upper deck. For more on crinoline-wearing female passengers, see Chapter 4.
48 It was apparently due to the pressures of fierce competition and floundering business that Baudry committed suicide in 1830 by shooting himself in the head in front of his stables (Gaillard, *Histoire des transports parisiens,* p. 18).
49 Papayanis, *Horse-Drawn Cabs,* p. 63.
50 Gaillard, *Histoire des transports parisiens,* p. 22.
51 Harvey, *Paris, Capital of Modernity*, pp. 113–15.

52 Gaillard, *Histoire des transports parisiens*, p. 43.
53 For newspaper accounts of these disputes, see the uncatalogued press clippings found in the department of 'documents éphemères' at the Bibliothèque Historique de la Ville de Paris.
54 The CGO developed an interest in autobuses (*omnibus automobiles*) from 1905. The first steam prototype vehicle was put in service in July 1905 on the Montmartre–St Germain line, and then in December of the same year, on the occasion of the Salon de l'Automobile, the CGO put in place a regular autobus service consisting of nine vehicles. For a complete history of the bus service in Paris, see Bellu, *Les Autobus parisiens*; on the first autobuses, see pp. 13–33.
55 'Il n'y a plus d'Omnibus à Paris' (12 January 1913).
56 *La Presse* (12 January 1913).
57 André Lang, 'L'omnibus se meurt! L'omnibus est mort!'.
58 For a brief analysis of the omnibus 'funeral', see Peter Soppelsa, 'The end of horse transportation in Belle-Époque Paris', *Interdisciplinary Studies in Literature and Environment*, 24:1 (2017), 113–29.
59 In considering different types of discourse together, I follow in the footsteps of scholars such as Priscilla Ferguson, Christopher Prendergast and Sharon Marcus, whose pioneering work on nineteenth-century Paris and its cultural production changed the way we approach representations and meaning of urban spaces. See Ferguson's seminal *Paris as Revolution*, Christopher Prendergast's *Paris and the Nineteenth Century* (Oxford: Blackwell, 1995) and Sharon Marcus's *Apartment Stories: City and Home in Nineteenth-Century Paris and London* (Berkeley, CA: University of California Press, 1999).
60 My book is in dialogue with a growing scholarship on literary representations of different forms of transport in modern British literature, including a recent volume edited by A. Gavin and A. Humphries, *Transport in British Fiction: Technologies of Movement, 1840–1940* (London: Palgrave, 2015), and Ian Carter, *Railways and Culture in Britain: The Epitome of Modernity* (Manchester: Manchester University Press, 2001).
61 Margaret Cohen, 'Panoramic literature and the invention of everyday genres', in Leo Charney and Vanessa Schwartz (eds), *Cinema and the Invention of Modern Life* (Berkeley, CA: University of California Press, 1996), p. 228.

Part I
Omnibus literature in context

1

Modernity in motion: omnibus literature and popular culture in nineteenth-century Paris

Setting the stage

On 25 May 1828, one month after the launch of Stanislas Baudry's omnibus service in Paris, a new vaudeville play premiered at the Théâtre de Vaudeville. Titled *Les omnibus, ou la revue en voiture*, the play portrays a bitter dispute between drivers of the newly introduced omnibuses and those of the individual vehicles for hire – *fiacres*, *coucous* and *cabriolets*[1] – that had previously dominated the Parisian transportation market. The drivers of vehicles for hire accuse the omnibus of unfairly luring customers away from other modes of transport, which are unable to compete with a fare of just 25 centimes.[2] In a parallel plot line, new popular theatres (such as le Théâtre du Gymnase, Le Cirque and the Théâtre de Vaudeville) engage in a fierce feud with the elite and aristocratic Théâtre de l'Opéra. While the popular theatres align themselves with the omnibuses, the Opéra sides with the more expensive vehicles for hire, representing social privilege. By masterfully weaving together these two seemingly unrelated strands of the plot, *Les omnibus, ou la revue en voiture* brings to the fore the nexus of public transport and popular culture, and thus the relationship between mass transit and mass entertainment.

Les omnibus, ou la revue en voiture was one among many works of popular literature that embraced the new form of mass transit as an archetypal modern subject that embodied many of the features of this very literature. An astonishing number of cultural documents published across the nineteenth century explored different aspects of the omnibus experience. These included a broad range of works of urban observation, literary guidebooks,[3] short stories, caricatures, vaudeville plays, society games and epic poems, as well as a number of works that are difficult to classify. Popular luxury volumes such as *Paris, ou le livre des cent-et-un* (1831–34), *Les Français peints par eux-mêmes* (1840–42), *Nouveau Tableau de Paris au XIXe siècle* (1834) and others included chapters on omnibus travel, while Edouard Gourdon devoted an entire *physiologie* – one of the most popular genres of the 1840s – to the topic (*Physiologie de l'omnibus*, 1842).

Beyond the middle decades of the nineteenth century, which saw the rise of popular print culture, the omnibus continued to fascinate writers long after it had lost its novelty. In the 1880s and 1890s, for example, there were scores of popular songs telling stories set on the omnibus. Writers such as Emile Dartès, a well-regarded editor of Victor Hugo's work, produced a three-volume humorous *Contes en omnibus* (1894), and as late as 1906 fin-de-siècle writers such as François Coppée, Jean Lorrain, Jules Clarétie and Octave Uzanne continued to publish tales set on the omnibus or wax nostalgic in the press about their experiences riding the vehicle in their youth.

In this chapter, I investigate the literary appeal of the omnibus – a seemingly mundane element of everyday life – and introduce many of the works to which I will return in later chapters. My argument here is twofold: first, I show how the omnibus fascinated nineteenth-century writers because it embodied the ideas of 'the popular' and 'the everyday'; second, I illustrate how this literature harnessed distinctive features of the omnibus – such as the diversity of the passengers, the idea of mixing different elements within the same space and the concept of the multiplicity of perspectives – to generate new modes of writing. *Omnibus literature*, as I call it, deployed the vehicle as an organising narrative and structuring principle, a means of depicting both the totality and the vicissitudes of the modern urban experience. In other words, the omnibus as a space of mixing and mobility provided a literary model for the writing of the everyday.

Paris on the page

Omnibus literature arose during a veritable revolution in the literary marketplace, beginning in the 1830s. The dramatic changes concerned both the kind of literature that was being written and consumed and the way it was produced and disseminated. Alongside the profound transformations of Parisian urban and social landscapes in the 1830s and 1840s emerged a broad array of new literary genres aimed at representing a society in transition. This lively urban literature became the hallmark of the mass literary market during the middle decades of the nineteenth century.[4] Described today as 'panoramic' (a term coined by Walter Benjamin), it sought to provide a seemingly objective, encyclopedic view of the city, its inhabitants and contemporary urban practices and trends – the kind of perspective afforded in the panoramas popular throughout Paris in the first half of the nineteenth century.[5] Different forms of panoramic literature targeted different types of audience. There were, for example, the widely popular and inexpensive *physiologies*, pocket-sized, easily consumable volumes that focused on a single social type or a particular urban location or phenomenon. Nearly 120 different *physiologies* were published between 1840 and 1842, predominantly by the publishing house Maison Aubert, with 500,000 copies sold at 1 franc each.⁶ A genre known for satirising contemporary mores, the *physiologies* offered remarkable insight into the social dynamics of the time while also providing the middle classes with a space for self-reflection. Similar to the *physiologies* in tone and aims – but different in looks and audience – were the upscale *tableaux de Paris*, or literary guidebooks. From *Paris, ou le livre des cent-et-un*, published between 1831 and 1834 and authored, as the title suggests, by 101 different writers, to the 1839–42 *Les Français peints par eux-mêmes* and numerous *nouveaux tableaux de Paris*, these books could be purchased in instalments or as elegantly bound complete editions and were usually geared toward a wealthier, middle-class public. Both the *physiologies* and the luxury volumes presented humorous, pseudo-sociological, episodic depictions of everyday urban phenomena (types, events, places, professions).⁷ Other cultural forms, such as the daily press, the serial novel (*roman-feuilleton*), the caricature and the popular theatre, emerged largely in response to the constantly changing, ephemeral pressures of the modern city.

The development of new literary forms took place against the backdrop of dramatic changes in the production and consumption of literature. Beginning in the 1830s, a number of technical innovations transformed both the printing process and paper production. Historian Martyn Lyons suggests that the 1830s saw the most significant changes to the publication process since the age of Gutenberg: 'In political terms, the Old Regime had ended in 1789, but the typographical Old Regime expired in the 1830s.'⁸ The industrialisation of book production, the launch of large-circulation daily newspapers, inaugurated by Emile de Girardin's *La Presse* and Armand Dutacq's *Le Siècle* in 1836, the introduction of advertisements and the invention of the railway, which facilitated distribution and marketing, all contributed to a fundamentally changing process of producing and reading literature, and to the advent of a mass literary market.

These new cultural forms did not limit themselves to depicting everyday experiences and urban phenomena: they aimed to classify, decipher and analyse the social class and moral standing of various Parisian types and to render legible and transparent the urban spaces they inhabited. This imperative to establish transparency stemmed not only from a reconfiguration of physical city spaces, increasing circulation of people and vehicles and a dramatic rise in population size in Paris but, even more importantly, from radical shifts in established social structures in post-Revolutionary France. To understand Paris meant to understand French history and society. As Priscilla Ferguson notes, 'Writers focused so obsessively on the city because it seemed to hold the key to an explosive past no less than to a bewildering future'.⁹ They saw a need to untangle the new cultural codes necessary to navigating a society in flux.

Omnibus literature in context

Yet, as scholars have pointed out, Paris was a difficult place to read.[10] Nineteenth-century Parisian urban spaces and the social landscapes associated with them refused clear interpretation. Indeed, urban observers who sought to make sense of Paris, to define or distil its identity, or to catalogue and classify it, were confronted with a decentred, unstable and multifaceted city. For writers interested in urban observation, 'reading' or 'writing' Paris was always problematised; the city, unsettled by accelerating circulation and social flux, seemed to elude understanding. As we have seen, though, the *raison d'être* of this array of specifically urban genres and texts was the ambition to give coherence and meaning to the instability of modern experience. Their proliferation reflected the desire to suspend and hold (and thus control) through writing the ever changing urban and social environment.

Within this context, the omnibus became a key object for representing the city and its inhabitants in all their complexity. Omnibus literature effectively taps into different connotations of the word *omnibus*. The term is, first of all, a neologism referring to a new mode of transport, a vehicle containing a heterogeneous group of people who are haphazardly thrown together and thus exposed to each other's gaze for an extended period of time. The diversity of passengers with respect to their social class, gender, comportment and attire, all contained within the same space, is central to the fascination the vehicle of mass transit exerted upon nineteenth-century writers and artists.

A drawing by M. Sahib from 1874 provides a vivid illustration of the heterogeneity that characterised the omnibus interior. It depicts a very crowded vehicle featuring passengers from a broad range of social classes (Figure 1.1). On the right, there is a working-class boy sitting next to a kitchen cook or a maid in a plaid shawl and a bonnet. Across from them is a fashionably appointed couple, whose clothes and stylish accessories clearly mark them as belonging to a higher social stratum. The lady's elegant coat adorned with a fur collar, her fashionable hat, handbag and gloves, as well as her companion's top hat and prominently displayed vest, made of an expensive material such as velvet, distinguish them from their surroundings. The man's long fingers casually hold the handle of his modish cane. Even their faces appear to be more refined than those of their fellow passengers. The dense class heterogeneity and crowdedness of the omnibus are palpable in this drawing. Every inch of this image appears to be filled with assorted human figures who dwarf the space of the vehicle itself. Omnibus literature thus borrows the concept of 'the omnibus' as a form holding together diverse pieces, a totality comprising a variety of distinct fragments, and puts it to narrative ends.

Later, the term 'omnibus' began to be used to characterise collections of disparate texts, inspiring a new way of gathering and disseminating writing. As a figure, the omnibus allowed urban writers to write about virtually everything, to broach every conceivable topic in a variety of registers, from the study

Modernity in motion

Figure 1.1 M. Sahib, 'L'intérieur d'un omnibus'. 1874.

of manners (*l'étude de mœurs*) to the analysis of type and character, from social satire to descriptions of changing urban landscape, and from caricature to philosophical meditations on time, space and the meaning of life. Like the vehicle, omnibus literature captured the heterogeneity of modern experience, making use of its 'omni-ness', or all-encompassing nature. Finally, the omnibus as a mode of representation was appealing because, as a vehicle intended 'for all', it embodied the concept of the popular, and thus was an ideal topic of popular literature. These deep connections between public transport and popular literature intended 'for all' shaped the literary corpus.

Performing the popular

As a subject of popular culture, the omnibus owes some of its popularity to what Margaret Cohen calls 'the conceptual emergence of the everyday' as a valid, and even privileged, topic of representation, and to the rise of the literature that focused on everyday social practices.[11] From its launch, the omnibus became a quintessential feature of the urban landscape, an indispensable part of the Parisian quotidian, the epitome of the everyday. Both the new conveyance itself and the novel forms of sociability that it engendered provided perfect fodder and form for what journalist Jules Janin, in his famous defence of popular literature, called 'une littérature pour tous les jours' (everyday literature). In arguing against what his opponent Désiré

Nisard called 'la littérature difficile' (difficult literature), Janin passionately advocated 'cultural democracy' (to use historian Mary Gluck's term), dismissing the idea that new popular literature was failing on both moral and aesthetic grounds.[12] Indeed, Janin called for a democratisation of literature for everybody: 'la littérature de tous à la portée de tous'[13] (everybody's literature accessible to all). Like the omnibus, a democratic vehicle meant for everybody, one that aimed (at least in principle) at a broad spectrum of the public, emerging popular literature was destined for a broad reading audience, rather than the elite alone. Thus, the omnibus and popular literature, as imagined by Janin and his fellow writers, shared the same public and participated in the production of a new kind of cultural modernity, in the streets, on the page and on stage.

For an example of how popular literature deployed the omnibus as a symbol of the popular, let us return to the vaudeville play *Les omnibus, ou la revue en voiture*. It is worth dwelling at some length on the very first play about the omnibus (and quite possibly the first literary text about it), because it perfectly articulates the association between public transit and popular culture. The play is a hilarious romp that taps into seemingly disparate but, in fact, deeply interconnected contemporary issues. First, it dramatises a turf war between private vehicles for hire and the newly introduced omnibuses, a conflict that featured in contemporary caricature as well (Figures 1.2 and 1.3). It also satirises a competition for theatre-going audiences between, on the one hand, the elite and stately Théâtre de l'Opéra, with its pedigree traced to the glory days of Louis XIV, and, on the other, the numerous popular theatres that sprung up during the first two decades of the nineteenth century. *Les omnibus, ou la revue en voiture* brilliantly captures the inherent link between popular entertainment and mass transit. The play explicitly identifies both the omnibus and the vaudeville as phenomena that benefit and represent the ordinary, middlebrow public ('les petits gens'), and places the idea of the popular, be it transit or entertainment, at the forefront.

At least three mid-nineteenth-century vaudeville plays centre their plots on the omnibus. As a genre, the *comédie-vaudeville* was preoccupied with capturing Paris at its most modern, and vaudeville playwrights were particularly interested in representing current events and everyday social conflicts. In the guise of slapstick comedy, vaudeville often exposed the underlying anxieties of the commercial middle class, the same class that constituted the majority of both omnibus passengers and vaudeville-goers. The omnibus and vaudeville, as both genre and experience, served as refracting mirrors for each other, shaping everyday social and cultural practices.

Vaudeville was by far the most popular form of public entertainment in Paris during the first half of the nineteenth century. By the 1840s, close to three million spectators a year attended vaudeville performances, and

Modernity in motion

Les cochers de fiacres aux prises avec ceux des Omnibus.

Figure 1.2 'Les cochers de fiacres aux prises avec ceux des omnibus'. c. 1830. This image shows drivers of the two types of vehicles, visible in the background, fighting in a boxing ring, with spectators – or passengers – watching intently.

vaudeville accounted for 56 per cent of all box-office receipts. Nearly 1,300 new vaudevilles plays were written and produced between 1815 and 1830 alone, and their popularity continued well into the nineteenth century.[14] As Jennifer Terni points out, both the rise of the public transportation system (specifically the omnibus) and the development of vaudeville contributed to the rise of a vibrant consumer culture during the July Monarchy and beyond.[15] A developing network of omnibus routes that catered to the commercial and entertainment centres of the city allowed a growing number of people to attend theatre performances. Spaces of leisure became more accessible to broader swathes of the population. At the same time, as a genre that drew on the latest urban trends and newest consumer practices, vaudeville deployed omnibus travel as both a frequent subject and as a plot device.[16] This

Omnibus literature in context

Figure 1.3 Jean Georges Frey, 'Les Dames Blanches et le fiacre: Y-s-auront le tems d'engraisser nos chevaux!!!!!'. 1828. This caricature highlights several contrasts. It shows a disgruntled-looking driver of a *fiacre* waiting idly, his horse seemingly hanging its head in despair, while in the background numerous elegantly dressed passengers are boarding an omnibus. The *fiacre* and its driver are in the shadow, depicted in dark, ominous colours. The omnibus, by contrast, is brightly coloured and lit. Finally, the omnibus driver is wearing an elegant coat and a top hat and looks dignified, whereas the *fiacre* driver is clad in rumpled clothing. The image appears to reverse the class association of two vehicles, coding the omnibus as a conveyance for the upper classes.

quintessentially popular form of mass culture was the first to grapple with the first vehicle of mass-transit.

From its very first lines, *Les omnibus, ou la revue en voiture* makes it clear that what is at stake here is not so much the vehicles themselves but the kind of people they represent. The opening song associates the omnibus with 'les petits gens':

> Les Omnibus c'est la voiture
> De la petit' propriété,
> Contre une avers', l'hiver ça vous assure,
> Et contre la poussière en été.
> Roulant comme les maîtres
> L'boulanger port' son pain,
> L'facteur porte ses lettres,
> Et dit en narguant le sapin:
>   Vivent, Vivent les Omnibus!
>   Roulons not' bosse

En carosse,
Cum jambis et pedibus,
A pied nous n'irons plus.[17]

(The Omnibus is the carriage
Of the little people
In the winter it protects you from the rain
And in the summer, from the dust
Rolling like masters
The baker is carrying his bread
The postman, his letters
And they all tease the policeman
In this way:
    Long live the Omnibus!
    Let's get our back rolling along
    Cum jambis et pedibus,
    No more going on foot!)

The song refers to a broad spectrum of ordinary working people (a baker, a postman, a seamstress, a young soldier, a bailiff and an office clerk) for whom the omnibus presents a unique opportunity of affordable urban transportation. It not only shields these people from the elements and provides very real comforts but, perhaps more importantly, allows them for the first time to feel like masters, with the line 'Roulant comme les maîtres' pointing to the essentially classed nature of urban locomotion. Thanks to the omnibus, 'Les petits gens ne s'rons plus victimes/ Du fier landau numéroté' (The little people will no longer fall victims/ to the proud numbered landau), suggesting a metonymic link between the landau, a luxury carriage, and its presumably privileged occupants, who literally splatter pedestrians with the mud that generously covered Parisian streets at the time. The mud also represents social oppression inflicted upon lower-class city dwellers by the upper classes.[18]

In a move typical of vaudeville plays, the song concludes with a satirical twist, proclaiming that now the ordinary people, just like polite society, can also happily run over those who are beneath them:

Nous pourrons à la ronde,
D'un air de dignité,
Ecraser l'pauvre monde
Comme la bonne société[19]

(Now, looking dignified
All around,
We, too, can run over little people
Just the way members of high society do)

The opening song thus establishes the play's problematic around questions of class and audience. It clearly privileges the 'ordinary' ('petits') people, the presumptive omnibus passengers, as well as vaudeville-goers, and hails the vehicle as a kind of equalising force, while at the same time reaffirming principles of social hierarchy.

The first scene features coachmen of various Parisian vehicles for hire – a *fiacre*, a *cabriolet* and a *coucou* – lamenting that the newly inaugurated omnibus is ruining their business ('La roue de la fortune a tourné, et les nôtres ne tournent plus'[20] (The wheel of fortune has turned, but ours now stay idle)). Their conversation is interrupted by the appearance of the Wandering Jew (a figure who embodies movement), who has returned to France after a two hundred-year absence.[21] In the play, the Wandering Jew is a pragmatic character who embraces progress and bestows the wisdom gained from his travels on the bewildered Parisians, helping them to make sense of their rapidly changing social and physical world.[22] The Wandering Jew begins by praising France for its commitment to progress ('Comme en France on avance'[23] (How things are moving along in France)). When coachmen offer him a ride, however, he is baffled by the outrageous prices. Popular legend has it that the Wandering Jew travelled with 5 *sous* in his pocket (corresponding to the five injuries he inflicted on Christ), a sum that, by happy coincidence, is equal to the omnibus fare. When an omnibus arrives, and the Wandering Jew learns about the fare, he immediately departs aboard the new vehicle, ignoring the coachmen's loud protestations.

The second plot line is introduced in the following scene, set in the waiting room of a courthouse, in anticipation of judicial proceedings. Here, the Wandering Jew meets the plaintiffs, the personified second-tier theatres ('les théâtres secondaires'), Le Gymnase, Les Variétés, le Vaudeville, les Nouveautés and la Gaïté. All of these theatres were well known for producing vaudevilles and other popular forms of entertainment. The personified theaters have come to plead their case against the oppressive 'tyrant de la rue Lepelletier [sic] . . . le grand Opéra'[24] (the tyrant of rue Le Pelletier. . . the great Opera). It appears that L'Opéra attempts to meddle with the kind of performances the other theatres like to stage. In a clever move, the Jew, while seemingly listing L'Opéra's objections, advertises the popular theatres, enumerating all the thrilling aspects of their performances: 'Je connais vos griefs!. . . on ne peut ni sauter, ni danser, ni valser, ni parler, ni mimer, ni monter à cheval, ni danser sur la corde, ni montrer les ombres chinoises, ni faire des tours de gobelets, ni avaler les sabres, ni assassiner, ni empoisonner, ni chanter juste, ni chanter faux. . .sans que l'Opéra ne se figure que ça le regarde.'[25] (I know your grievances!. . . L'Opéra takes it upon himself to interfere every time you wish to jump, or dance, or waltz, or talk, or mime, or mount a horse, or dance on a rope, or show Chinese shadow play, or show magic tricks with glasses, or swallow swords, or assassinate, or poison, or sing in key, or sing off key.)

Here we see a clear juxtaposition of mass and elite cultures: the second-tier theatres represent the middlebrow crowd, while L'Opéra personifies high art, ancien régime aristocracy and wealth.[26] 'Nous arrivons en Omnibus, pour plaider; tous les petits-Théâtres se sont levés en masse' (We arrive on an omnibus to plead our cause; all the second-tier Theaters are rising up), declares Le Vaudeville, making clear the connection between the public conveyance and popular entertainment. When their opponent, L'Opéra, comes on stage, the Wandering Jew remarks, 'Ah ça, il n'est pas venu en Omnibus, celui-là!'[27] (Ah! This one didn't come on an Omnibus). Indeed, the actor playing L'Opéra makes his entrance on stilts, literally representing high art and high society; at the same time, the association of stilts with the circus, perhaps the lowest form of popular entertainment, contributes to ridiculing L'Opéra, who in this performance becomes a source of physical comedy (in other words, becomes 'vaudevillesque'). The vaudeville's audience could certainly relate to – and enjoy – such mockery of high art.

The two plot lines converge in the last act of the play, which is set in front of the Palais de Justice. With the rain that has begun to fall, the coachmen of the vehicles for hire are eagerly anticipating customers. We understand that the court proceedings have concluded when, according to stage directions, the second-tier theatres triumphantly pour outside armed with umbrellas (*parapluies*) and depart on an omnibus. They are followed by L'Opéra, carrying an elegant but useless *ombrelle* (parasol). We can assume that he lost his case: L'Opéra 'se sauve à toutes jambes'[28] (runs off as fast as his legs would carry him). In the nineteenth century, the parasol was associated with the elite leisure classes and was unambiguously coded as feminine. That L'Opéra, played by a male actor, is carrying a feminising *ombrelle* adds insult to injury in mocking this character and, by extension, the kind of audience associated with elite entertainment.[29]

Having thus established the unquestionable advantage of popular theatres, the action of the play then shifts back to the conflict between the coachmen of the vehicles for hire and the omnibus drivers. In the final scene, the Wandering Jew settles their dispute and brokers peace between the two groups by calling on them to share the streets of Paris. Appealing to the coachmen's business acumen, he reminds them that, in fact, the omnibuses and the vehicles for hire do not compete for the same passengers: 'ceux qui sont montés en Omnibus ne seraient montés ni en fiacre, ni en cabriolet, d'après leurs facultés pécuniaires'[30] (those who take the omnibus would not ride in a *fiacre* or a *cabriolet* anyway, in accordance with their financial abilities). All ends well as the entire cast of characters – the coachmen, the theatres and the Wandering Jew – joyfully depart the stage in an omnibus. Class tensions are successfully resolved within the safe space of the theatre stage, as the Wandering Jew re-establishes order and reminds the audience of existing social hierarchies. In the concluding song, the Wandering Jew recalls once more the parallel between vaudeville and the omnibus, and invites the audience to treat them in the same way:

> La mode en Omnibus s'installe,
> De public ils sont tous pourvus;
> Faites, Messieurs, que votre salle
> Chaque jour soit un omnibus...
>
> (The fashion for Omnibus is established
> They all are supplied with public
> Make it so, Messieurs, that your theatre
> Be 'an omnibus' every day...)

L'omnibus ou la revue en voiture cleverly uses the innovation in public transit to make an argument about innovative theatre practices, at the same time using the vaudeville theatre, beloved by the middlebrow public, to promote the omnibus. Both the transport and the art form, the play argues, ultimately benefit the middlebrow public and represent its values. The play captures the deep connection between the popular theater – and, more broadly, popular literature – and the omnibus: both appealed to a similar public and reflected a shift toward the democratisation of public life, whether in entertainment or transport. In doing so, the omnibus and its representations in popular literature participated in articulating 'cultural modernity', as defined by Sharon Marcus: both the cultural form and the form of transport revealed a keen awareness of the new.[31] As we shall see, other popular genres engaged with omnibus travel, drawing on its salient characteristics to generate new forms of writing.

Surfing the omnibus literature

In a sense, omnibus literature became the medium *par excellence* for representing modern urban experience. It explicitly takes the characteristics of the omnibus – such as the concept of mixing diverse elements under a unified form, or the multiplicity of voices and perspectives one associates with this vehicle – and turns them into writing strategies. In what follows, I offer a brief introduction to some of the main texts of omnibus literature and an analysis of ways in which they deployed various features of the vehicle and put them to literary use.

Omnibus literature was quintessentially what Margaret Cohen calls literature of the everyday, and it is to her classic analysis of key features of this literature that I now turn. Focusing on a number of works of panoramic genres, such as *tableaux*, *physiologies*, literary city guides and volumes such as *Paris, ou le livre des cent-et-un*, *Les Français peints par eux-même* and *Le Diable à Paris*, Cohen reveals how they rely on 'micronarratives with no continuity from plot to plot', usually presented from the viewpoint of a single narrator.[32] These brief snapshots of everyday happenings assemble a variety of modern urban experiences, subjects and characters. Multiple authorship is another prominent feature of panoramic genres, contributing to the range of voices and viewpoints typical of this literature,[33] and the diversity of contributing authors – from well established through up-and-coming to virtually unknown – complements the diversity of topics. Finally, panoramic literature is characterised by what Cohen aptly terms 'heterogenericity', a wide range of genres and registers within the same text.

These concepts are particularly useful in considering omnibus literature, which deployed them well beyond the lifespan of the panoramic literature of the July Monarchy, and used them self-reflexively, linking formal literary strategies with the vehicle's features. While the authorial and generic diversity of panoramic texts relates to their panoptic aims, within the genre of omnibus literature it reflects the 'omni-ness' of texts that take this new mode of mass transit not merely as a topic but also as a narrative organising principle. In other words, the form and the content mirror one another: these popular texts use the 'omnibus' structure to make sense of a broad range of modern experiences and to work through the tensions and complexities of their contemporary urban environment and shifting social structures.

The reliance on micronarratives is perhaps the most salient characteristic of numerous works in the corpus. Consider, for example, how one of the first works of omnibus literature, the anonymous *Les omnibus. Premier voyage de Cadet la Blague de la place de la Madeleine à la Bastille et retour* (1828), makes use of micronarratives organised around the flow of passengers on and off the vehicle.[34] In this satirical work, the narrator deploys many of the comical ingredients of vaudeville theatre – slapstick humour, chance encounters, reversals of fortune – to convey the chaotic happenings that he observes during a ride. Here are just a few examples. The first vignette involves a drunkard harassing a proper bourgeois woman travelling with her husband; the husband defends his honour with his fists, and in the process both the husband and the drunkard tumble out of the omnibus. The wife follows but misses the step 'et tomba la tête la première sur le boulevard, les jambes en l'air, et montrant ce qu'on a l'habitude de cacher'[35] (and fell head first on the boulevard, legs in the air, and showing that which one usually conceals). In the next episode, three ladies of easy virtue (or, as the narrator calls them, 'les nymphes') and their male companions make their entrance, and the narrator recognises one of the ladies as his friend's mistress. And in another scene, a family with children, dogs and a gigantic leg of lamb (*gigot*) causes tremendous chaos and disorder through a series of predictable mishaps (the little boy urinates in his father's lap; the dog pilfers the leg of lamb; the narrator tries to extricate the leg from the dog, who ends up biting him; the narrator throws the dog out on to the boulevard, etc). Upon noticing this group about to board the omnibus, the narrator anticipates that their presence will provide him with a good story: 'Je me doutais que ses originaux nous fourniraient quelque scène nouvelle, et je ne me trompais pas'[36] (I suspected that these characters would supply me with some new stories, and they didn't disappoint). In the end, the passengers get arrested for causing a public disturbance, but upon their release they all go out to dinner, and social and narrative order is restored.[37] The entire work thus uses omnibus travel as an organising narrative principle: each episode centres on a group of passengers, and the episode's beginning and end correspond to the journey's beginning and end.

We find a similar structure in a text published at the end of the nineteenth century. Emile Dartès organises the three chapters comprising his *Contes en omnibus*[38] (first published as three separate volumes in 1893, and then again as one volume in 1894) around the comings and goings of passengers as observed by a first-person narrator, with each chapter named after an omnibus line (Madeleine–Bastille, Montrouge-Gare de l'Est and Batignolles-Clichy-Odéon). Thus, omnibus travel explicitly supplies the narrative structure of the work as a whole. The episodes include mundane observations of conversations among passengers, 'shaggy dog' stories, including slapstick humour about passengers falling into each other's laps, and an extended sequence about a mother, her baby and a wet nurse (which I will analyse in greater detail in Chapter 4). At the end of the third tale, the narrator concludes that while the omnibus is neither the fastest nor the most comfortable mode of transportation, it is a literary gold mine for a writer, as he lists all the fascinating and diverse characters he had the chance to observe during his journey, and who now will provide fodder for his stories:

> Quant à moi, pour six sous, j'ai été voituré une heure durant, à trois chevaux s'il vous plaît, avec cocher devant, laquais derrière, et j'ai vu trente-six choses émouvantes ou simplement intéressantes: un huissier arrêté, spectacle aussi rare que réjouissant; un piou-piou qui m'a rappelé Cambronne, de glorieuse mémoire, ce qui m'a fait revivre une page de l'Histoire; j'ai vu défiler tous les échantillons de l'espèce parisienne: des bourgeois, des filles, des ouvriers, des gommeux, voire même des Anglaises qui personnifient l'espèce londonienne; [. . .]Bref, je n'ai pas eu une minute d'ennui.[39]

> (As for me, for 6 *sous* I was ferried around for a whole hour, pulled by three horses if you please, with a coachman in front and a valet in the back, and I saw thirty-six things that were touching or simply interesting: a bailiff getting arrested – a sight as rare as it is joyous; a soldier who reminded me of Cambronne, of glorious memory, making me relive a page from history; I saw numerous examples of Parisian types parade before me: the bourgeois, the prostitutes, the workers, the fops, even the Englishwomen embodying the London type. In short, I wasn't bored even for a minute.)

It is clear, then, that the omnibus continued to supply narrative form well into the nineteenth century. The vehicle brings together a number of unrelated plot lines and highlights the dynamics between, on the one hand, the variety of characters and plots, and, on the other, the capacity of the omnibus as a narrative device to unify them into a single whole. In this sense, many works set on an omnibus become themselves 'omnibus' texts, or 'works comprising several different items'.

Much more than a background or setting, the omnibus provides essential structural elements around which these works are organised. It naturally lends itself to episodic narratives that begin when a passenger boards the vehicle and ends when the passenger descends; temporally, each episode lasts the length of a ride. There is no need for a formal transition between episodes; all the author needs to do is usher one or more passengers out of the vehicle before moving on to the next story. While the episodes usually centre on thematically diverse topics, the setting delivers both narrative transitions and unity.

Multiple authorship and heterogeneity are other prominent traits of omnibus literature. Several important multi-authored volumes from the 1830s, 1840s and 1850s included texts about the omnibus by well-known writers of the time. An early example is Ernest Fouinet's 'Un voyage en omnibus de la barrière du Thrône à la barrière de l'Etoile' (1831) from *Paris, ou le livre des cent-et-un*, which aimed to provide moral insights into the social topography of Paris through satirical observations. 'Un voyage en omnibus' is a first-person narrative in which the narrator recounts what he observes during a ride across the city. His observations include descriptions of sites he sees from the window and comments on a wide range of passengers (a flirty *grisette*; an old dowager; a peasant; a beautiful, delicate young lady who captivates the narrator; an appalling drunk smelling of tobacco and alcohol). As in other texts, the stories about each passenger are short and episodic, lasting only the duration of the ride, and Fouinet intersperses these passenger tales with philosophical musings that showcase how the omnibus captured writers' imagination by providing them with a metaphor of life: 'L'omnibus est l'image du monde; on vient, on s'en va: qui s'en occupe? A moins que vous ne soyez le Roi, le premier enfant qu'attend une jeune mère, ou le célibataire que guettent ses collatéraux, le prêtre qui enterre, vous regarde-t-on entrer, vous regarde-t-on sortir?'[40] (The omnibus is the image of the world: you get on, you get off – who cares? Unless you're the king, the baby expected by a new mother, an old bachelor whose heirs await his death, or a priest officiating at a funeral, does anyone care whether you come or go?)

Similarly, Louis Huart's 'Les voitures publiques', from *Nouveau Tableau de Paris au XIXe siècle* (1834), offers an overview of different Parisian vehicles, a short typology of vehicle drivers, a meditation on the speed of modern life, a biting analysis of social hierarchy as embodied by various types of conveyances and, finally, a philosophical vision of an omnibus as a metaphor of life:

> Car notre vie est-elle rien autre chose qu'un voyage en omnibus ? Comme les voyageurs d'omnibus, nous arrivons tous on ne sait d'où; nous prenons la place

à côté de ceux qui sont installés; nous faisons quelques connaissances avec les personnes qui voyagent de concert avec nous. – Si elles descendent en route, leur souvenir est bien vite effacé de notre mémoire par les autres voyageurs qui viennent prendre leur place; puis, dans l'omnibus comme dans le monde, nous nous marchons sur les pieds les uns des autres, parce que partout les rangs sont pressés, et que nous cherchons à faire notre chemin sans penser à nos voisins; puis enfin l'omnibus étant arrivé à sa station, au terme de la course, chacun de ces voyageurs venus *on ne sait d'où*, se dispersent et disparaissent pour aller *on ne sait où*.[41]

(For is our life not an omnibus journey? Like omnibus passengers, we all arrive from we don't know where; we take our seat next to those who are already there; we make acquaintance of some of our fellow travellers. If they get off along the way, their memory is quickly erased by other passengers who come to take their place. Then too, on the omnibus as in life, we step on each other's feet because people everywhere are in a rush, and we seek to make our way without giving a thought to those around us. Finally, when the omnibus arrives at the final destination, and the trip comes to an end, each one of the passengers who had come *from we don't know where*, will now disperse and disappear – *we don't know where*).

The tone of this meditation on life and death and the meaning of social interactions stands in stark contrast to the rest of Huart's essay, which is either dry and factual or satirical.

Both multiple authorship and heterogeneity are at work in the 1854 *Paris-en-omnibus*. This text was produced by a trio of writers renowned in the world of popular press: Taxile Delord, editor-in-chief of *Le Charivari*, Arnould Frémy, also involved with *Le Charivari*, and Edmond Texier, editor-in-chief of *L'Illustration*.[42] *Paris-en-omnibus* was part of *Les Petits Paris*, a series of fifty short illustrated volumes investigating different aspects of Parisian life.[43] In the tradition of the *physiologie* of the 1840s, the titles in the *Petits Paris* series ranged from those focused on a specific type (*Paris-Grisette, Paris-Voleur, Paris-Prêtre, Paris-Notaire, Paris-Fumeur*) to those centred on a specific space (*Paris-Restaurant, Paris-Boursier*). The price for one volume was 50 centimes, and they could be purchased individually or as a series subscription. Their in-octodecimo format also replicated the size and look of the *physiologies*. *Paris-en-omnibus* consists of thirty short chapters widely varying in tone and subject, ranging from a straightforward history of the omnibus service in Paris ('De l'omnibus et son origine') to lengthy disquisitions on omnibus horses and their upkeep ('Le Palais des chevaux' and 'De la sociabilité du cheval d'omnibus'), and from reflections on the melancholy of the regular omnibus passengers ('Les mœurs de l'habitué de l'omnibus') to satirical tales of encounters with prostitutes who use the omnibus to fetch clients, and of improbable on-board childbirths ('La femme qui accouche').⁴⁴ *Paris-en-omnibus* also contains what can be called *mini-physiologies*, typological studies of the omnibus driver and the omnibus conductor, as well as other types frequently found aboard the conveyance. For example, one chapter is about the 'omnibus farceur', a joker who causes mayhem by sitting on the lap of another passenger, or even on top of an old lady, or pretends to have an attack of cholera. At the end of the chapter we learn that 'les farceurs d'omnibus sont excessivement rares. On peut même dire réellement qu'il n'existe plus' (the omnibus jokers are exceedingly rare. You can in fact say they no longer exist), and so it becomes clear that the entire vignette is a joke.⁴⁵ In addition, we find diverse approaches to typologising: while the chapter on the conductor is a third-person 'objective' observation, the chapter dedicated to the driver ('Grandeur et décadence du cocher') is a first-person narrative written from the perspective and in the voice of the *cocher* himself.

The tone and register of the chapters in *Paris-en-omnibus* vary extensively. Some present short humorous mises-en-scène in the mode of slapstick comedy (such as the vignette about the omnibus joker cited above). Others are almost philosophical in tone. Consider, for example, a chapter called 'Des mœurs de l'habitué d'omnibus'. In this chapter, the narrator describes his experience as a regular omnibus passenger and highlights the modern urban subject's sense of alienation and estrangement:

> Rien ne porte à la tristesse et à la mélancolie comme de voyager souvent en omnibus. L'habitué d'omnibus, à quelque sexe qu'il appartienne, est un être sombre, silencieux, concentré en lui-même. L'omnibus rend farouche et misanthrope. J'ai fait pendant deux ans le trajet de Paris à Saint-Cloud par les omnibus de la rue de Bouloi. Je partais par le dernier départ de minuit le quart. Quand on parcourt la même route deux années de suite, on finit par connaitre le personnel des voyageurs. Ce sont presque toujours les mêmes personnes qui se retrouvent. Vous croyez qu'on va faire connaissance; ah! bien oui! On s'assoit à coté les uns des autres sans rien dire; les femmes abaissent leurs voiles, les hommes ramènent leurs chapeaux sur les yeux. [...] Qu'un voyageur candide et novice essaye d'entamer la conversation, on lui répond d'abord par monosyllabes, puis on finit par ne plus répondre du tout.⁴⁶

(Nothing predisposes toward sadness and melancholy more than frequent omnibus travel. A regular omnibus rider, no matter what sex, is a sombre, quiet person who turns inward. The omnibus makes you mistrustful and misanthropic. For two years, I took the omnibus of rue de Bouloi from Paris to Saint-Cloud. I took the last omnibus at quarter past midnight. When you make the same trip for two years, you end up recognizing your fellow passengers. It's almost always the same ones. You'd think people would get to know each other. Ha! Think again: you sit next to one another without saying a word. Women lower their veils; men pull their hats over their faces. When a novice traveller attempts to start a conversation, at first people respond with monosyllables and then end up not responding at all.)

With the images of silent passengers pulling their hats over their eyes and their veils over their faces, this passage perfectly captures the disconnection and alienation that were a fundamental part of cultural understanding of the modern urban environment and that contributed to anxieties about modernity. The presence of such a poignant and keen reflection in a work that is predominantly satirical and tongue-in-cheek in tone is particularly jarring.

Heterogeneity is also at work in Charles Soullier's 1863 *Les Omnibus de Paris, pièce curieuse et utile à l'usage des voyageurs dans Paris*.[47] This text opens with a polemical poem praising the omnibus as a symbol of innovation and progress, of social equality and class inclusiveness. The poem is followed by several pages of a straightforward history of public transportation in Paris. The book's last and longest section is a detailed guide to the Parisian omnibus lines, their itineraries, transfers and other practical matters. Such a dizzying breakdown of generic boundaries was likely to produce what Cohen calls 'epistemological chaos', or readerly confusion, as to how to approach such a text. Just as the omnibus-vehicle erased boundaries while simultaneously establishing hierarchies among its passengers, the omnibus-text collapsed a broad range of different types of writing between its covers.

Perhaps the most emblematic work of omnibus literature is Edouard Gourdon's 1842 *Physiologie de l'omnibus*. While written by a single author and following the conventions of this genre, Gourdon's *Physiologie* displays a remarkable diversity of tone, style, register and subject matter.[48] The thirty chapters comprising this work include detailed descriptions of the vehicle and the omnibus station; typological portraits of passengers as well as the conductor and the omnibus bureau chief (*le buraliste*); several humorous mises-en-scène that stage dialogue among passengers and explore various comical situations; a love poem; a lengthy list of advertisements one finds in the station; and satirical essays on a variety of topics, from doctors' investment habits to men's facial hair.

Most *physiologies* provide a satirical portrait of just one urban type (such as the *grisette, flâneur* or *bourgeois*) or phenomenon. But the conceit of the omnibus allows Gourdon to mock a great variety of types. There is, for example, a vignette about a young poet, who, having failed to publish his poetry, comes up with a clever scheme to ride the omnibus in order to both distribute his verses and use them for seduction: 'Il voyage depuis six mois, distribuant de droite et de gauche ses épîtres amoureuses, épiant avec l'attention d'un ruse chasseur, le gibier qu'il convoite, qu'il plume quelquefois, ayant grand soin de n'offrir ses strophes et son cœur qu'à des femmes mariées ou veuves.'⁴⁹ (He has been riding omnibuses for the past six months, distributing his love epistles left and right, spying his coveted prey – which he occasionally fleeces – with the attention of a keen hunter. He makes sure to only offer his verses and his heart to women who are married or widowed.) This vignette includes the actual lengthy love poem purportedly written by the aspiring poet, and thus makes particularly visible the generic diversity of this text.

Another chapter satirises greedy doctors who allegedly put their gain above their patients' interests. Gourdon jokingly claims that doctors were prime investors in omnibus companies because frequent accidents involving the conveyance supplied them with a steady stream of clients: 'Tout calcul fait, il a été prouvé que trois cents voitures à six sous équivalent presque à un huitième de cholera permanent... Le médecin affectionne donc l'omnibus plus que toutes autre voiture, non pour lui, il ne sort jamais qu'en coupé ou en cabriolet, mais pour la société entière qu'il porte dans son cœur, sur laquelle il est appelée à veiller, et puis un peu aussi – j'allais dire beaucoup – pour sa caisse qu'il est appelé à remplir.'⁵⁰ (To sum up, it was proven that three hundred vehicles at 6 *sous* are equivalent to one eighth of permanent cholera... The doctor is fond of the omnibus more than of any other vehicle, not for himself – he only travels in a carriage or a cabriolet – but for the sake of the entire society which he holds dear in his heart, and over which he is called to keep watch. And also a little bit – I would even say a lot – for the sake of his cash box that he is called to fill.)

In addition, the *Physiologie de l'omnibus* features many humorous scenes that the narrator observes during his omnibus ride, which allows him to ridicule different types of greedy, immoral or otherwise outlandish behaviour. There is, for instance, a story about a woman who tries to avoid paying the fare for her ten-year-old child by pretending that he is only three years old: 'Le tableau est pittoresque. Imaginez une femme d'une taille excentrique, tenant sur ses genoux un gros garçon de dix ans qu'elle espère sauver à la perspicacité du conducteur.'⁵¹ (The scene is picturesque: imagine an eccentric-looking woman holding on her lap a big ten-year-old boy she is hoping to hide from the conductor's vigilance.)

In another mise-en-scène, we find an amusing dialogue between two former lovers who run into each other on the omnibus:

-Comment, c'est toi!
-Comment c'est vous!
[...]
-Ah! Octavie!
-Tu n'as donc pas oublié mon nom?
-Ni ton adresse. Où demeures-tu?
-21 bis au troisième, la porte à gauche.

-Ah bien, j'y suis! Faut-il toujours toucher le bouton avant d'entrer?
-Oui légèrement, j'ai des voisins. Et toi?
-J'en ai aussi.
-Ce n'est pas ce que je te demande. Où demeures-tu?[52]

(-It's you!
-It's you!
[...]
-Ah! Octavie!
-So you haven't forgotten my name?
-Nor your address. Where do you live?
-21 bis on the third floor, door on the left.
-Great, I'll be there. Do you still need to push the button before coming in?
-Yes, but lightly – I have neighbours. And you?
-I have them too.
-That's not what I am asking! Where do you live?)

Although this humorous dialogue does not appear to contain a lot of information, it allows the reader to glean quite a bit about the two characters involved (for example, the man's caddish behaviour is made clear by the fact that he doesn't remember his former mistress's address). Another episode features a beautiful young woman with whom the narrator begins to flirt. The reader expects a development of the flirtation story. Instead, the story is interrupted by a chapter-long digression on moustaches, highlighting the unexpected turns that urban travel sometimes takes. Indeed, the topics and tone of the *Physiologie de l'omnibus* capture and reflect the diversity of the omnibus experience. With its panoramic scope – the passing scenes and the fragments of conversation overheard – the *Physiologie* gets to the heart of the idea of this vehicle as engine of modernity. The omnibus doesn't merely represent change, motion, and flux: it embodies it.

If the *Physiologie* is full of omnibus statistics, omnibus vignettes, omnibus jokes and omnibus quips typical of this satirical genre, it concludes with a strikingly poetic and disquieting image of a nocturnal omnibus as a mythological creature, a shape-shifting 'monstre fantastique' (fantastic monster) that glides through the night:

> Les lanternes de l'omnibus jettent sur les voyageurs des reflets verts et jaunes qui s'attachant çà et là sur un visage, un chapeau, un profil, une cravate, une main, les dessinent vigoureusement dans la nuit. Ce sont des caprices bizarres et toujours en mouvement, c'est une page d'Hoffmann, une esquisse de Rembrandt ou de Caillot; voici des chiens et de chauves-souris, des serpents et des loups, un rocher velu, un pont et des nuages.... Mais voici bien autre chose: l'omnibus vient de croiser un réverbère, et la silhouette entière du monstre, chevaux et cocher,

voiture et voyageurs, conducteur et marche-pied, s'est accrochée aux aspérités d'une muraille blanche, et s'y reproduit comme dans un miroir... Puis tout cela se dilate peu à peu, les roues s'écartent, s'étendent, les chevaux maigrissent et s'allongent à vue d'œil, les voyageurs chevauchent sur un énorme manche à balai dont le conducteur tient le gouvernail. Nous sommes devenus lilliputiens, puis quelque chose de noir et d'uniforme, puis rien du tout: les rayons de la lanterne ne nous atteignent plus.[53]

(The omnibus lights throw green and yellow reflections upon the passengers. They dwell here and there on a passenger's face, a hat, a profile, a tie, a hand – they sketch them sharply in the night. It's always a bizarre whim that is always in motion. It's a page from Hoffmann, a sketch by Rembrandt or Caillot. Here come dogs and bats, snakes and wolves, a mossy rock, a bridge and clouds.... But here is something else: the omnibus went by a street light, and the silhouette of the monster in its entirety – horses and coachman, vehicle and passengers, conductor and step – clings to the rough surface of a white wall, and is repeated as in a mirror... Then all this expands little by little: the wheels move aside, stretch out, the horses grow thin, and lengthen in front of us; passengers ride on an enormous broomstick handle with the conductor at the rudder. We have become Lilliputians, then something black and uniform, and then – nothing at all. The light of the lantern no longer reaches us.)

This passage reveals an acute awareness of what will later become dominant themes of modernity: anonymity, alienation, mutability. The passengers of Gourdon's omnibus are first changed to Lilliputians, then to a uniform anonymous mass and, finally, to 'nothing at all', signalling a progressive dwarfing of humanity in the face of the modern machine. Gourdon shows how this new vehicle of public transit perfectly captured what Baudelaire would famously call 'le transitoire' (the transitory).

Omnibus literature emerges as a quintessential genre of the middle decades of the nineteenth century. The nineteenth-century urban authors I have examined in this chapter – and to whose works I will return throughout this book – used the omnibus as both form and content to represent their fluid cultural moment, capitalising on the 'omni-ness' of the vehicle, on its capacity to contain manifold experiences of the urban everyday. Taken as a whole, nineteenth-century omnibus literature mirrors the way the vehicle encompassed the dizzying diversity of urban experiences. Omnibus literature thus serves as a lens through which to analyse the emergence of Paris as a modern city, probe its constitutive parts and give form to the complexities of French society in post-Revolutionary France.

The omnibus didn't simply offer urban writers a fruitful topic: it helped shape the literature of the time. Akin to the public-transit experience itself, omnibus literature offered snapshots of everyday life, capturing its provisional, fluid, transitory nature: as in Baudelaire's 'Une Charogne', images both sublime and grotesque appear for a brief moment only to be swept away by the city in motion.[54] Ultimately, the omnibus became a literary form through which urban writers engaged with central aspects of nineteenth-century modernity: circulation, mobility and flux, both literal and figurative; alienation as a defining feature of modern urban experience; chance encounters and momentary connection; and the breakdown of boundaries – between social classes, between sexes and between literary categories and genres.

Notes

1 For descriptions of these vehicles, see p. 12.
2 For comparison, the fare for a *cabriolet* ride started at 1 franc 25 and increased depending on the length of the ride.
3 A term coined by Ferguson in *Paris as Revolution*, p. 55.
4 In recent decades, the genre of panoramic literature has enjoyed renewed attention from literary scholars and cultural historians. These studies include (but are not limited to) the following: Hahn, *Scenes of Parisian Modernity*; Susan Hiner, *Accessories to Modernity: Fashion and the Feminine in Nineteenth-Century France* (Philadelphia, PA: University of Pennsylvania Press, 2010); Martina Lauster, *Sketches of the Nineteenth Century: European Journalism and its Physiologies, 1830–50* (Basingstoke: Palgrave Macmillan, 2007); Judith Lyon-Caen, 'Saisir, décrire, déchiffrer: les mises en texte du social sous la monarchie de Juillet', *Revue Historique*, 306:2 (2004), 301–30; Marcus, *Apartment Stories*; Catherine Nesci, *Le flâneur et les flâneuses. Les femmes et la ville à l'époque romantique* (Grenoble: Ellug, 2007); Anne O'Neil-Henry, *Mastering the Marketplace: Popular Literature in Nineteenth-Century France* (Lincoln, NE: Nebraska University Press, 2017); Nathalie Preiss, *Les Physiologies en France au XIXe Siècle* (Mont-de-Marsan: Editions Inter-Universitaires, 1999); Richard Sieburth, 'Same difference: the French *Physiologies*, 1840–1842', in Norman F. Cantor (ed.), *Notebooks in Cultural Analysis: An Annual Review* (Durham, NC: Duke University Press, 1984), pp. 163–99; Valérie Stiénon, 'La vie littéraire par le kaléidoscope des Physiologies', in *La Vie littéraire et artistique aux XIXe siècle* (2011) and 'Le canon littéraire au crible des physiologies', *Revue d'Histoire Littéraire de la France*, 114:1 (2014), 131–41; Victoria Thompson, *The Virtuous Marketplace: Women and Men, Money and Politics in Paris, 1830–1870* (Baltimore, MD: Johns Hopkins University Press, 2000); Judith Wechsler, *A Human Comedy: Physiognomy and Caricature in Nineteenth-Century Paris* (Chicago, IL: University of Chicago Press, 1982).
5 While I use Benjamin's foundational term 'panoramic literature' as the accepted way to refer to these texts, my understanding of these works follows recent scholarship that invites us to rethink Benjamin's somewhat reductive approach, specifically his wholesale dismissal of genres such as *physiologies* as inconsequential. For example, Martina Lauster argues for the central importance of what she calls 'metropolitan sketches' as a form of knowledge during the middle decades of the nineteenth century, while Valérie Stiénon proposes the model of kaleidoscope (rather than of panorama) for understanding these texts. See also O'Neil-Henry's contribution to this discussion in *Mastering the Marketplace*.

6 Sieburth, 'Same difference', p. 163. The Maison Aubert, run by Gabriel Aubert and Charles Philipon, also produced lithographic prints, caricatures and the well-known satirical journals *La Caricature* and *Le Charivari*.
7 Victoria Thompson outlines the commercial aims of different types of urban literature, distinguishing cheaper, smaller *physiologies* from more luxurious tomes: 'While those in its upper ranks bought the lavishly bound multi-authored *tableaux*, the inexpensive *physiologies* had a broader middle-class audience' ('Telling spatial stories: Urban space and bourgeois identity in early nineteenth-century Paris', *Journal of Modern History*, 75:3 (2003), 524). For an extensive discussion of differences between cheap *physiologies* and luxury volumes, see also O'Neil-Henry, *Mastering the Marketplace*, especially chapter 1.
8 Martyn Lyons, *A History of Reading and Writing in the Western World* (New York: Palgrave, 2010), p. 137.
9 Ferguson, *Paris as Revolution*, p. 1.
10 Christopher Prendergast, for example, notes in his groundbreaking study of nineteenth-century Paris that 'problems of readability and interpretation... are... in varying degrees of severity, problems in the history of the city throughout the whole of the nineteenth century'. See his *Paris and the Nineteenth Century*, p. 11.
11 Cohen, 'Panoramic literature', p. 228. Cohen points out that this literature not only offers objective information about details of everyday life but also, and perhaps more importantly, rhetorically performs this attention to detail: 'Giving texture to the tiniest corners of daily life, it conveys a sense of the density of everyday experience, of its lived complexity' (p. 231).
12 Gluck, *Popular Bohemia*, p. 39. My discussion here draws on Gluck's excellent analysis of the aesthetic debates pitting high culture against emerging popular culture in the 1830s. Gluck argues that these debates were inextricably linked to diverging conceptions of modernity: 'The debate raised for the first time essential questions about the nature of cultural modernity in a postromantic age. On the one side was a bourgeois conception of the modern, which valorized moral control and social deference; on the other was a frankly popular vision, which celebrated the emancipatory potential of commerce and everyday life' (p. 41).
13 Jules Janin, 'Manifeste de la jeune littérature: réponse à M. Nisard', in response to Désiré Nisard's 'D'un commencement d'une réaction contre la littérature facile', in *La Revue de Paris* (December 1833), and Sainte Beuve, 'De la littérature industrielle', in *Revue des deux mondes* (1839).
14 For a stimulating discussion of the relationship between vaudeville and melodrama, see Gluck, *Popular Bohemia*.
15 Terni, 'A genre for early mass culture', 227.
16 For an analysis of other vaudeville plays featuring the omnibus, see Chapter 3.
17 Charles Dupeuty, Frédéric De Courcy and Espérance Lassagne, *Les omnibus, ou la revue en voiture* (Paris: J.-N. Barba, 1828), p. 4.
18 Mud as a symbol of social injustice recalls Balzac's use of this metaphor in *Le père Goriot*. The landau was a vehicle known for its luxury and was associated with high aristocracy; its structure, including a convertible roof, made for maximum visibility of its occupants. The landau is still used by the British royal family on ceremonial occasions.

19 Dupeuty *et al.*, *Les omnibus*, p. 5.
20 Dupeuty *et al.*, *Les omnibus*, p. 6.
21 Richard I. Cohen explains that the figure of the Wandering Jew was widespread in France from the late eighteenth century and throughout the nineteenth century. The Wandering Jew gained particular currency during the Restoration period, becoming a veritable stock figure, with numerous images circulating in print. Eugène Sue's 1844 hugely popular novel *Le Juif errant* is the best-known example. Cohen shows that in many of these representations, the Wandering Jew appears to transcend his religious or specifically Jewish associations and instead is used to reflect social and cultural concerns of the time (p. 147). This is clearly what is in play in *L'Omnibus ou la revue en voiture*. See Richard I. Cohen, 'The "Wandering Jew" from medieval legend to modern metaphor', in Barbara Kirshenblatt-Gimblett and Jonathan Karp (eds), *The Art of Being Jewish in Modern Times* (Philadelphia, PA: University of Pennsylvania Press, 2008), pp. 147–75.
22 The play highlights the fact that its Wandering Jew is a figure from popular culture, recycled from iconography: when he first appears on stage, a coachman immediately recognises him: 'C'te tête là, je l'ai vue peinte… / Dans un'vieille complainte… / Mais vraiment, mais vraiment, C'est le Juif errant' (Dupeuty *et al.*, *Les omnibus*, p. 9) (This face, I have seen it painted somewhere/ in a medieval lament/ Look, look, it's the Wandering Jew).
23 Dupeuty *et al.*, *Les omnibus*, p. 10.
24 Dupeuty *et al.*, *Les omnibus*, p. 30.
25 Dupeuty *et al.*, *Les omnibus*, p. 30.
26 L'Opéra, along with Le Théâtre des Italiens, was frequented by 'les gens du monde', or members of high society. Anne Martin-Fugier points out that a ticket for a performance at the Opéra cost 9 francs, a sum affordable only by the very privileged. Martin-Fugier, *La Vie élégante*, p. 312.
27 Dupeuty *et al.*, *Les omnibus*, p. 32.
28 Dupeuty *et al.*, *Les omnibus*, p. 35.
29 On the social valence of the *ombrelle*, see Hiner, *Accessories to Modernity*, pp. 107–44. Unlike the *ombrelle*, the *parapluie* was firmly associated with petit-bourgeois mentality: it served 'a purely utilitarian end' and proclaimed 'ignominiously both the absence of carriage and the pedestrian bourgeois concern for protecting one's garment' (p. 113).
30 Dupeuty *et al.*, *Les omnibus*, p. 38.
31 Marcus, 'Transparence de l'appartement parisien', pp. 397–8. For more on cultural modernity, see the Introduction.
32 Cohen, 'Panoramic literature', p. 232.
33 Cohen, 'Panoramic literature', p. 232.
34 *Les omnibus. Premier voyage de Cadet la Blague de la place de la Madeleine à la Bastille et retour* (Paris: Chez Chassaignon, 1828).
35 *Les omnibus*, p. 8.
36 *Les omnibus*, p. 14.
37 It is, of course, difficult to know how popular or widely read a text like *Premier voyage* was at the time of its publication and afterwards. Yet we can surmise that

it was at least somewhat well known: Octave Uzanne, popular writer and trend-setter of the late nineteenth century, refers to this work in his beautifully illustrated history of transport, *La Locomotion à travers le temps* (1900).
38 Although not a bestseller by any means, this work appears to have enjoyed moderate success with the reading public, as evidenced by two successive editions by Flammarion (the three volumes came out in the in-octavo format in 1893, while the following year the work was published as a single in-sixteenmo volume). Short *réclames*, or advertisements, were placed in popular publications such as *Gil Blas*, *Le Rappel*, *Le Matin* and *La Nouvelle revue*. The text of the *réclame* appears to be identical across different publications. For example, the one in *Gil Blas* reads as follows: '*Contes en omnibus*, le nouveau volume d'Emile Dartès, paru chez Flammarion dans la collection des "Auteurs gais," mérite bien le succès que lui fait le public. Rien n'est amusant comme ces scènes que retrace l'auteur, comme ces petites intrigues qu'il révèle. Ajoutons que les dessins de Gorguet, Métivet et Vogel qui mettent tout cela en relief sont ravissants' (*Contes en omnibus*, the new volume by Emile Dartès, published by Flamarion in their 'Auteurs gais' series, deserves the success it enjoyed with the public. Nothing more amusing than the scenes depicted by the author, than the plots he reveals. Let us add that the illustrations by de Gorguet, Métivet and Vogel that highlight the stories are lovely) (*Gil Blas*, 18 July 1894).
39 Emile Dartès, *Contes en omnibus* (Paris: Ernest Flammarion, 1894), pp. 163–4.
40 Ernest Fouinet, 'Un voyage en omnibus de la barrière du Thrône à la barrière de l'Etoile', in *Paris, ou le livre des cent-et-un* (Paris: C. Ladvocat, 1831–34), p. 74.
41 Louis Huart, 'Les voitures publiques', p. 177.
42 Taxile Delord (1815–77) was a well-known publicist and man of letters. In addition to serving for many years as editor-in-chief of the pre-eminent satirical magazine *Le Charivari*, he contributed to such well-known collective works as *Les Français peints par eux-mêmes* and *Le Diable à Paris*. He also authored a multi-volume *Histoire du Second Empire*.
43 The authors' names do not appear on the cover. The cover simply indicates 'par les auteurs des *Mémoires de Bilboquet*'. This seems to presume that *Les Petits Paris* addresses readers familiar with popular literary productions of the time and who have already read a previous satirical work by the authors.
44 These and other stories will be discussed in detail in Chapter 4.
45 Taxile Delord, Arnould Frémy and Edmond Texier, *Paris-en-omnibus* (Paris: Librairie d'Alphonse Taride, 1854), p. 72.
46 *Paris-en-omnibus*, pp. 54–6.
47 Charles Soullier, *Les omnibus de Paris, pièce curieuse et utile à l'usage des voyageurs dans Paris, contenant une liste alphabétique des 31 omnibus, avec leurs parcours, etc., accompagnée de notes historiques et statistiques très intéressantes et d'un indicateur général des monuments, musées, etc.* (Paris: Cordier, 1863).
48 For a fascinating discussion of the instability of literary categories and generic boundaries during the July Monarchy, see O'Neil-Henry, *Mastering the Marketplace*.
49 Edouard Gourdon, *Physiologie de l'omnibus* (Paris: Terry, 1842), p. 75.

50 Gourdon, *Physiologie de l'omnibus*, p. 51.
51 Gourdon, *Physiologie de l'omnibus*, p. 86.
52 Gourdon, *Physiologie de l'omnibus*, pp. 20–1.
53 Gourdon, *Physiologie de l'omnibus*, p. 116.
54 'Les formes s'effacent et n'étaient plus qu'un rêve,/Une ébauche lente à venir,/ Sur la toile oubliée, et que l'artiste achève/Seulement par le souvenir.' Charles Baudelaire, 'Une Charogne', in *Œuvres complètes*, p. 43.

2

Transitory tales: reading the omnibus repertoire

In an 1883 article in the *Journal des Demoiselles*, writer Lucien Griveau declares that omnibus travel is essential to understanding Paris and Parisians:

> J'aime l'omnibus pour lui-même, pour sa physionomie particulière tout à fait humaine. Il est rare que je le quitte sans qu'il m'ait fourni un sujet d'observation ou de songerie. Il est un des pistons par quoi fonctionne une machine comme Paris, un des multiples agents qui concourent à son mouvement et à sa vie. Tout le jour, dans le lourd véhicule, la société défile avec sa diversité de types, chacun le souci au front ou souriant à une espérance, et, pour quiconque se plaît à rêver, une philosophie se dégage de cette gerbe de destins épars qui viennent là se nouer d'un lien léger, se toucher et se confondre une minute dans un même balancement de tête sous la trépidation des vitres.[1]

> (I like the omnibus for its own sake, for its particular physiognomy that is entirely human. It is rare that I leave it without a topic of observation or reverie. It is one of the pegs which make the machine of Paris work, one of the great agents that contribute to its movement and its functioning. Every day, the entire society and its diverse types parade through the omnibus, each with a worried face or with a hopeful smile; if you're inclined to dream, you will perceive a philosophy that emerges from this bundle of disparate destinies that come together, connect with a light bond, and mesh together for a brief moment in a matching swaying of heads, to the rattle of the windows.)

The mixed metaphors in Griveau's text illustrate some of the ways the vehicle of mass transit was deployed in omnibus literature. The personified 'human physiognomy' of the omnibus metonymically links the vehicle to its passengers, suggesting that the main interest resides in the dynamics of their fleeting interactions, in the diversity of human types from all walks of life gathered aboard, in the titillation of discovering their live stories ('destins'). From this sample of society in miniature, Griveau tells us, emerges 'une philosophie', a deeper understanding of modern life. At the same time, Griveau reminds us that the omnibus is not simply a vehicle but an essential part of the great 'machine' of Paris, fundamental to the workings of the metropolis. This passage is emblematic of how writers who invested in urban observation, such as Griveau, perceived the omnibus: as a treasure trove of storytelling material, as a boundless source of characters and plots and as a literary device to organise them. In the seemingly chaotic randomness of city life, writers found multitudes of stories about a wide range of human types all conveniently gathered along the vehicle's seats. The omnibus allowed writers to dissect the Parisian social body in all its diversity while providing an insider's guide to the changing city itself.

If the omnibus literature included a broad array of genres (city guidebooks, panoramic texts, vaudeville plays, poetry, fiction and journalism), it shared a number of features and topoi that constitute what I call the 'omnibus repertoire'. This repertoire consists of characters, scenarios or situations that were recycled in different texts across the nineteenth century. In this chapter, I focus on a selection of exemplary recurring features from the omnibus repertoire through which we can read key themes of urban modernity. From Ernest Fouinet in 1831 to Octave Uzanne in 1900, writers put the figure of the omnibus to productive literary use as a rich source for understanding and representing both the rapidly changing physical landscape of Paris and the shifting nature of post-Revolutionary French society.

The first feature I consider in this chapter is an omniscient first-person narrator I will call the 'omnibus flâneur': a character instrumental in shaping perspective and in structuring narratives that use the omnibus as their setting. The omnibus flâneur displays similar characteristics across texts and emerges as a distinct urban type. A second commonly recurring feature is the trope of the omnibus journey as a narrative vehicle to explore the changing urban environment and to give the reader a textual tour of Paris. Travelling aboard the omnibus affords the narrator an entirely fresh vision of the city. At the same time, an omnibus journey gives rise to the most common topos of the omnibus literature: using the interior as a space for social observation and the study of manners (as Griveau's passage shows). This is arguably the central aspect of omnibus literature, as it provides urban writers with a tool to showcase their skill at 'reading' the city. What is more, the omnibus setting allows for a study of multiple social types all at once. I conclude with a discussion of the omnibus as a site of chance encounters. While this type of encounter in any setting is a literary commonplace,[2] the texts that I consider here convey a broader vision of the modern urban environment as either a space of connection or estrangement.[3]

These features of omnibus literature evoke larger questions about the preoccupations and agitations of the nineteenth century: change, social flux and the instability of modern experience. The omnibus repertoire was developed in the vehicle's early years in response to transformations in the physical aspects of the city and in the social structure of post-Revolutionary France, as well as to the anxiety that these changes provoked. But even when the omnibus as a mode of transportation became outmoded, it continued to function as a medium of literary representation of the city, as shorthand for Parisian modernity with all its paradoxes. The omnibus repertoire, established during the middle decades of the century, was recycled and deployed in works through the 1880s, 1890s and into the first decade of the twentieth century. In other words, it became a topos, a literary commonplace that readers readily associated with urban observation and modernity. What is more, tales of omnibus travel allowed late-nineteenth-century writers to forge a connection with the earlier phenomenon of panoramic literature, thus granting them legitimacy as urban observers. Authors such as Guy de Maupassant, Octave Uzanne and François Coppée used omnibus travel in their works to nostalgically evoke the city of their childhood, to (sometimes ironically) appeal to readers' sense of recognition by recycling familiar tropes and to inscribe their writing within the tradition of urban literature.[4]

The omnibus flâneur

In sketching the portrait of a model flâneur in his *Physiologie*, Louis Huart writes: 'Le flaneur compose tout un roman, rien que sur la simple rencontre en omnibus d'une petite dame en voile baissée.'[5] (The flâneur makes up an entire novel from a mere trifle, like meeting a woman on the omnibus, her face covered with a veil.) It is no coincidence that Huart chooses the setting of the omnibus to describe his character's keen talent for social observation and his ability to spin a narrative out of a small detail, such as a flash encounter on a public conveyance. The omnibus flâneur can be described as a first-person male narrator-passenger through whose eyes and voice the reader textually experiences the ride. This figure is key to understanding the narrative strategies of much of the omnibus literature. The omnibus flâneur is at once familiar and new: a subset of the classical nineteenth-century figure who haunts a wide variety of nineteenth-century works of literature and visual culture, he uses mass transit as a privileged vantage point for urban observation and social commentary and for its storytelling possibilities.[6]

The flâneur hardly needs an introduction: no figure embodies nineteenth-century urban experience more fully. As Priscilla Ferguson reminds us, he is 'an emblematic representative of modernity and personification of contemporary urbanity'.[7] A detective, a leisurely city stroller, an artist and an astute reader and decipherer of the rapidly changing urban and social landscape, the flâneur was a focal point of much of the urban literature on Paris, as well as of contemporary scholarly commentary on it.

In the section of *The Arcades Project* devoted to the rich archive of nineteenth-century flâneur writing, Walter Benjamin was the first to implicitly suggest a deep link between this figure, the act of urban strolling and the experience of public transport. Over fifteen references to the Parisian omnibus appear in the 'Flâneur' section (Konvolut M), drawing on a variety of nineteenth-century French and German sources as well as Benjamin's own commentaries.[8] The omnibus flâneur not only goes 'botanizing on the asphalt', to use Benjamin's famous formulation, but also deploys the omnibus to construct a complementary vision of the city, one that brings into sharp relief a connection between the advent of early public transport and the rise of urban modernity.

In *Paris as Revolution*, Ferguson offers a compelling genealogy of the flâneur, showing how this figure's cultural valence changes over time.[9] From a negatively valued urban personage in the early nineteenth century, the flâneur evolves into a central character of the panoramic literature flourishing in the 1830s and 1840s. During this period, the flâneur becomes associated with the figure of the writer, one who possesses the superior art of observation and who, like the panoramic writer himself, is capable of deciphering the rapidly changing metropolis and unifying its disparate parts.[10]

This association reaches its apex, of course, in the work of Charles Baudelaire, for whom the flâneur is a quintessential modern poet, a privileged yet alienated interpreter of the city. However, as Ferguson shows, by mid-century and in the context of the Haussmannisation, the flâneur becomes problematised, as he now embodies the malaise and anxiety of the artist confronting urban modernity.[11] By the final decades of the nineteenth century, the association between flânerie and writing wanes, and the flâneur loses his aura of superiority and distinction. If this figure becomes democratic, it is also, to a large extent, rendered banal. As we shall see, late-nineteenth-century authors such as Maupassant used the flâneur ironically in the context of omnibus stories, uncoupling this character from writerly associations.

With this background in mind, the flâneur featured in most omnibus literature showcases his mastery over the urban and social space through narrative control. The power of the omnibus flâneur depends on his superiority in relation to his subjects (passengers, conductors and drivers), a superiority that omnibus texts establish more than one way. Unlike others who find themselves aboard public transport out of necessity, the omnibus flâneur's journey is often quite explicitly *not* motivated by a need to travel; rather, it is fuelled by a desire to observe and to explain the dramas that emerge from the interactions of the passengers within the omnibus. Consider the narrator of Edouard Gourdon's *Physiologie de l'omnibus*, who frames his stories as a type of sociological or ethnographic research, using the word 'études' (a study) or 'étudier' (to study). Introducing the omnibus station as his case study, he writes: 'Sur la rive gauche de la Seine... il est un bureau d'omnibus-modèle que j'ai souvent étudié, et que j'espère étudier longtemps encore'[12] (On the left bank of the

Seine... there is an exemplary omnibus station that I have often studied, and that I hope to study in the future). In this context, the station is not utilised for its intended purpose – waiting for public transport – but for its observational and storytelling potential. The narrator uses the word 'study' again to describe the ride: 'Comptons nos voisins et commençons nos études'[13] (Let's count our neighbours and begin our studies). He then informs his readers of his plans to dine in luxury in Neuilly, with champagne, before embarking on a leisurely stroll back home, clearly establishing his class advantage vis-à-vis other passengers and omnibus workers, for whom this would likely be unaffordable. For Gourdon, the omnibus is a vehicle of urban observation rather than transportation.

Similarly, in 'Un voyage en omnibus', Ernest Fouinet presents his upcoming journey as a tour for exploring what he calls the 'vaste repertoire-omnibus' (a vast repertoire-omnibus), the human comedy of errors he is about to observe: 'Ainsi je me préparais à ma tournée historique, philosophique et morale, en montant le marchepied de l'omnibus solitaire de la barrière du Trône.'[14] (And so I was preparing for an historical, philosophical and moral tour as I was going up the steps of a solitary omnibus at the Barrière du Trône.) The role and prerogative of the omnibus narrator are thus to bring narrative order to the chaos and dislocation of the urban environment. As Ferguson points out, 'narrative control is a function of urban possession'.[15] The omnibus interior, where passengers of different genders and social classes are thrown haphazardly together, is emblematic of urban chaos. Through his astute exploration of the social body assembled on the omnibus, the narrator-flâneur effectively achieves mastery over the otherwise disparate and anxiety-provoking crowd.

Keenly invested in investigating the everyday, fascinated with 'the moment', the omnibus flâneur successfully engages in what David Frisby calls 'a form of ethnography', excavating the hidden knowledge about the city and the metropolitan masses who inhabit it.[16] Similar to Gourdon's well-to-do flâneur-narrator, the narrator of Emile Dartès' *Contes en omnibus* (1894) descends from the omnibus at the end of each *conte* and takes a hackney cab back to his home located near the Luxembourg Gardens. Having accomplished what he set out to do, collecting material for his tales, he can now afford the luxury of taking a cab, thus distancing himself from the other passengers – the objects of his tales – who perhaps have no such choice because of their generally lower social and economic status. Dartès privileges the experience of the ride – rather than the destination – because of the storytelling possibilities he finds within. As late as 1906, in an article about omnibus conductors, poet and dramatist François Coppée explicitly presents his omnibus journey not as a necessity but as a form of social observation: 'Je prends, le plus souvent que je puis, les voitures publiques. Je les prends quand j'ai du temps devant moi, et surtout pour le plaisir de voir et d'observer les visages, car je ne connait encore rien de plus intéressant que la figure humaine.'[17] (I take public transportation as often as I can. I take it when I have a lot of time on my hands, and especially for the pleasure of seeing and observing faces, since there is nothing more interesting than a human face.) In all these instances, the omnibus flâneur casts himself as a kind of ethnographer of local culture, an explorer observing modern Paris as if it were an exotic locale. Defamiliarising the familiar allows the narrator to take a critical look at the aspects of omnibus travel that may have initially appeared too common.

Another way in which the omnibus flâneur asserts his power is by physically positioning himself in a place from which he commands an omniscient view of the interior. Ernest Fouinet, in 'Un voyage en omnibus', tells us that 'pour mieux examiner, je m'assis sur le strapontin qui est au fond. J'étais donc le *président*, c'est le terme dont se servent les habitués d'omnibus'[18] (to better examine everything, I sat on the jump-seat that is in the back. I was thus *the president*: that's the term used by regular omnibus passengers). Here Fouinet repeatedly insists on making visible the power structures that place him literally above the others, conferring authority on his observations.[19] This superior position affords him a totalising, even panoptic view: 'Je suis *président*: je vois de haut. Chef d'orchestre, régisseur de la troupe dramatique de l'omnibus, aucun son faux, aucun mauvais geste ne m'échappe'[20] (I am *president*: I see from above. Orchestra conductor, director of the omnibus theatre troupe – no false note or gesture can escape my eye). Beyond the spatial positioning of the omnibus flâneur, his power and presumption to narrate are predicated upon his often explicitly stated unrivalled capacity for social observation: a 'professional decipherer' (to use Martina Lauster's term), he knows how to read the crowd, and thus no false sound or wrong gesture escapes his critical gaze.[21]

The omnibus flâneur thus emerges as an urban type in his own right. Through his astute and frequently satirical storytelling, the omnibus flâneur establishes his authority to control both the stories and their subjects. At once part of the omnibus crowd and above it, his main task and prerogative are to interpret and render legible the often-chaotic space of the modern public conveyance and, beyond it, the modern city itself. Indeed, numerous works of popular literature deployed omnibus travel as a way to represent the changing city of Paris.

Looking out

In *Le Diable à Paris* (1846), Balzac invites his reader on a journey to explore the Parisian boulevards: 'Maintenant prenons notre vol comme si nous étions en omnibus, et suivons ce fleuve, cette seconde Seine sèche, étudions-en la physionomie'.[22] (Now let us take our flight as if we were in an omnibus, and let us follow this river – this other Seine that is dry – and let us study its physiognomy). Balzac's use of the omnibus metaphor suggests that the omnibus ride was an established trope that furnished writers with an ideal vehicle for depicting Paris, and one that offered readers a textual guided tour of streets, buildings and monuments. Omnibus literature teems with narrators and characters who embark on journeys through the streets of Paris, describing the neighbourhoods and landmarks they behold from the windows.

Indeed, descriptions of Paris through the device of omnibus travel became a regular component of the omnibus repertoire. As early as 1829, Madame de Flesselles's posthumously published didactic guide to Paris for young visitors, *Les jeunes voyageurs dans Paris*, uses this device to describe and explain famous Parisian monuments that young protagonists observe from the vehicle – an educational agenda conveyed through the playful medium of the omnibus ride. Similarly, an anonymous 1869 guidebook, *Paris en omnibus*, uses travel along the thirty-one omnibus lines as the book's organising principle. Each chapter of this pocket-size book is structured around a particular itinerary. The author sets out to create a panoramic and encyclopedic vision of the city:

> Noter, - dans un style simple et même familier, à l'occasion, – la physionomie de Paris, celle de ses différents quartiers, celle de ses monuments, celle de ses rues anciennes ou modernes; noter cette physionomie, non pas seulement au point de vue des allures, des mœurs, des habitudes, de l'industrie ou de commerce de tel ou tel quartier; rechercher quand il y a intérêt la physionomie ancienne, et même quelquefois l'histoire, mais l'histoire que tout le monde connaît et non celle qui se cache dans les manuscrits poudreux des premiers âges.[23]

> (To note – in a simple and occasionally even colloquial style – the physiognomy of Paris, that of its different neighbourhoods, its monuments, its old and new streets. To study this physiognomy from the point of view of appearance, customs, habits, industry and commerce of each neighbourhood. To research, when needed, its former appearance and even history – the history that everyone knows, rather than the one that's buried in dusty manuscripts from the olden days).

The trope of omnibus travel allows this narrator to collect and organise images of the recently Haussmannised Paris, as he painstakingly describes what he sees from the omnibus window. As an urban historian and ethnographer, he offers detailed accounts of each neighbourhood, its character and its monuments, as well as small details of everyday life. In depicting the dramatically changing city, the narrator brings out the differences and tensions between the old and the new, the past and the present, just as he emphasises the distinctly modern nature of his writing enterprise, one that privileges 'l'histoire que tout le monde connaît' (the history that everyone knows), befitting the modernity of the omnibus itself.

Written in the present tense, *Paris en omnibus* recreates in language the physical experience of touring the city from the vehicle. The narrator-observer addresses readers directly as if they were at his side, as he points out various monuments and asks them to 'look' along with him:

> Nous voici sur la Place de la Concorde; vous la connaissez de reste, aussi les Champs-Élysées.... Au point de vue de la majesté, observez un moment cette interminable avenue, la plus belle entrée de Paris. Au bout est l'Arc-de-Triomphe, et, à travers son portique, vous apercevez la statue de Napoléon Ier debout au sommet du plateau de Courbevoie. Au point de vue simplement pittoresque, remarquez, je vous prie, cette nuée continuelle de voiture qui montent ou descendent l'avenue des Champs-Élysées.[24]

> (Here we are at the Place de la Concorde; you know it well, along with the Champs-Elysées.... Observe for a moment this majestic, never ending avenue, the most beautiful entryway to Paris. At the end, there is the Arc de Triomphe, and, through its portico, you can catch sight of the statue of Napoleon I standing at the top of the Courbevoie plateau. If you would like to see something simply picturesque, ladies and gentlemen, please note the continuing flow of carriages that ride up and down the Champs-Elysées.)

Beyond this, the narrator explains the capacity of both the omnibus-vehicle and the omnibus-text to encompass the city as a transparent and visible whole, and the ambition of the omnibus-text to render it legible: '*Paris en omnibus* – du moins nous le pensons – est tout aussi lisible pour le lecteur qui veut rester chez lui; seulement pour celui-ci, ce sera *Paris dans un fauteuil*, mais le lecteur n'en aura pas moins sous les yeux tous les aspects de la grande ville'[25] (*Paris en omnibus* – at least that's what we think – can be understood by the reader who wants to stay at home; only for him it will be *Paris in an armchair*, yet he will nonetheless see all the aspects of the big city right before his eyes). In other words, the text and the city, the reader and the urban stroller, become one and the same. The reader can experience the city in real time by reading the omnibus-text just as well as by riding the omnibus-vehicle.

An 1867 thirty-one-volume series of guides to Paris by Lasserre (*Paris en omnibus, itinéraire pittoresque, historique et industriel*, likely produced for that year's World's Fair) uses a similar structure: each volume follows the itinerary of one of the omnibus lines in order to depict city sights. The conceit of one volume, for example, is that the narrator describes aloud what he sees from the omnibus for the benefit of other passengers, capitalising on having a captive and ever changing audience:

> Voilà, me dis-je, la chair véritablement populaire que je cherchais depuis si longtemps, la chair mouvante où se succède un auditoire sans cesse renouvelé, un auditoire qui peut vous donner son temps et vous prêter son oreille, un auditoire que vous pouvez désennuyer en l'occupant, que vous charmerez en l'instruisant.

Auditoire immense comme la ville elle-même, auditoire universel et démocratique dans le meilleur sens du mot, car le riche et le pauvre, l'avocat, l'homme de lettres, l'artisan se rencontrent tous sur cet égalitaire terrain.²⁶

(Here, I said to myself, is a really popular carriage for which I have been searching for a long time. The audience here succeeds one another constantly, and is endlessly renewed, an audience able to lend you its time and its ear, an audience you can entertain, keep busy, that you will enchant and educate all at once. An audience as big as the city itself, universal and democratic in the best sense of the word; everyone – the rich and the poor, a solicitor, a man of letters and an artisan – all meet on this egalitarian terrain.)

This innovative technique in Lasserre's text and other such guidebooks brings together visual and verbal modes of perception and collapses temporal distance between past and present, producing the effect of spatial presence for the reader.²⁷

Still other writers adopted the device of the public transport journey to describe and understand the city. Ernest Fouinet's 'Un voyage en omnibus' is explicitly structured as a journey between the two landmarks of the title: barrière du Thrône and barrière de l'Étoile.²⁸ The narrator provides a running commentary on the sites and curiosities he observes as the vehicle crosses the entire length of the city's right bank from east to west, wondering, for instance, about the origin of the 'appelation étrange' (strange name) of the rue Picpus, or noting the famous Elephant statue on the Place de la Bastille.²⁹ Likewise, in Victor Fournel's 1858 meditation on *flânerie*, *Ce qu'on voit dans les rues de Paris*, the narrator uses the omnibus passenger's vantage point to describe shop signs and posters visible through the windows as the vehicle makes its way across the city. Observations of such seemingly banal sights enable him to bring out the beauty of the quotidian, to 'découvrir le beau côté des choses'³⁰ (discover the beautiful side of things). His verbalised journey through the urban landscape presents the city as a legible text, open to deciphering and interpretation.

The omnibus journey was thus established as a way to textually explore Paris in urban literature from the 1830s through the 1860s and became a veritable topos in later decades of the nineteenth century. We find it most prominently in the writings of Octave Uzanne. Although this fin-de-siècle writer is especially known for his interest in fashion and for his involvement with book culture, he was also deeply engaged with the themes of modern locomotion.³¹ For Uzanne the omnibus represented both a relic of the past and a prism through which to reflect upon questions of tradition and modernity and the ways in which these two intertwined. What is more, Uzanne consciously exploited topoi of omnibus travel developed in the earlier omnibus literature in order to convey nostalgia for the past. At the same time, by reusing omnibus imagery recognisable from the literature of earlier decades, he recovered and perpetuated the omnibus as a mode of representing the city and its social landscape. The omnibus remained a metaphor for the literature of the city even as it was soon to become obsolete as a mode of transportation.[32]

Consider, for instance, Uzanne's 1900 article 'Omnibus de Paris' from *Le Monde Moderne*. The piece opens with a reflection on travel as pastime, stating that for many, exploring their own city is far superior to other kinds of travel: 'Nombreux sont les voyageurs de *Paris pour Paris*, qui, épris d'observation personnelle, et d'explorations inédites, estiment pouvoir découvrir tout en une ville'[33] (Numerous are travellers from Paris to Paris who, enamoured with personal observation and previously unseen explorations, reckon that they can discover everything in one city.) Like earlier commentators, Uzanne's narrator embarks on a kind of ethnographic journey of discovery via the omnibus. It offers him a superior vantage point for urban observation: 'Nous n'avons qu'à regarder pour tout découvrir et observer sur un simple parcours d'omnibus'[34] (All you need to do is look to discover and observe everything during a simple omnibus ride). Lamenting that the emergence of mass tourism trivialised travel to far-flung places, he proposes that one may as well explore Paris instead: 'il nous reste la possibilité d'aiguiser nos observations sur les choses pittoresques à notre portée' (we can always sharpen our observation skills on the picturesque within our reach). In fact, Uzanne claims that 'il n'est peut-être rien de supérieur au voyage trans-parisien dans nos lourdes diligences urbaines'[35] (there is perhaps nothing better than a trans-Parisian voyage in our heavy urban carriages). Through recycling of the omnibus voyage trope, Uzanne perpetuates the idea of this vehicle as a mode of 'looking out'.

The *impériale* offered the omnibus narrator a different vantage point. Once again, contemporary writers understood well the poetic potential of this method of seeing the city. In *Paris-en-omnibus* (1854), Taxile Delord evokes Victor Hugo's famous description of Paris in *Notre-Dame de Paris*, proposing a competing view of the city from the *impériale*: 'Un grand poète a donné une description de Paris *à vol d'oiseau*. Quel charmant chapitre ne ferait-on pas intitulé: *Paris du haut d'une impériale d'omnibus*! Car le boulevard, depuis la Madeleine jusqu'à la Bastille, c'est le vrai Paris, c'est Paris tout entier avec ses théâtres, ses cercles, ses cafés, ses promeneurs, ses femmes élégantes, sa population bariolée!'[36] (A great poet gave us a bird's-eye-view description of Paris. One could write a charming chapter called *Paris from the upper deck* of *the omnibus*! For the boulevard, from Madeleine to Bastille, is the real Paris, the Paris with all the theatres, rings, cafés, ramblers, elegant women and all its colourful inhabitants!) The *impériale* also allowed the narrator to peek voyeuristically inside the open windows of the buildings that line the streets, as we see in François Coppée's 1902 article 'Croquis parisiens: l'omnibus'. Here Coppée nostalgically recalls his travels on the *impériale* in his youth, travels that he claims later inspired his interest in writing about the poor whose lives he could glean through the windows:

> Ici, on dinait en famille, sous la suspension, tous les nez baissés dans la fumée de la soupe. Plus loin, un couple s'était déjà levé de table et mis à l'aise, et l'homme, à bras de chemise, fumait sa pipe, accoudé à la fenêtre auprès de sa bourgeoise, en camisole. Dans chaque intérieur, un détail, rapidement aperçu – une machine à coudre, deux verres sales près d'une bouteille, des livres sur une planche, un portrait d'homme célèbre accroché au mur – révélait toute une existence.[37]

> (Here, you see a family dining under a ceiling light, all noses inhaling the fragrance of the soup. Further on, a couple that has already left the table and made themselves comfortable, a man in shirtsleeves smoking a pipe, leaning out the window next to his spouse in a nightshirt. In each apartment, a detail quickly noticed – a sewing machine, two dirty glasses next to a bottle, some books on a shelf, a famous man's portrait on the wall – revealed life in its entirety.)

The fleeting images that the narrator glimpses through the windows supply him with material for storytelling; future stories will emerge from such details, like a pair of dirty glasses on the table, or a sewing machine. Here the omnibus is presented as a conduit to a kind of (hidden) knowledge, otherwise inaccessible.

In his 1885 short story 'Le père Mongilet', Guy de Maupassant complicates the by then accepted tropes of the omnibus flâneur and *impériale* travel as a way of exploring the city. Although the eponymous protagonist engages in flânerie, he is not a typical flâneur: a man of quality, merit and with a keen sense of vision. Here the story seems to take a mocking view of the flâneur figure: the old Mongilet is no poet, but an ordinary office clerk, one of many populating Maupassant's œuvre. There is nothing remarkable or incisive about this character – even his comically sartorial name underscores his banality, and he possesses none of the superiority of a mid-century flâneur. Here Maupassant seems to ironically appropriate the flâneur figure and his presumptive elevated artistic status by replacing him with this unexceptional character, thus subverting the figure of the omnibus flâneur with which the reader would have been familiar.

Yet flânerie is precisely the activity in which Mongilet engages from the *impériale*, where he regularly spends his leisure time: 'je grimpe sur mon impériale, j'ouvre mon ombrelle, et fouette cocher. Oh ! J'en vois, des choses, et plus que vous, allez ! Je change de quartier. C'est comme si je faisais un voyage à travers le monde, tant le peuple est différent d'une rue à une autre. Je connais mon Paris mieux que personne'[38] (And then I climb up on top of the omnibus, open my umbrella and off we go. Oh, I see lots of things, more than you, I bet! I change neighbourhoods. It is as though I were taking a journey across the world, people are so different from one street to another. I know my Paris better than anyone). Thanks to a ride on the *impériale*, Mongilet traverses the city not only geographically but also socially, as he gains privileged access – however fleeting – to neighbourhoods that people of modest station such as himself rarely penetrate.

In addition to his ironic treatment of the flâneur figure, Maupassant adds a twist to the trope of 'looking out' by reversing it: while the riders on the *impériale* enjoy the view of the city, the pedestrians, café-goers and people looking out of their apartment windows enjoy the view of the *impériale* riders. If the omnibus passengers are looking out on to the city, then the city is looking back at them, collapsing the divide between spectator and spectacle. Mongilet peers through the windows in order to witness dramas of domestic life: 'Ce qu'on voit de choses là-dedans, d'un homme qui crie; on rigole en passant devant les coiffeurs qui lâchent le nez du monsieur tout blanc de savon pour regarder dans la rue.'[39] (You would not believe what one sees in there at a glance. You can guess a scene simply by seeing the face of a man shouting; you are amused on passing by a barber's shop to see the barber leave his customer all covered with foam to look out on to the street.) I would like to dwell for a minute on this fleeting image, which perfectly captures the complexities of modern urban experience. If Mongilet looks inside a barbershop, voyeuristically seeking pleasure in random snapshots of everyday life, the barber returns his gaze, attracted by the sight of the vehicle and its passengers. Both Mongilet and the barber, the omnibus and the shop, are part of the modern urban spectacle, one in which the subject and the object of the gaze become interchangeable, and the boundaries between spectacle and spectator are irrevocably blurred. Such blurring is even more evident when we turn to another key aspect of the omnibus repertoire: the study of the omnibus interior.

Looking in

'Semblable à certains fruits dont l'écorce est rude, peu agréable à l'œil, et le Cœur savoureux et parfumé, l'omnibus renferme tous ses trésors, tout son intérêt sous sa carcasse' (Like that fruit that has a harsh and disagreeable exterior, but delicious and fragrant flesh, the omnibus conceals all its treasures, all its significance inside its frame), proclaims Gourdon in the *Physiologie de l'omnibus*.[40] Indeed, if the topos of omnibus travel is often used to describe cityscapes and to give the reader a sense of the immediate in experiencing the city, the true object of fascination is the passengers assembled inside. As a setting, the omnibus is unique in that it allows a writer to gather a wide variety of characters and plot lines within a contained space. The stream of passengers of different sexes and classes who come and go, the endless variety of human types, the vicissitudes and permutations of their often fraught interactions with each other and the fleeting glimpses of their life stories provide priceless material to the storyteller. Authors explicitly articulated the literary value of the omnibus as a space of social observation, and the stories of what transpires aboard constitute a key aspect of nineteenth-century omnibus repertoire.

Edouard Gourdon, for example, declares that the omnibus station (*bureau d'omnibus*) is far superior to other public city spaces (such as cafés, restaurants or theatres) as a setting for social observation: 'Que si, à votre arrivée dans un bureau de correspondance, vous jetez les yeux sur les personnages qui vous entourent, j'ose vous promettre, pour peu que vous ayez la bosse de l'observation, une galerie de portraits que vous chercheriez vainement autre part et des charges qui danseront longtemps dans votre esprit.'[41] (When, upon arriving at the omnibus station, you look at all the characters that surround you, I would bet you that in the event that you have a knack for observation, you will find a gallery of portraits and caricatures you would be hard-pressed to find elsewhere that will be rattling around in your mind for a long time.) The passengers here are presented as objects of scrutiny – characters, portraits – and also of satire, as the word 'caricatures' indicates, inviting in advance the reader's judgement and laughter. What distinguishes the omnibus (and omnibus station) is that the people assembled there are thrown together by chance and by necessity, rather than by choice; and so the interactions among them promise to be livelier than elsewhere.

Offering a more global vision, Emmeline Raymond notes in 'L'Omnibus', from *La Mode illustrée* (1862), that the omnibus contains a representative and comprehensive sample of the entire Parisian society, a modern-day Noah's ark:

> L'omnibus parisien est l'arche moderne; si un cataclysme quelconque venait à engloutir Paris, en respectant les omnibus qui sillonnent en tous sens, on retrouverait dans le personnel qu'ils contiennent la plupart des types humains. Toutes les races du globe, toutes les classes de la société, comme un flot continu, sans cesse renouvelé, passent dans ces voitures consacrées à *tout le monde*, ainsi que leur nom en fait foi.[42]

> (The Parisian omnibus is a modern-day ark. If one day a cataclysm engulfed Paris but spared the omnibuses that run in all directions, you would find most human types among its passengers. All races of the world, all social classes pass through these vehicles in a continuous flow that is constantly renewed – vehicles destined for *all*, as inscribed in their name.)

Raymond somewhat hyperbolically conjures up an image of the vehicle that encompasses 'tout le monde' and highlights the ever changing composition of the interior ('sans cesse renouvelé'). Yet this hyperbole is typical of the nineteenth-century conception of the 'omni-ness' of the omnibus, of its capacity to contain all of society's elements, even the most unexpected. Even Raymond's

Omnibus literature in context

assertion about racial diversity, which may at first appear far-fetched, is in fact corroborated by a nearly contemporaneous caricature by Daumier depicting a Turco soldier from North Africa surrounded by curious Parisians on a crowded omnibus (Figure 2.1). The image, inspired by a real-life regiment of Turco soldiers stationed near Paris in 1859, portrays the Turco soldier in exotic garb and typically exaggerated fashion, his extreme blackness contrasting with the whiteness of his fellow passengers, whose reactions range from fear (the little girl recoiling from him) to curiosity (two women leaning toward him). The image presents the omnibus as a space that throws the French and the foreigner together yet at the same time highlights their differences and keeps them apart.[43]

Figure 2.1 Honoré Daumier, '–N'est-il pas vrai, brave turco, que vous préférez les Françaises aux Africaines? –Chut! ... ma bonne... tu vois bien que tu vas le faire rougir!'. *Le Charivari*, 31 August 1859.

Later in the century, Octave Uzanne recycles the by then familiar image of the vehicle as a favoured site of social observation and inquiry for artists and writers:

> Les peintres y notent des expressions de physionomies variées, des attitudes, des détails de mouvements, des colorations des costumes à la mode, et les romanciers y découvrent de nombreux types vivants en qui ils incarnent leurs héroïnes; car il est peu d'endroits où l'observation des êtres soit plus facile et moins indiscrète.[44]

> (There, artists find varied facial expressions, attitudes, details of movements, colours of fashionable clothing; novelists discover numerous real-life types upon which they model their heroines; for there are few other places where observing people is easier and less indiscreet.)

Through the use of vocabulary that characterised earlier texts of urban observation – 'physionomies', 'types', 'observation' – Uzanne both evokes the conventions of panoramic literature and implicitly inscribes his own text within this tradition. He introduces a character he calls 'un voyageur-amateur', who can clearly trace his lineage to the omnibus flâneur of the 1830s and 1840s, and who undertakes the journey because of the omnibus's potential as a space of observation, noting once again that this is where society in its entirety is gathered:

> Toute la société s'y trouve plus ou moins bien échantillonnée, et l'observateur ne tarde pas à entrer en contact avec chacun des sujets qui peu à peu révèlent leur individualité par leurs gestes, leur langage, leurs façons de réclamer la correspondance, de payer, de lire le journal ou de descendre de voiture.[45]

> (All of society is more or less represented there, and an observer can quickly come into contact with each of the subjects who, little by little, reveal their personality through gestures, language, the way they ask for a transfer, pay the fare, read the newspaper or alight from the vehicle.)

Echoing Baudelaire's famous description of the flâneur's experience of the crowd in 'Les Foules',[46] Uzanne depicts the interaction of the omnibus flâneur with other passengers as a way to commune with the masses: 'au lieu de se concentrer en soi, il s'extériorise en entrant dans la vibration d'une collectivité d'individus d'autant plus intéressants qu'ils restent davantage dans le mystère de leur anonymat'[47] (instead of focusing on himself, he exteriorises by joining the community of individuals who are that much more interesting because they maintain the mystery of their anonymity). Here Uzanne revisits classic themes of modernity – crowds, anonymity – in order to draw a connection between past and present. And like his predecessors writing in the middle decades of the nineteenth century, he sets out to render legible the human 'text' he encounters on the omnibus.

Indeed, explicit references to reading and interpreting the social body gathered aboard the vehicle are a key aspect of the omnibus repertoire. The omnibus passengers, who embody the city in all its diversity, constitute the most important 'text' to be read. This aspiration to lay bare and render legible the complex fabric of the city's social composition is evident in numerous caricatures that represent the cross-section of the omnibus interior, exposing the passengers to the viewer's direct scrutiny (Figures 2.2 and 2.3). In works of popular literature, it is by focusing on small gestures, details of dress or seemingly insignificant interactions among the passengers, or by classifying passengers and omnibus workers into easily recognisable types, that narrators guide readers in understanding the complexity of the modern city.

In Gourdon's *Physiologie de l'omnibus*, for example, the narrator boasts his talent for interpreting minute signs and for deciphering the social and moral standing of omnibus passengers. He informs the reader that on a weekday it is easy to distinguish passengers from different neighbourhoods and thus from different social classes based on their attire and demeanour: 'Le voyageur de la Chaussée d'Antin n'est pas celui du Marais; le voyageur du Faubourg Saint-Germain n'est pas plus celui de la banlieue que celui de la Cité.'[48] (The passenger from the Chaussée d'Antin is not the same as the one from the Marais; the passenger from the Faubourg Saint-Germain is not the same as the one from the suburbs or the Cité.) However, on Sundays their sartorial differences are no longer obvious, and thus the lines of propriety often become scandalously blurred. The omnibus flâneur's sharp eye and keen intelligence are required to distinguish a woman of easy virtue behind the veneer of proper dress: 'L'œil exercé de l'observateur peut seul alors distinguer dans la foule les personnages qu'il cherche.'[49] (Only a well-trained observer's eye can tell the difference among a crowd of characters.) In this instance, what betrays the *lorette* (a woman of dubious virtue), he tells us, are her dirty ears, only half-concealed behind the fashionable *chapeau Herbaut*.[50] The omnibus narrator thus positions himself not only as an excellent interpreter of social clues but also as someone who upholds the established moral order by exposing those attempting to mask their lack of social and moral standing behind fashionable clothing.

In another instance, it is by 'reading' another passenger's face that Gourdon's narrator deduces her aristocratic origins, despite her modest dress: 'C'est une femme de cinquante ans; la régularité de ses traits, la finesse de son profil, révèlent une de ces noblesses d'ancienne date, dont nous ne rencontrons plus les types que dans les portraits des règnes de Louis XIV et Louis XV.' (It was a woman fifty years of age. The regularity of her facial traits, the delicacy of her profile revealed an old-line nobility, the kind we now only see in the portraits dating back to the reigns of Louis XIV and Louis XV.) The woman's mere presence aboard the public conveyance suggests that her fortunes have suffered

Transitory tales

Figure 2.2 M. de Penne, 'Le public des omnibus dans les bureaux de correspondence'. *L'Illustration*, 31 July 1868. This image represents a cross-section of omnibus stations in different Parisian neighbourhoods and brings to the fore the class diversity of passengers.

Omnibus literature in context

Figure 2.3 Honoré Daumier, *En omnibus*. 1864. In this image, Daumier stages the rich complexity of the modern experience of public transport. The viewer is placed inside the vehicle, face to face with the passengers.

dramatically in the new post-Revolutionary world order. Her countenance and comportment lead Gourdon's narrator to evoke the entire traumatic history of France following the Revolution of 1789. This is not simply a story of one woman who has likely gone from riding glamorously in 'un carrosse blasonné' (emblazoned carriage) in her youth to breathing 'l'air respiré par seize personnes plus ou moins polies et bien nées, qu'elle ne connaît pas' (the air inhaled by sixteen strangers more or less polite, more or less well born with whom she is not acquainted). The visual contrast between the mother and her daughter, seated side by side on the omnibus bench, conjures up the stark contrast between modernity and history, between past and present: 'C'est l'histoire d'une societé nouvelle greffée sur les troncs mutilés d'une societé ancienne.'[51] (It is the history of a new society grafted upon the mutilated trunk of society of the past.) Gourdon not only deftly extracts an individual history of this one passenger by treating her as a legible space, a page to be read, but also gestures to the history of an entire generation of aristocratic daughters who fell down the social ladder in the aftermath of the Revolution. In what Martina Lauster called 'the dynamic interplay between surface and depth', Gourdon expands his observations of the everyday, based on reading the surfaces (here human faces and figures, gathered aboard an omnibus), into a deeper discussion of historical forces agitating France at the time.[52]

In a similar fashion, Lucien Griveau structures 'En omnibus' to showcase the narrator's superior talent for observation and interpretation. The story focuses on the misfortunes of a young woman and her young child left destitute after the death of her husband. But even before the young woman tells her story to a compassionate *voisine d'omnibus* – and before the narrator recounts it to the reader – he infers (or imagines?) her life story by merely looking at her: 'Jeune, mais l'air fatigué, elle avait au front une ride précoce.... des traits plus fins que n'en ont généralement les filles du peuple. Mais la figure allongée, alanguie par les veilles et portant la trace des souffrances qu'amènent l'abandon et la misère, laissait deviner quelque catastrophe qui, survenues peut-être au moment où elle allât être mère, l'avait fanée avant l'âge.'[53] (Young but tired-looking, she had an untimely wrinkle across her forehead.... her face was more delicate than usually found among working-class women. But her thin face, withered by sleepless nights and bearing traces of suffering brought on by neglect and poverty, let you surmise a tragedy which perhaps struck her when she was about to become a mother, and which aged her before her time.) As a true *physionomiste*, the narrator asserts his ability to *read* the young woman's appearance for clues of not only her social class but her entire life, peeking behind the surface of her sad countenance. The rest of the story is then spun out of this brief moment of observation. Just as the young woman is a readable object of the narrator's gaze, the story of her misfortunes becomes the object of his tale.

What makes such interactions particularly seductive for the urban observer is their voyeuristic overtones. Indeed, many private human dramas played out on an omnibus are often not intended for the narrator's eyes or ears. Yet he derives a particular pleasure from the fact that the stories are surreptitiously gleaned from his fellow passengers. Seizing on the paradoxical nature of the omnibus interior that is at once public and curiously intimate, Griveau articulates the narrator's ambition and his powerful ability to uncover the secrets of other people's lives: 'Peut-être est-ce quelque drame intime qui vient s'asseoir à coté de vous. En coudoyant toutes ces existences parties de tous les bouts de l'horizon pour se rencontrer à ce point d'intersection banal, il me semble toujours être au milieu de livres fermés dont j'aurais envie de soulever la couverture.'[54] (Perhaps it is an intimate drama that just sat beside you. By rubbing shoulders with all these lives that came from all corners of the world in order to meet at this banal junction, I always feel like I am surrounded by closed books, the covers of which I wish to lift.) The narrator's role thus consists in rendering transparent and visible that which otherwise remains hidden and private: he is the one who lifts 'la couverture' and lets the reader peek under. Here Griveau seems to be playing on the double meaning of 'couverture', both 'book cover' and 'blanket', or 'bedspread.' The titillation of this 'couverture' about to be lifted is suggestive of the sexual charge that inflects both the omnibus interior where passengers congregate close together, and the omnibus narratives that delight in exploring it.

The final aspect of the omnibus repertoire focusing on the interior is the typologies of passengers and omnibus workers. Classification of social types based on observations was a hallmark of urban literature of the

1830s and 1840s. By simplifying the multiplicity of human experiences to what Judith Wechsler calls 'the satirical presentation of typical characters in everyday situations',⁵⁵ omnibus texts sought to make sense of complex modern phenomena and to control the (potentially menacing) crowds. Unlike the genre of *physiologies*, where each text focuses on a single social type (e.g. *Physiologie de l'épicier*, *Physiologie de la lorette*), or works such as *Les Français peints par eux-mêmes*, which devote a separate chapter to each type (e.g. 'La Femme adultère', 'L'Epicier'), omnibus literature is a kind of super-*physiologie*: the concept of the omnibus brings together a broad variety of social types. Once again, Gourdon's *Physiologie* is exemplary in how it presents a number of types the narrator encounters aboard the omnibus or at the station. He first affirms a kind of friendly complicity with the intended reader, presumably male and bourgeois like himself, to whose observation skills he directly appeals: 'vous le reconnaitrez sans peine'⁵⁶ (you will recognise him right away). One such type is 'le monsieur aux cheveux gris' (gentleman with grey hair), an older gentleman who spends 'les cinq sixième de sa vie en omnibus' (five sixths of his life on an omnibus) because he creepily enjoys the proximity of female passengers whose knees he can touch or whose handkerchiefs he can pick up: 'Le mouvement c'est sa vie; mais au milieu du mouvement, dans ses courses perpétuelles, il a su se créer des jouissances à lui connues, une vie pleine de péripétie, d'aventures et de far-niente à la fois.'⁵⁷ (Movement is his life; and in the midst of movement, during his perpetual rides, he managed to create pleasures known to him, a life full of adventures and of *far-niente* all at once.)

Another type we find in Gourdon is 'un poète' (a poet), a young man foisting his unpublished writings on unsuspecting female passengers. But Gourdon also ironises the very concept of type when he introduces 'Le monsieur qui fait passer l'argent' (gentleman who passes the change): '*Le monsieur qui fait passer l'argent* est un des bons types de l'omnibus. Il est jeune ou vieux, l'âge n'y fait rien. S'il a vingt-cinq ans, il porte des gants citrouille, et l'on est bien tenté de croire que c'est pour mieux les montrer qu'il avance sans cesses la main. . . . S'il a de quarante à soixante ans, le monsieur qui fait passer l'argent porte des gants de filoselle ou n'en porte pas du tout.'⁵⁸ (*Gentleman who passes the change* is a good omnibus type. He is young or old; the age doesn't matter. If he is 25 years old, he wears pumpkin-coloured gloves, and one is tempted to believe that it is in order to better show them off that he keeps extending his hand. If he is between 40 and 60 years old, the *gentleman who passes the change* wears embroidered gloves or no gloves at all.) While appearing to fit neatly into a 'type', he can in fact be anybody.

Emmeline Raymond also uses the omnibus setting to sketch a series of urban types: a polite gentlemen who helps to pass the fare and assists ladies on and off the vehicle; then his foil, 'l'égoïste renfrogné' (surly egoist), who is an inconsiderate brute ('qui essaie de se caser selon ses goûts, sans tenir compte de ses voisins; il ouvre ou ferme la vitre sans consulter la convenance d'autrui; il se pose en biais, il se penche, il s'accoude etc' (who tries to get comfortable without regard to his neighbours; he opens or closes the window without asking if it's convenient to others; he leans over, he stretches out, he sticks out his elbows, etc)); followed by 'l'homme important' (a man of importance), obsessed with making an impression on his fellow passengers. Female passengers are divided in two categories: 'celles qui parlent et celles qui ne parlent pas'[59] (those who talk and those who don't talk). But her purpose here is different from Gourdon's: if his types are satirical in nature, Raymond's have clear didactic undertones. She uses descriptions of types to critique certain kinds of behaviours in a public space and to offer prescriptive models of comportment. This take on typology befits her role as the editor-in-chief of *La Mode Illustrée*, a fashion magazine that played a central role in the articulation of ideals of bourgeois femininity in the second half of the nineteenth century. Although her regular readership was overwhelmingly female, in this article Raymond goes beyond offering advice on proper behaviour to women only and extends it to male passengers as well.

Octave Uzanne both recycles and extends a familiar topos by developing an extensive typology, first of the different types of omnibus lines and then of their passengers. He begins by introducing different types of omnibus lines. There is, for example, 'L'omnibus *populo*', which transports primarily working-class passengers. Then there is a line that Uzanne designates as '*demi-chic*, c'est-à-dire populaire au point de départ et se mondanisant, s'embourgeoisant en arrivant au centre de Paris' (*demi-chic*: that is, it is working-class at the point of departure but gentrifies when it arrives in the centre of Paris). But the omnibus that Uzanne declares his favourite is the Batignolles-Clichy–Odéon line, because it serves as a unifying link between the artistic and the aristocratic parts of Paris that are normally separated by geographic, economic and social distances; this line 'réconcilie Montmartre avec le faubourg Saint-Germain, le quartier Latin et la rue des Martyrs' (reconciles Montmartre with the faubourg Saint-Germain, the Latin Quarter and the rue des Martyrs). In doing so, it serves as a kind of bridge between different social worlds: 'Le grand transurbain, qui va du second au premier théâtre français, du restaurant *Foyot* au *Père Lathuille*, du Luxembourg à la place Clichy'[60] (The great trans-urban vehicle that travels from second-tier theatres to those of the first tier, from the restaurant *Foyot* to *Père Lathuille*, from Luxembourg to Place Clichy). The classification of the vehicle is followed by a detailed typology of the omnibus driver ('le muet et le bavard' (the mute and the chatty)), the conductor ('le poli, le gallant, le sans-façon, le débraillé, puis l'ahuri' (the polite, the courteous, the cavalier, the dishevelled, the halfwit)) and the passengers.[61] Among the male passengers Uzanne notes 'de grognons, d'expansifs, de familiers, d'impénétrables'[62] (the grumblers, the effusives, the informals, the inscrutables). He singles out his preferred type, '*le plate-formiste*, l'amateur spécial de la plate-forme, considérant ce *look-out* comme le poste le plus favorable à l'observation et à l'occasion' (*the platformist*, an enthusiast of the platform, who considered this *look-out* as a post particularly favourable to observation), a character not unlike the omnibus flâneur himself, who uses the vehicle's landing for watching other passengers, and women in particular. As for the women passengers, Uzanne offers an unapologetically gendered typology, classifying them according to their attitudes or responses to the attention bestowed upon them by fellow male passengers:

> *L'indifférente*, habituée aux hommages, et qui ne semble plus avoir conscience des regards qui la dévisage; puis *la timide*, qui ne sait où se fourrer, rougit, pâlit, prend des attitudes gauches exprimant son trouble et qui finit, pour échapper à ces yeux braqués vers elle, par feindre le sommeil ou la lecture passionnante; enfin, *la coquette*, qui, selon ses avantages, pose volontiers devant les objectifs, de profil ou de face, soupirant doucement, ôtant ses gants, montrant ses doigts fuselés chargés de bagues, s'appliquant à augmenter encore davantage l'admiration qu'elle sait inspirer.[63]

> (The *indifferent*, one who is used to compliments, and who seems not to notice the stares she is attracting; then the *shy* one, who doesn't know where to hide, who blushes, turns pale, who takes awkward poses that express her discomfort and who, in order to avoid all those eyes glued to her, ends up faking sleep or reading. Finally, the *flirt*, who, depending on what charms she possesses, gladly poses before the cameras, in profile or *en facei*, sighing gently, taking off her gloves, showing off her slender fingers adorned with rings, and seeking to amplify even more the admiration that she inspires.)

The final type Uzanne introduces is the *plongeur*. The *plongeur* is a kind of urban observer who likes to peek in the windows of apartment buildings lining the streets: 'le voici... Plongeant dans les intérieurs des maisons, assistants aux fins diners en bras de chemises, aux lits préparés, aux étranges ombres chinoises projetées sur les rideaux lumineux des fenêtres closes, aux déshabillés imprévus, à toute la fantasmagorie de la vie des autres fortuitement surprise au passage' (here he is... Plunging his gaze inside houses, joining fancy dinners in shirtsleeves, joining beds that are all ready, attending strange Chinese shadows projected upon drawn window curtains, catching unexpected glimpses of flesh and all the phantasmagoria of the lives of others fortuitously gleaned in passing). The omnibus provides a privileged vantage point for this visual penetration into domestic interiors. Yet, Uzanne claims (rather disingenuously), the *plongeur* is not a voyeur or a libertine but rather an observer interested in a broad range of human experiences: 'Tout en fumant son cigare, dans une rêverie de digestion, il se croit un petit Asmodée pénétrant de ménage en ménage, chez le riche et chez le pauvre, partout insoupçonné, dans ces magasins ou ces entresols où chacun se croit si bien à l'abri des indiscrétions'[64] (Smoking a cigar and absorbed by the digestion, he fancies himself a little Asmodeus who goes undetected to households both rich and poor, and to shops and mezzanines where one believes to be sheltered from indiscretions.) A devil-like figure who first appears in Lesage's 1707 *Le Diable boiteux*, where he peeks inside Parisian houses by removing their roofs, Asmodeus was a frequent reference point for urban literature of the 1830s and 1840s. This figure encapsulated the idea of rendering visible and legible that which was otherwise hidden to the eyes of the uninitiated, revealing the city's secrets through visual superiority. By gesturing toward this iconic figure, Uzanne inscribes his text within the lineage of earlier literature of urban observation.[65]

In addition to the typology of passengers, the omnibus repertoire includes that of omnibus workers, such as the conductor, the ticket master (*le buraliste*) and the driver, as well as of passengers.[66] Like the vehicle itself, these occupations were new and modern when they began to appear in literature, and they thus elicited both fascination and discomfort. In particular, the conductor became a popular subject, providing important clues to cultural anxieties about new modes of labour and the rise of industrialisation that the omnibus emblematised. The conductor is often represented as a small, dehumanised peg in an enormous urban machine; more than any other character, he embodies the excesses of rising capitalism. For example, Charles Friès in 'Le Conducteur d'omnibus' (from *Les Français peints par eux-mêmes*), highlights the dreary monotony and repetitive nature of the conductor's work, comparing his fate to that of a galley slave:

> C'est une triste destinée que celle du conducteur d'omnibus. D'un bout de l'année à l'autre, on le voit, rivé à son marche-pied comme le forçat l'est à sa chaîne, poursuivre son éternel pèlerinage à travers les mêmes rues, les mêmes quais, les mêmes boulevards. La pluie, le vent, le froid, la grêle, rien n'arrête dans sa course ce juif errant d'un nouveau genre. Pour lui, jamais de répit ! Marche ! Marche ! tel est le cri qui bourdonne sans relâche aux oreilles de ce malheureux qu'on a plaisamment qualifié d'image vivante du *repos* dans le *mouvement*.[67]

> (The fate of the omnibus conductor is a sad one. From the beginning of the year to the end, we see him cling to the running board like a convict to his chain, carrying on his eternal pilgrimage along the same streets, the same embankments, the same boulevards. Rain, wind, cold, hail – nothing stops in his course this new kind of Wandering Jew. For him, not a moment of rest! Go on! Go on! This is the scream that rings relentlessly in the ears of this wretched man who is pleasantly described as the picture of *rest* in the midst of *movement*.)

Taxile Delord paints a similar image of the conductor in *Paris-en-omnibus*, depicting him as a depressive type: 'Je conçois la morne tristesse et l'abattement dans lesquels les conducteurs d'omnibus sont presque constamment plongés'[68] (I appreciate the dreary sadness and despondency in which omnibus conductors are almost always immersed). And, as late as 1906, François Coppée devotes an entire article to the conductor in which he too bemoans his fate and praises him for deep devotion to his job. Coppée particularly admires the conductor's endless patience and civility even when faced with the most difficult work conditions: 'Et cela dans les pires circonstances, même sous l'averse diluvienne, quand les voyageurs à parapluie attaquent la voiture, pareils aux légionnaires romains donnant l'assaut à l'abri de leurs boucliers et exécutant la célèbre manœuvre de la tortue'[69] (And this even under the worst of circumstances, even under diluvial downpour, when umbrella-wielding passengers attack the vehicle, similar to Roman legionnaires attacking under the cover of their shields and executing the famous tortoise formation.) It is as if the conductor became the receptacle of all of urban misery, aggression and anomie. Unlike many other omnibus types, the conductor is often represented with a great degree of empathy, reflecting perhaps the authors' own anxiety about changing labour practices ushered in by modernity.

Writers from across the nineteenth century put the omnibus to literary use as a medium of social observation and a tool to render legible the changing urban environment reflective of a society in flux. These modes of writing constituted essential elements of the omnibus repertoire. Other features of this repertoire bring into relief the modern city and modernity by holding the tension between connection and estrangement, social bonds and alienation.

Connection and estrangement

The omnibus repertoire includes recurring scenarios indicative of broader visions of Parisian urban space, and what we find is two diametrically opposed approaches to the urban environment. For some, Paris was a place of alienation and disconnection, a city dominated by a breakdown of communication and social relationships, a place where inhabitants came into fleeting contact only to never see each other again. For others, on the contrary, it was a world where individual connections and felicitous chance encounters were possible and led to lasting attachments.[70] It was through the figure of the omnibus that urban writers could propose these two contrasting visions of the modern city – and, more broadly, modernity – that were key to the nineteenth-century cultural imaginary. If some works of omnibus literature represented Paris as a space of estrangement, characterised by indifference, alienation and dislocation, others depicted it as a place of connection, full of (often happy) coincidences epitomising the interconnectedness of individuals of all walks of life. These two competing visions were represented by scenes of chance encounters on the omnibus, sometimes within the same text.

In the first scenario, encounters between strangers lead to a momentary connection – or the potential for connection – that lasts as long as the omnibus ride. The speed, motion, flux and anonymity associated with modern transport work to preclude deep human bonds, and so unrealised connections became a key feature of the omnibus repertoire. A vignette in Fouinet's 'Un voyage en omnibus' exemplifies the vision of the city as a space of estrangement. This vignette evokes the fleeting nature of omnibus encounters as the narrator describes a beautiful young woman who boards the vehicle and immediately captures his imagination. She seems like a magical apparition: 'Une femme aux cheveux châtains-bruns, aux yeux noirs, au teint pâle, vêtue d'une robe de mousseline claire, de couleur tendre; un petit être délicat, vaporeux, svelte créature, qu'un poète, un peintre aurait à peine besoin d'idéaliser pour en faire une bonne fée ou un ange.'[71] (A woman with light-brown hair, black eyes, pale skin, clad in a light-coloured muslin dress; a delicate little person, a diaphanous, slender creature; a poet or an artist would not need to idealise her to turn her into a good fairy or an angel.) She is described as an ideal beauty with pale skin and dark hair and her clothes and the light colours of her dress suggest elegance and virtue. The young woman affects the narrator not only visually but olfactorily as well: 'et de sa robe, de ses cheveux, de son mouchoir... montait jusqu'à moi un léger parfum de vétiver, de portugal, de violette, un parfum végétal'[72] (from her dress, her hair, her handkerchief emanated a light perfume of vetiver, portugal, violet, a perfume of plants). These flowery and exotic scents stand in sharp contrast with the reality of public transport.

Fouinet's narrator delights when their hands touch as he asks the lovely passenger to pass the fare to the conductor. When she drops the change in his hand, he vows to use it exclusively for the 'achat d'un objet parfumé, élégant' (the purchase of a perfumed, elegant object) such as a bottle of perfume or gloves for a ball. He then describes his anguish when a red-faced drunkard places himself too close to her: 'Cette figure d'un rouge livide, aux traits déformés par la débauche, si près de ce visage d'une blancheur transparente.... Hideuse alliance! Un beau rayon de soleil sur une mare fangeuse! Une chenille, un scarabée sur une rose ou une sensitive.'[73] (This livid, red figure, with features distorted by debauchery, so close to the transparent whiteness of her face! Hideous alliance! A beautiful ray of sun on a muddy pond! A caterpillar, a beetle on top of a rose or a mimosa.)

Eventually the anonymous beauty steps off the omnibus, and the narrator, in the throes of deep melancholy, is left to ruminate about the encounter in terms strikingly anticipating Baudelaire's 'A une passante', the best-known poem of chance encounter and unrealised, unrequited urban love: 'Pourquoi étais-je triste? Avait-elle seulement fait attention à moi? J'avais fait attention à elle, j'avais été heureux de la voir; c'en était assez pour que je regrettasse de la perdre, presque sûr de ne plus la retrouver.' (Why was I sad? Did she even pay attention to me? I paid attention to her; I was happy to behold her; this was enough for me to regret losing her, almost certain to never see her again.) This experience of loss is by no means unique, Fouinet writes. Rather, it is emblematic of the alienation of urban life, where a momentary promise of happiness comes to naught: 'Qui n'a pas vu passer dans sa vie, une femme dont il s'était dit:- Je l'aimerais à jamais. –Et il revenait cent fois sur le chemin où il l'avait rencontrée, et vainement toujours.' (Is there a man who has not experienced seeing a woman pass by, thinking to himself that he could love her forever. And he would return a hundred times to the spot where he had met her, and always in vain.) Ultimately, the omnibus serves as a metaphor for life, in all its isolation and indifference: 'O omnibus! quel philosophe tu es!'[74] (Oh omnibus! You are so philosophical!). And the narrator too moves on to the next object of observation.

A whimsical short story by Paul Gavarni titled 'Une aventure d'omnibus' offers a satirical yet bitter view on the romantic potential of omnibus encounters.[75] In this story, the protagonist, a poet named Numance, meets a beautiful, witty aristocratic lady aboard an omnibus, where both have been summoned by the Devil, who momentarily takes the conductor's place. The poet follows the lady when she leaves the omnibus and asks her for a rendezvous, which she reluctantly grants. When Numance arrives at the assignation, he is handed a note from his beloved which reads: 'Un des plus doux plaisirs d'une femme est de faire un regret.'[76] (One of the sweetest pleasures a woman can have is to cause a regret.) While Numance is consumed with humiliation and despair ('il crut un instant qu'il allait pleurer' (he thought for a moment that he was going to cry)), the narrator tells us that the lady, who happens to be a duchess, has but one eye, a detail that escaped the young lover even though he was sitting right next to her on the omnibus: 'La duchesse de Margueray est borgne du côté droit; mais elle a le profil délicieux, et Numance était placé à sa gauche dans la voiture.' (The duchess of Margueray was blind on the right side; but she had a lovely profile and Numance was sitting to her left in the vehicle.) The story not only exemplifies a sense of alienation, separation and the fleeting nature of romance in the urban environment but also illustrates the unknowability of others: although Numance sat right next to the lady, she remained an enigma to him, concealing her name, her social status and her deformity.[77]

By contrast with these plots of dislocation, alienation and romantic failure, other documents used the omnibus to illustrate their vision of the city as a space of connections, full of unexpected associations and possibilities. In this scenario, the compact area of the omnibus and the physical intimacy it creates foster human relations. As the city of Paris grew exponentially over the course of the nineteenth century, perhaps this was a way to make the growth and constant influx of population less menacing. Here I want to focus on two recurring scenarios of the omnibus repertoire: a chance meeting between a creditor and a debtor, and a romantic chance encounter leading to marriage.

The omnibus as a setting for chance meetings between a creditor and a debtor trying to dodge payment was used to comic effect across a variety of popular genres. Its first mention appears virtually at the same time as the omnibus itself, in Léon Gozlan's 1828 poem *Le Triomphe des Omnibus*: 'Cette porte béante incessamment ouverte/ Au pauvre débiteur à deux doigts de sa perte/ Quand un dur créancer, la sentence à la main,/ Escorté d'un recor, parait sur son chemin'[78] (This door constantly wide open/ To a poor debtor two steps away from his downfall/ When a harsh creditor, a verdict in hand/ Blocks his way). The social worlds of the young dandy living beyond his means and the merchants who supply his luxury articles did not typically overlap, and the delinquent dandy ran no risk of ever having to face his creditors. The omnibus by its very nature, however, brought together individuals of different social strata. It thus became a convenient trap for the dandy, who usually boarded the omnibus when he lacked funds for a cab, and so was forced to confront his irate supplier under circumstances from which he cannot escape. In 'Un voyage en omnibus', Fouinet imagines the unfolding of this encounter as a theatrical mise-en-scène:

> Un débiteur va se trouver nez à nez avec son créancier qu'il fuyait depuis un an. N'est-il pas divertissant de voir toutes les ruses pour cacher sa figure: c'est l'œil droit, c'est l'œil gauche; le nez à essuyer, un mal de dents subit qui le force à couvrir sa joue de son mouchoir; mais le créancier à la piste, qui reconnaîtrait son débiteur dans une ride comme Cuvier reconnait un animal antédiluvien dans un ossement, le créancier le saisit au collet: dialogue chaud, animé, brûlant.[79]

> (A debtor finds himself face to face with his creditor, whom he has been avoiding for a year. Isn't it entertaining to see all the ruses he deploys to hide his face: he turns this way and that way; a nose to blow or a sudden toothache force him to cover his cheek with a handkerchief. But the creditor on his trail recognises his debtor like Cuvier recognises an antediluvian animal in a fossil; the creditor grabs him by the collar: a heated, lively, burning dialogue ensues.)

Here the debt dodger goes to great lengths to hide from his nemesis, but the space of the omnibus does not allow this. The narrator clearly delights in the scene, which he finds 'divertissant' both for other riders and for readers. A visual pendant to Fouinet's account can be found in Daumier's 1843 caricature 'Une Rencontre désagréable' (Figure 2.4), featuring a fashionable young gentleman confronted by his tailor: '–Je ne me trompe pas! . . . c'est M. Alfred . . . pourriez-vous me dire quand vous me donnerez un acompte sur la petite note de neuf cent francs que vous me devez depuis trois ans? . . . . –Que le diable emporte l'omnibus et le tailleur! . . . j'aurais bien mieux fait de prendre un cabriolet!' (I am not mistaken. . . this is Monsieur Alfred. . . could you

Figure 2.4 Honoré Daumier, 'Une rencontre désagréable'. *La Comédie humaine*, 1843.

please tell me when you will be so kind as to settle the little bill for 900 francs you've owed me for three years? ... To hell with the omnibus and the tailor! ... I should have taken a cab!)

The image draws a sharp visual contrast between the young man's stylish white coat and black vest, and the tailor's black coat and white vest, presenting them as each other's foil. While the tall young dandy is carefully coiffed, sports fashionable accessories (the cane, the hat, elegant shoes) and dominates the image through both size and colour, the tailor literally shrinks into his seat, looking frumpy with his wrinkled clothes and balding head, as he modestly clutches his hat on his lap. The young man clearly attempts to ignore the tailor by turning his head away from his nemesis and toward his seatmate on the other side. Yet, with his hand creeping toward the dandy as if to grab him, it is the tailor who has the advantage in this situation, for the young man is obviously held captive by the moving vehicle. Daumier's caricature visually reiterates the scenario we find in literature. Depicted as a space of connection, the omnibus throws together people belonging to different social spheres, here against one of them's wishes.[80]

A different take on the omnibus as an urban space of connection involves budding romance that leads to marriage. While the omnibus was most often associated with illicit female sexuality, such as adultery and prostitution,[81] the 1880s and 1890s see a veritable explosion of popular songs about strangers who fall in love during a journey, with a happy marriage to follow. We find variations on this scenario in several songs intended for cabaret and café-concert performances, such as 'Le Conducteur et la couturière' (1892), 'L'Omnibus des Amours' (1886) and 'Les Amours d'un cocher d'omnibus' (1886). 'Le Conducteur et la couturière' tells a predictable story of a romance between an omnibus conductor and a dressmaker who rides to work every morning. After months of mutual silent admiration, the two protagonists confess their love to each other. Their marriage speedily follows:

> Sans plus tarder, ils s'épousèrent,
> Et si tendrement ils s'aimèrent,
> Qu'en trois ans il eur' quatre enfant
> Telle est l'histoire simp'e et belle
> D'un' couturièr, d'un conducteur,
> Qui, s'aimant d'un amour fidèle,
> Sur la ligne Panthéon-Courcelles,
> Tous deux ont trouvé le bonheur![82]

> (Without tarrying they married
> And loved each other so well
> That in three years they had four kids
> Such is this story, simple and lovely
> Of a seamstress and a conductor
> Who loved each other well
> On the Pantheon-Courcelles line
> They found their happiness!)

Sometimes the omnibus quite literally brings the lovers together. In 'Un mariage en omnibus' (1882), a young woman meets her future husband when the omnibus stops short and she stumbles into his arms: 'J'étais près de la sonnerie,/ Près d'un jeune homme en chapeau rond,/ Assez gai de physionomie/ Soudain un choc m'envoie sur lui'[83] (I was next to the bell,/ Next to a young man in a round hat,/ Looking content / Suddenly a jolt sends me toward him) (Figure 2.5). With the next jolt, it is the young man who falls into her arms. At the end of the suggestively bumpy ride, the young man helps the young lady down from the vehicle and is ready to propose: 'Je viens de vous offrir ma main, Voulez-vous m'accorder la vôtre?' (I just offered you my hand,/Would you

Figure 2.5 'Un mariage en omnibus'. 1882. Cover, sheet-music score.

grant me yours?). The song playfully if improbably suggests that the omnibus can breed lasting relationships. In 'Mon voisin d'omnibus' (1888), the female protagonist, on her way to visit her aunt, realises in dismay that she left her purse at home.[84] An obliging young man offers to pay her fare while confessing his instant love to her: 'Mon voisin m'a dit tout bas: je t'aime! Voilà six sous' (My seatmate whispers quietly: I love you! Here are 6 *sous*). The young lady never makes it to her aunt that day, and although the lyrics imply that their love is improperly consummated ('Et je pris le parti de rire, en remettant

Figure 2.6 'Mon voisin d'omnibus'. 1888. Cover, sheet-music score.

au lendemain, D'aller chez ma tante' (I decided to have fun, and postponed the visit to my aunt till the next day)), the image that accompanies the song depicts a wedding, suggesting that all ends well, and social order is restored[85] (Figure 2.6). The proliferation of songs thematising chance encounters on the omnibus testifies to just how ingrained this idea was in the cultural imagination by the end of the century.

From the first days of omnibus travel, authors of urban literature used the vehicle to engage with the city in transition and with a dramatically shifting social landscape. The tropes and figures examined in this chapter emerged as part of the vibrant panoramic literature of the 1830s and 1840s that deployed the omnibus as a mode of representation, a form through which to capture multiple aspects of the modern and the everyday. Writers across genres and styles adopted the omnibus as a way to communicate their vision of Paris. The omnibus penetrated the French literary and cultural imagination, becoming an integral concept and topos for addressing key questions about contemporary life. And nineteenth-century writers understood well the value of the omnibus, capitalising on it to appeal to popular audiences. Emile Dartès proclaimed that had the omnibus not existed, it would have been necessary to invent it: 'Ainsi je conclurai en disant que l'institution des omnibus parisiens est une noble institution qu'il faudrait inventer s'il n'existait pas.'[86] (And so I conclude by saying that the institution of the Parisian omnibus is a noble one, and had it not existed already it would have had to be invented.)

If the omnibus texts share a common repertoire, they also share cultural and social preoccupations key to understanding nineteenth-century French society: social mobility and elusive class equality, as well as shifting gender relations and the impact of the changing urban environment on women's place in society. As we shall see in the following chapters, the omnibus was a figure through which different forms of popular literature grappled with tensions generated by these questions.

Notes

1 Lucien Griveau, 'En omnibus', *Journal des Demoiselles*, 51:2 (1883), 48.
2 For a stimulating discussion of the topos of the chance meetings in carriages in literature from the eighteenth to the twentieth centuries, see Carsten Meiner, *Le carrosse littéraire et l'invention du hasard* (Paris: Presses Universitaires de France, 2008).
3 In an article on Galdós's 'La novella en el tranvía', Elizabeth Amann proposes that nineteenth-century works about public transit are organised around the following four dichotomies: inside/outside, small/large world, sound on/off and legible/illegible. Amann also rightly states that Galdós's novella (set in Madrid), published in 1871, draws on the nineteenth-century French literary tradition of representing public transport. See Elizabeth Amann, 'Reading (on) the tram: Benito Péres Galdós's "La novella en el tranvía"', *Orbis Litterarium*, 69:3 (2014), 193–214, especially 195–6.

4 Here I focus on the aesthetic and ideological aspects of the omnibus repertoire. But there were certainly economic reasons for literary recycling of the omnibus topos. Throughout the nineteenth century, writers deployed the device of the omnibus because they knew that it appealed to readers and therefore their works would sell well. For a lively discussion of the place of recycling in the literary marketplace, see O'Neil-Henry, *Mastering the Marketplace*.

5 Louis Huart, *Physiologie du flâneur* (Paris: Aubert, 1841), p. 55. Note the spelling of the word 'flâneur'. According to Priscilla Ferguson, in the early nineteenth century, when the word 'flâneur' first emerged, it appeared without the circumflex. The early iterations of this character have almost universally negative connotations. However, the flâneur soon changes both connotation and spelling: 'The circumflex accent that the word usually acquires signals a redefinition through a change of perspective. Instead of prompting a negative moral judgement, the flâneur's conspicuous inaction comes to be taken as positive evidence of both social status and superior thought.' Ferguson, *Paris as Revolution*, pp. 82–3. *Physiologie du flâneur* must have appeared on the cusp of this transition. I maintain the circumflex in the English translation for the sake of consistency.

6 Here my analysis diverges from that of Karlheinz Stierle. Although Stierle identifies the omnibus and the flâneur as two phenomena that embody the essence of the city during the July Monarchy, he makes a sharp distinction between the experience of public transport and that of a flâneur: 'En refusant l'expérience de la ville que permet l'omnibus, le flâneur acquiert son profil spécifique. Le flâneur est ce promeneur citadin philosophe, qui se refuse par principe au transport collectif en omnibus. Tandis que le passage d'omnibus est défini par son but et que le chemin de ce but ne signifie pour lui qu'une distance abstraite, c'est le chemin lui-même qui est le but pour le flâneur.' (By refusing the experience of the city afforded by the omnibus, the flâneur acquires his specificity. The flâneur is an urban philosopher-stroller who rejects, on principle, public transportation such as the omnibus. While the omnibus trajectory is defined by its destination, and the path to this destination is but an abstract distance, for the flâneur the path itself is the destination.) Karlheinz Stierle, *La Capitale des signes: Paris et son discours* (Paris: La Maison des Sciences des Hommes, 2001), p. 127. My analysis of the crucial link between the flâneur and the omnibus and the material I present in this book offer a necessary correction to this view.

7 Priscilla Parkhurst Ferguson, 'The flâneur on and off the streets of Paris', in Keith Tester (ed.), *The Flâneur* (London: Routledge, 1994), p. 22.

8 Walter Benjamin, *The Arcades Project*, trans. Howard Eiland and Kevin McLaughlin (Cambridge, MA: Harvard University Press, 2002), pp. 424–34.

9 Ferguson, *Paris as Revolution*, pp. 80–106.

10 Ferguson writes: 'It was not by chance that the flâneur appeared on the streets and in the narratives of early nineteenth-century Paris. The post-Revolutionary city both invited and required new urban practices. The disarray engendered by continually shifting political and social bases, like the incertitude fostered by a constantly fluctuating population, undermined the sense of the city as a whole. The narratives of a ubiquitous flâneur joined otherwise separate parts.' *Paris as Revolution*, p. 112.

Omnibus literature in context

11 Although the discussion of the concept of the flâneur goes beyond the scope of this chapter, it is worth mentioning that this figure came to signify different things for different scholars. For Elisabeth Wilson, the flâneur is a 'mythological or allegorical figure who represented what was perhaps the most characteristic response of all to the wholly new forms of life that seemed to be developing: ambivalence' (p. 96), rather than a description of male experience of/in the city. Wilson sees the flâneur as a figure of ambiguity and of anxieties about modern experience, and even of the crisis of masculinity; for Griselda Pollock, the flâneur is the embodiment of patriarchal power; and for Priscilla Ferguson, the flâneur is a strategy of representation. See Elisabeth Wilson, 'The invisible flâneur', *New Left Review*, I:191 (1994), 90–110; Griselda Pollock, *Vision and Difference: Femininity, Feminism and the Histories of Art* (London: Routledge, 1988); Ferguson, *Paris as Revolution*. For recent discussions of sensory aspects of the flâneur experience, see 'Le flâneur and the senses', Aimée Boutin (ed.), *Dix-Neuf: Journal of the Society of Dix-Neuviémistes*, 16:2 (2012); and Aimée Boutin, *City of Noise: Sound and Nineteenth-Century Paris* (Urbana, IL: University of Illinois Press, 2015).
12 Gourdon, *Physiologie de l'omnibus*, p. 18.
13 Gourdon, *Physiologie de l'omnibus*, p. 68.
14 Ernest Fouinet, 'Un voyage en omnibus', p. 62.
15 Ferguson, *Paris as Revolution*, p. 93.
16 David Frisby, 'The flâneur in social theory,' in Tester (ed.), *The Flâneur*, p. 97. Frisby uses the term to draw a parallel between Benjamin's approach to archival research and the work of a nineteenth-century flâneur himself.
17 François Coppée, 'Physionomies parisiennes: le conducteur de l'omnibus', *Les annales politiques et littéraires*, 1200 (24 June 1906).
18 Fouinet, 'Un voyage en omnibus', p. 67. Italics in the original.
19 Although the word 'président' did not have the modern connotation of political power when Fouinet's text was written, it nevertheless denoted a person in a position of authority.
20 Fouinet, 'Un voyage en omnibus', p. 69. Italics in the original.
21 Lauster, *Sketches of the Nineteenth Century*, p. 9.
22 Honoré de Balzac, 'Histoire et physiologie des Boulevards de Paris. De la Madeleine à la Bastille', in *Le Diable à Paris*, 2 vols (Paris: Hetzel, 1845–46), vol. 2 (1846), p. 92.
23 *Paris en omnibus. Guide familier dans le Paris de 1869 (Paris Ancien et Paris Nouveau) par un simple voyageur en omnibus, en chemin de ceinture et en bateau mouche indiquant les rencontres et les correspondances de ces divers modes de locomotion dans Paris* (Paris: Chez les principaux libraires et dans tous les bureaux d'omnibus, 1869), p. v.
24 *Paris en omnibus*, pp. 261–2.
25 *Paris en omnibus*, p. v.
26 Lasserre, *Paris en omnibus, itinéraire pittoresque, historique et industriel. Ligne H, de l'Odéon à Clichy* (Paris: A. Parent, 1867), p. vii.
27 In her chapter on 'The mobile observer: sketches and optical media' in *Sketches of the Nineteenth Century*, Lauster shows the connection between travelogues of the 1830s and 1840s and popular forms of entertainment such as panoramas and

dioramas. She argues that these contemporary visual media served as intertext for some of the descriptive texts of Paris.

28 Barrière du Thrône (located near the current Place de la Nation) and barrière de l'Etoile (located near Place de l'Etoile) were built as entry points for royal processions.
29 Ernest Fouinet, 'Un voyage en omnibus', pp. 63, 67.
30 Victor Fournel, *Ce qu'on voit dans les rues de Paris* (Paris: Delahays, 1858), p. 284.
31 On Uzanne, see Willa Silverman, *The New Bibliopolis, French Book Collectors and the Culture of Print, 1880–1914* (Toronto: University of Toronto Press, 2008).
32 Uzanne wrote extensively about transportation. In 1895, he published 'Perspective d'avenir: la locomotion future' (illustrated by Albert Robida) in *Le Monde Moderne* in which he expressed his admiration for the automobile as a vehicle of the future. In 1900, he published *La Locomotion à travers le temps, les mœurs et l'espace. Résumé pittoresque et anecdotique de l'histoire générale des moyens de transports terrestres et aériens* (Paris: Librairies Paul Ollendorf, 1900), a beautiful luxury volume with numerous illustrations and engravings, containing an overview of different modes of transportation throughout history. That same year, Uzanne published a long essay titled 'Omnibus de Paris' in *Le Monde Moderne*. Both pieces appeared in anticipation of the World's Fair of 1900, an event aimed at showcasing technological achievements of the final years of the nineteenth century, including the Paris metro, moving pictures, electric trains and motorcars, and ushering in a new century that promised to build on these successes. Uzanne's writings about transportation fit in well with his aesthetic and intellectual interests, such as fashion. Like fashion, locomotion engages with the past, present and future all at once, and implies both permanence and change. Writing about locomotion allowed Uzanne to express his ambivalent attitude toward technology, and modernity itself. As Willa Silverman points out, throughout his career Uzanne's work displayed 'a tension between modernism and anachronism that would characterise his attitude toward technology as well' (*The New Bibliopolis*, p. 23). Writing about transportation allowed Uzanne, a 'reactionary modernist', to use Silverman's term, to reflect on the themes of passage of time and contingencies of modern life (*The New Bibliopolis*, p. 23).
33 Octave Uzanne, 'Omnibus de Paris', *Le Monde Moderne*, 1:28 (1900), 482.
34 Uzanne, 'Omnibus de Paris', 484.
35 Uzanne, 'Omnibus de Paris', 484.
36 Delord *et al.*, *Paris-en-omnibus*, p. 78.
37 François Coppée, 'Croquis parisiens: l'omnibus', *Les annales politiques et littéraires* (7 September 1902), 147–8.
38 Guy de Maupassant, 'Le père Montgilet', *Gil Blas* (24 February 1885), n.p.
39 Maupassant, 'Le père Montgilet', n.p.
40 Gourdon, *Physiologie de l'omnibus*, pp. 55–6.
41 Gourdon, *Physiologie de l'omnibus*, pp. 17–18.
42 Emmeline Raymond, 'L'Omnibus', *La Mode Illustrée* (27 October 1862), 351–2. Raymond (1824–1902) was a prolific author of novels, conduct manuals and numerous translations. She was best known as the founder and editor-in-chief of a weekly fashion magazine, *La Mode Illustrée: Journal de la famille*, which she directed for forty years. Beyond setting fashion trends, Raymond used

the magazine to promote bourgeois ideology of womanhood. See Susan Hiner, 'Terre à terre: domesticating fashion with Emmeline Raymond', conference paper presented at the Nineteenth-Century French Studies Colloquium, Brown University, 26–29 October 2016.
43 For a detailed analysis of this image, see Elizabeth C. Childs, *Daumier and Exoticism: Satirizing the French and the Foreign* (New York: Peter Lang, 2004).
44 Uzanne, 'Omnibus de Paris', 485.
45 Uzanne, 'Omnibus de Paris', 485.
46 'Le promeneur solitaire et pensif tire une singulière ivresse de cette universelle communion. Celui-là qui épouse facilement la foule connaît des jouissances fiévreuses, dont seront éternellement privé l'égoïste, fermé comme un coffre, et le paresseux, interné comme un mollusque. Il adopte comme siennes toutes les professions, toutes les joies et toutes les misères que la circonstance lui présente.' Charles Baudelaire, 'Les Foules', in *Œuvres complètes*, p. 420. ('The solitary and thoughtful stroller draws a unique intoxication from this universal communion. He who easily espouses crowds knows feverish delights, of which the selfish will be eternally deprived, locked up like a chest, and the lazy, confined like a mollusk. He adopts as his every profession, every joy and every misery circumstances place before him.' Charles Baudelaire, *The Parisian Prowler*, trans. Edward Kaplan (Athens, GA: The University of Georgia Press, 1989), p. 21.)
47 Uzanne, 'Omnibus de Paris', 485.
48 Gourdon, *Physiologie de l'omnibus*, p. 42.
49 Gourdon, *Physiologie de l'omnibus*, p. 42.
50 For a discussion of fashion accessories and their relation to changing social structures and emerging modernity, see Hiner, *Accessories to Modernity*. She writes: 'The *lorette*'s manipulation of the material of luxury points to a cultural shift in value lamented by many of the physiologists and novelists of the period: her identity resides in her display of luxury and not in the cult of origins to which luxury used to refer; her capital is her costume – the fragile and fleeting ephemera of fashion – and lacks the stable value of the traditional standards of gold and land' (p. 39).
51 Gourdon, *Phyiologie de l'omnibus*, pp. 93–4.
52 Lauster, *Sketches of the Nineteenth Century*, p. 94.
53 Griveau, 'En omnibus', p. 48.
54 Griveau, 'En omnibus', p. 48.
55 Wechsler, *A Human Comedy*, p. 14.
56 Gourdon, *Physiologie de l'omnibus*, p. 71.
57 Gourdon, *Physiologie de l'omnibus*, pp. 70–1.
58 Gourdon, *Physiologie de l'omnibus*, pp. 84–5.
59 Raymond, 'L'Omnibus', 352.
60 Uzanne, 'Omnibus de Paris', 486. Foyot was a high-end restaurant frequented by aristocracy, while Père Lathuille, a restaurant located in Clichy (and made famous by Manet), was associated with the modest classes.
61 Uzanne, 'Omnibus de Paris', 488.
62 Uzanne, 'Omnibus de Paris', 491.
63 Uzanne, 'Omnibus de Paris', 491–2.

64 Uzanne, 'Omnibus de Paris', 492.
65 Jules Janin, in the preface to *Paris, ou le livre des cent-et-un*, compares the representational strategies of the book's contributors to those of Asmodeus. For a discussion of the devil in European urban literature, see Lauster, *Sketches of the Nineteenth Century*, especially chapter 4.
66 Gourdon devotes several pages to the 'buraliste' (Gourdon, *Physiologie de l'omnibus*, pp. 11–16); Victor Fournel, in *Ce qu'on voit dans les rues de Paris*, asserts that the character of a driver depends on the vehicle that he drives, as he analyses different Parisian conveyances (Fournel, *Ce qu'on voit dans les rues de Paris*, p. 274).
67 Charles Friès, 'Le Conducteur d'omnibus', in *Les Français peints par eux-mêmes* (Paris: Curmer, 1840–42), p. 102.
68 Delord *et al.*, *Paris-en-omnibus*, pp. 39–40.
69 François Coppée, 'Physionomies parisiennes', 24.
70 See Amann, 'Reading (on) the tram', 195.
71 Fouinet, 'Un voyage en omnibus', p. 70.
72 Fouinet, 'Un voyage en omnibus', p. 70.
73 Fouinet, 'Un voyage en omnibus', p. 76.
74 Fouinet, 'Un voyage en omnibus', p. 77.
75 For a detailed analysis of this story, see Elizabeth Amann, 'The devil in the omnibus: from *Le Charivari* to *Blackwood's Magazine*', *Nineteenth-Century Contexts*, 39:1 (2017), 1–13.
76 Paul Gavarni, 'Une aventure d'omnibus', *Le Charivari* (26 August 1840), n.p.
77 Amann reminds us that according to the Goncourt brothers' account, the story is loosely based on Gavarni's own experience. A high-society lady (who, unlike the one in the story, had both her eyes) he met on the omnibus refused to give him her name. She did, however, mention that her husband subscribed to *Le Charivari*. Gavarni published the story to attract the woman's attention, and, in fact, proceeded to have a relationship with her. See Edmond de Goncourt and Jules de Goncourt, *Journal*, vol. 1, 1851–3, A. Ricatte (ed.) (Paris: Flammarion, 1959), pp. 72–3. See also Amann, 'The devil in the omnibus', 2.
78 Léon Gozlan, *Le Triomphe des Omnibus* (Paris: Abroise Dupont, 1828), p. 5.
79 Fouinet, 'Un voyage en omnibus', pp. 61–2.
80 This scenario is also at the crux of *Mon voisin d'omnibus*, a vaudeville play in which the entire plot is predicated on the encounter between the creditor and his debtor, who then unravels an entire complicated plot aimed at making sure he gets paid. See Chapter 3 for a detailed analysis of the play.
81 See Chapter 4 for a discussion of this association.
82 Durand-Dahl, music by H. Noyrd, *Chansons de Zig et Zag* (Paris: George Ondet, 1892).
83 'Un marriage en omnibus', lyrics by Villemer-Delormel, music by Franz Liouville.
84 'Mon voisin d'omnibus', lyrics by A. Jambon, music by Emile Bouillon.
85 Virtually the same scenario plays out in *Un coup de foudre en omnibus*, an 1889 chamber play intended for amateur performances. Marcel, a young bachelor, lends some change to a young woman who finds herself aboard an omnibus without her purse. Marcel, of course, falls deeply in love. The couple is reunited when the woman brings to Marcel's house the money lent to her for the fare. The ending

suggests that matrimony will soon ensue. *Un coup de foudre en omnibus* plays with the idea of a chance encounter on an omnibus but domesticates it by bringing together two characters who are socially well suited to each other, making the play acceptable to the respectable bourgeois audience for whom it was intended. See P. Darasse, 'Un coup de foudre en omnibus', in *Comédies pour salons et théâtre*, 2nd edn (Paris: impr. de la Publicité générale, 1889).
86 Dartès, *Contes en omnibus*, pp. 164–5.

Plate 1 Omnibus de la Companie des 'Dames Blanches'. 1828.

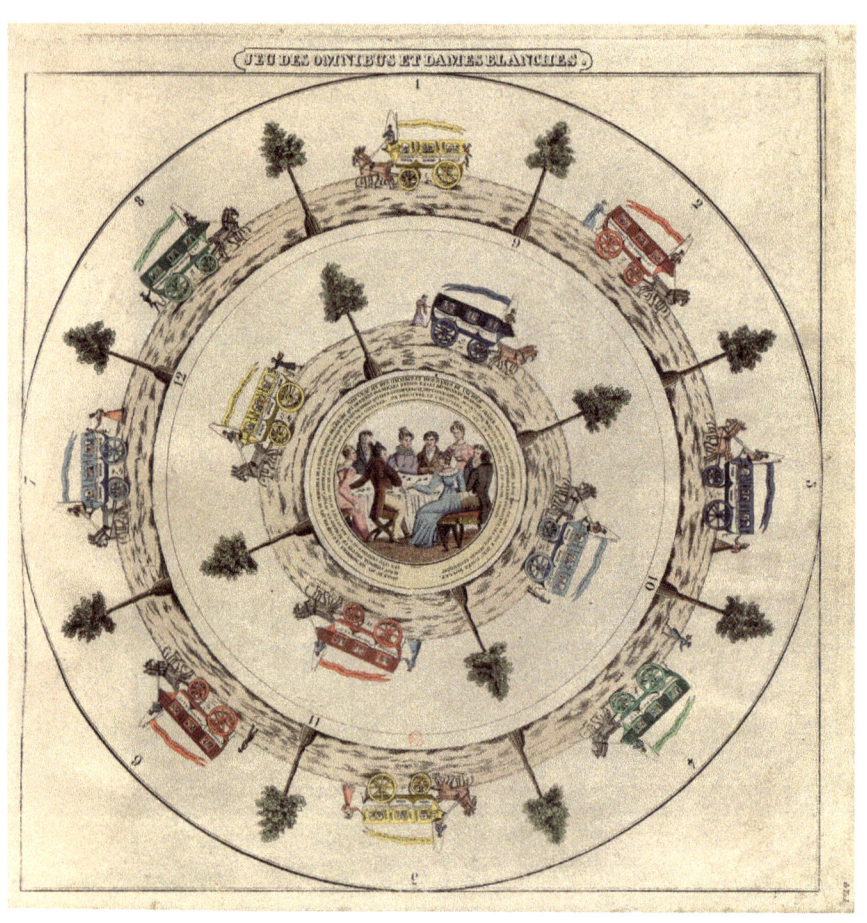

Plate 2 *Jeu des Omnibus et Dames Blanches*. 1828. This board game became the design for the first iconic Hermès silk scarf, released in 1937.

Plate 3 Camille Pissarro, *Boulevard des Italiens, soleil du matin*. 1897. Oil on canvas. This late-nineteenth-century painting depicts several crowded omnibuses among the bustle of the busy boulevard.

Plate 4 Victor Ratier, 'Un banc d'Omnibus. Trois, six, et trois… huit, encore une place! serrez-vous, Messieurs et Dames'. 1829.

Plate 5 J.J. Grandville, 'Comment, ces gens-là vont monter aussi? – Omnibus!! Madame!', *Les Métamorphoses du jour*. 1828–29.

Plate 6 Victor Ratier, 'Echantillons de mœurs Parisiennes. Un banc d'Omnibus de la Madelaine à la porte St Martin. Pour deux... Fait historique, dessiné d'après nature. Maris honnêtes garde à vous!'. 1829.

Plate 7 Maurice Delondre, *En omnibus*. 1880. Oil on canvas.

Plate 8 Mary Cassatt, *En omnibus*. 1890–91. Colour print.

Part II
Class, gender and locomotion: social dynamics on the omnibus

3

Circulation and visibility: staging class aboard the omnibus

> Le voyage en omnibus unit toutes les classes sociales sans distinction ni division. De tous les milieux parisiens où l'on se puisse rencontrer, la voiture d'omnibus est évidemment celle qui offre la plus parfaite image de démocratie et de fraternité courtoise. Ouvriers, boutiquiers, rentiers, savants, poètes, financiers, comédiens et comédiennes, domestiques et maîtres, musiciens et chanteurs, académiciens et ramasseurs de bouts de cigare s'y coudoient chaque jour quelques courts moments dans le plein air de l'impériale, l'étranglement de la plateforme, sinon sur les coussins du box intérieur.
>
> Octave Uzanne[1]

Writing at the turn of the century, Octave Uzanne paints an idealised picture of the omnibus interior, one where people from all walks of life and diverse social classes happily commingle and coexist in harmony, cheerfully sharing the omnibus bench with one another. Yet this romanticised and nostalgic vision of the omnibus as a 'perfect image of democracy and fraternity' stands in opposition to many of its textual and visual representations throughout the nineteenth century. As a unique space of class mixing – its name embodying the elusive democratic promise of post-Revolutionary France – the omnibus generated complex and often conflicting commentaries.

Some nineteenth-century observers celebrated the omnibus as a quintessentially democratic vehicle, one that became a focal point for the breakdown of social hierarchies and embodied both revolutionary change and a promise of social mobility. Others focused on the shortcomings of the vehicle's democratic potential, highlighting instead how the modest fare still excluded certain populations. Finally, some observers expressed discomfort about the inevitable class mixing aboard the omnibus. This discomfort emerges in stories and images that span the nineteenth century and tell the tale of a society attempting to make sense of its rapidly changing social structures, one in which different groups sought to define and assert their class identity and belonging.

When the omnibus service was first proposed in 1827–28, it was intended primarily for a broad range of working-class patrons, or 'industrial classes', as they were called at the time. Nicholas Papayanis reminds us that the omnibus companies 'wished to cast a wide net that would take in all respectable and employed people who needed to commute long distances but would not normally engage cabs'.[2] But it was precisely the idea of class mixing that delayed the introduction of the vehicle in Paris. Guy Delaveau, the conservative police prefect, rejected nearly three hundred applications to start an urban coach service, in part because he was apprehensive about a vehicle open to all classes. Moreover, he was concerned that gathering together a large number of lower-class people could lead to public unrest and social disorder. Maxime Du Camp asserts that city officials during the Restoration feared 'a political danger in the circulation of coaches destined for all classes of society'.[3] In addition, the background of Stanislas Baudry, the entrepreneur who eventually launched the first omnibus service (L'Entreprise générale d'omnibus), played a role in the police prefect's repeated rejection of his application: his revolutionary background, his service in Napoleon's army and his alleged involvement with Carbonarism were deemed suspect.[4]

When an urban coach service was finally authorised in January 1828 by a new (and more liberal) police prefect, the most striking and distinctive feature of the conveyance was that it was by law open to everyone regardless of class, wealth or social status. This legal inclusiveness distinguished the nineteenth-century omnibus from its seventeenth-century predecessor, *la carrosse à cinq sous*, which excluded people of lower classes.[5] Although the omnibus conductor was empowered to reject those who might disturb other passengers, were drunk, wore inappropriate attire or had a dog, no one could be excluded solely based on rank or social station, and anyone able to pay the fare was allowed on board as long as there were seats available.

But was the omnibus truly 'for all'? By most historical accounts, the actual class composition of the omnibuses until the late nineteenth century fell far short of the ideal of universal inclusiveness. For one thing, the wealthy and status-conscious travellers eschewed it in favour of private carriages or individual carriages for hire. For another, poor and working-class city dwellers could not afford even the initial low fare of 25 centimes, which was raised to 30 centimes in 1830. Additionally, the system of free transfers between the lines (*correspondances*) was not established until 1834, so the cost of crossing the city could amount to as much as 60 centimes, a sum beyond the reach of most working poor. The *impériale* was more affordable at 15 centimes, but it was not introduced until 1855. Even at that price, it was not affordable to everyone. An image by Darjou (Figure 3.1) illustrates this well: the conductor explains that while for 4 *sous* you can ride on the *impériale*, the fare of 3 *sous* allows you the privilege of chasing after the omnibus on foot.

Circulation and visibility

Figure 3.1 A. Darjou, 'Actualités. – Oui Messieurs c'est quarte sous l'impériale; pour trois sous vous n'avez plus que le droit de suivre en courant'. n.d.

According to historian Michel Margairaz, urban transit did not truly become 'mass transit', open to all levels of society, until the late nineteenth century, when the fares were reduced as a result of negotiations between the Companie Générale des Omnibus and the municipal authorities, which at the time were dominated by radical republicans with socialist leanings.[6] Furthermore, historian David Pinkney notes that omnibus service did not begin until 8 am, 'a genteel hour that indicates how little the buses were intended for the mass of working Parisians';[7] and the placement of initial omnibus lines clearly privileged neighbourhoods on the Right Bank where wealth and commerce were concentrated. As a result, in those early years commercial and other petit-bourgeois passengers were most likely the majority, and the class composition of the vehicle's interior was less heterogeneous than the omnibus literature suggests.[8] And yet, more than any other aspect of the omnibus, it was the *potential* for class inclusiveness that captured the imagination of contemporary commentators. Despite historical evidence to the contrary, textual and visual representations of the omnibus interior consistently place travellers of widely diverse social classes within the confined space of the vehicle.

My central claim in this chapter is that the omnibus served as a complex and equivocal symbol of social class in nineteenth-century popular literature, rather than a straightforward emblem of class inclusiveness as the vehicle's name asserts. What the omnibus meant as a class signifier in cultural representations was often inconsistent and contradictory, and it could not be contained in a single model. Indeed, the omnibus provided social observers and urban writers with multiple ways of thinking about social class. First and foremost, social commentary focused on class mixing inside the vehicle and the ways this mixing threatened – or promised, depending on the author's perspective – to upend existing social hierarchies. At the same time, the omnibus's potential as a socially diverse space provided an ideal setting for the performance of class identity at a time when it was continuously being negotiated and contested. In addition, the very mobility of the omnibus symbolically embodied the potential of social mobility, as the vehicle literally traversed differently classed neighbourhoods in Paris, offering the modest classes the possibility of circulation through parts of the city previously unavailable to them.

Indeed, urban space played a central role in shaping middle-class identity in nineteenth-century France. Historian Victoria Thompson traces shifts in how Parisian middle classes experienced urban spaces, suggesting that 'space was used by members of the middle class to craft a distinctive and authoritative urban identity', especially around the time of the July Revolution of 1830.[9] Following the Revolution of 1789, there was a clear connection between social and spatial relations in the urban context; Thompson shows that in the earlier decades of the nineteenth century, popular literature about Paris presented different social groups as occupying the same spaces in unproblematic ways: 'Although these texts depicted a city that was socially segregated, urban topography and social stratification worked together to give the impression that the organisation of Parisian society was orderly and stable.'[10] However, Thompson identifies a marked shift after the July Revolution: it was around urban spaces that bourgeois fears of social and political upheavals crystallised. At the same time, urban spaces emerged increasingly as sites where the middle classes could differentiate themselves from popular classes in everyday practices and artistic representations.

The omnibus was among these sites, both aboard the actual Parisian omnibus and especially in the pages of popular literature. Because its enclosed space was in principle open to everyone, the middle classes experienced potential class mixing and exposure to the lower classes as particularly anxiety-provoking, while the working classes saw the omnibus as an arena especially suited to asserting their claim on urban space and, by extension, their place in society. The unique omnibus seating arrangement, with benches or stalls along the walls of the vehicle, exposed passengers to each other's unrelenting gaze for the duration of the trip. This was perhaps the only urban space where such prolonged exposure was not only possible but unavoidable: in other public urban sites, such as parks, cafés and museums, people were free to move and circulate. But it was difficult if not impossible to avoid others' inspection aboard an omnibus. Confined to a small, circumscribed space, omnibus passengers' every word and gesture was open to interpretation and scrutiny by their fellow passengers. Passengers' dress and demeanour, the crucial markers of one's social status and respectability, were subject to continuous inspections by others. Even more so than café-goers later in the century, they were captives of each other's gaze.[11]

This chapter traces the complex ways in which omnibus literature deployed the figure of the omnibus to stage class relations and the performance of class identity in the virtual space of the page. If the actual omnibus offered less class diversity than this literature might suggest, the omnibus *imaginaire* construed it as a defining feature of urban life, and as an emblem of changing social structures. The different cultural documents that I study in this chapter, from panoramic and didactic texts and vaudeville theatre of the 1820s, 1830s and 1840s to Second Empire lithographs and Third Republic fiction, express the sensibilities of the middlebrow public, which constituted both the intended readership of this literature and the intended ridership of the omnibus. Omnibus literature did more than reflect on the reality of class relations in the everyday experience of the omnibus: it articulated and shaped bourgeois anxieties and perceptions about class within the newly established urban spaces.

Equality in motion

Many nineteenth-century observers enthusiastically embraced the democratic nature of the omnibus. In *Physiologie de l'omnibus* (1842), Edouard Gourdon envisions the vehicle as a kind of miniature model of society as a whole:

> Je cherche une personnification de la société, je la trouve entière, vraie et juste, avec ses anachronismes, ses non-sens, son crétinisme, sa sottise et son amour-propre, dans l'omnibus. L'omnibus est un échantillon d'autant plus fidèle qu'il varie sans cesse. C'est un miroir où toutes les silhouettes, grandes et petites, sombres et bouffonnes, viennent se décalquer, où le ridicule et ses mille nuances se montrent de grandeur naturelle, de pied en cap. Tout le monde passe par l'omnibus; faire l'histoire de l'omnibus, c'est faire l'histoire de la société.[12]

(Looking for a personification of the society, I find it in its entirety – with all its anachronisms, its nonsense, its stupidity and self-centredness, I find all of it on the omnibus. The omnibus is a particularly faithful representation precisely because it is constantly changing. It is a mirror in which all the silhouettes, big and small, gloomy and comical, are reflected, where the absurd and its thousand nuances reveal themselves in their natural grandeur. Everyone passes through the omnibus. To write the history of the omnibus is to write the history of society.)

For Gourdon, the omnibus embodied the mobility and flux of post-Revolutionary French society. Old class categories no longer held true, and social mobility seemed possible. With its promise of equality, the omnibus served as a figure of progress and democratic spirit. If the mania for *physiologies* was linked to the frenzied attempt to describe and understand a society that was undergoing dramatic changes, morphing beyond recognition before writers' very eyes, it is easy to see why a writer like Gourdon would seize upon the omnibus as its image.

In the view of many well-known writers and journalists, the omnibus was an idealised space where established social hierarchies were suspended. For example, in *Paris-en-omnibus* (1854) Taxile Delord equates the vehicle with democratic progress itself: 'Il est certain que l'omnibus est un agent de progrès démocratique. L'omnibus rapproche les distances, confond toutes les classes de la société, mêle tous les rangs. Il a réalisé ce qu'on pourrait appeler le *droit à l'équipage.*' (There is no doubt that the omnibus is the agent of democratic progress. The omnibus diminishes distances, combines all social classes, mixes up all the ranks. It created what may be called *the right to carriage.*) He then asserts semi-ironically that the absence of an omnibus service is a sure sign that a city is out of step with progress: 'Il n'y a pas d'omnibus à Rome, à Naples, à Florence: aussi le peuple de ces villes est-il considérablement arriéré'[13] (There is no omnibus in Rome, Naples or Florence, which suggests that the people of these cities are considerably backwards). Charles Friès, in the 1842 'Le Conducteur d'omnibus', from *Les Français peints par eux-mêmes*, refers to the *cadran*, the conductor-operated device to count passengers, as a 'symbole éclatant d'égalité sur lequel le riche et le pauvre sont cotés au même taux'[14] (shining symbol of equality which counts the rich and the poor at the same rate). Similarly, Edmond Texier, in the 1853 *Tableau de Paris*, writes that 'L'omnibus, c'est la démocratisation du véhicule, l'extension illimitée du droit de se faire voiturer au plus bas prix'[15] (The omnibus is a democratisation of vehicle, an unlimited extension of the right to be driven at the lowest cost). And the anonymous author of an 1843 article from *Le Magasin pittoresque* insists that the class inclusiveness of the omnibus leads passengers of different walks of life to treat each other with equal respect, calling the vehicle a true 'école de politesse' (school of manners). Not only does the omnibus 'sauvegarde contre les boues de Paris la très nombreuse classe des gens qui n'ont pas équipage' (preserve against the mud of Paris numerous groups of people who do not own a carriage), but also, most importantly, it fosters proper codes of conduct in a public space:

> Il ne permet point aux élégants de développer leurs poses, ou d'étaler leurs grâces sur les coussins; mais il apprend à tout le monde comment il faut se tenir le corps droit, n'occuper au plus que sa place, relever les basques de l'habit ou les bouts d'une écharpe, serrer les coudes contre le corps, retirer les genoux en arrière, et surtout ramener ses pieds sous la banquette.[16]

> (It does not allow people of means to put on airs or to spread out on the seat cushions; instead, it teaches everyone how to keep oneself straight, to occupy no more than one seat, to gather coat tails or the end of a scarf, to keep elbows to oneself, to pull back one's knees and especially to place one's feet under the bench.)

In this view, the omnibus is a form of social policing, imposing corporeal control and restraint upon passengers' bodies and even their clothing. The author then points out that in addition to fulfilling the didactic function of educating city dwellers in proper public comportment, the omnibus serves a larger common good for all social classes: 'C'est qu'elle est une institution véritablement populaire, créée en vue d'intérêts généraux; c'est qu'elle prend son point d'appui dans la satisfaction légitime des besoins de toutes les classes de la société qui peuvent disposer de trente centimes.' (This is a truly popular institution, created for the sake of general interest; it's based on the legitimate satisfaction of the needs of all social classes who are able to spare 30 centimes.) In fact, the author credits the omnibus with myriad recent advances in urban development, such as 'polices des rues, amélioration de la voie publique, tendance au nivellement du prix des loyers entre les faubourgs et le centre'[17] (policing of streets, improvement in road conditions, a levelling of rent prices between city centre and the suburbs).

Likewise, Emmeline Raymond hails the omnibus and omnibus stations as exemplary social spaces of class equality, and as models of fairness. She notes that while getting a seat on an omnibus is a daunting task because these conveyances are typically overcrowded, when it came to allocating seats, strict order reigned in omnibus stations, an order that had nothing to do with the passengers' social standing and everything to do with their place in line:

> Mais une égalité inexorable préside à la distribution des places disponibles, et, quelle que soit la position sociale du numéro 10, il ne passera pas avant le numéro 9, celui-ci fut-il vêtu de la blouse la plus modeste. L'omnibus n'examine pas les individus, il tient compte seulement des chiffres; il n'admet aucun privilège, et ne reconnait qu'un droit, égal pour tous, préservé contre tout subterfuge par la surveillance générale, gardienne jalouse de l'équité, qui ne pourrait être violée en faveur d'un seul sans être atteinte dans la personne de tous.[18]

(An inexorable equality reigns over the distribution of available seats, and whatever the social position of number 10, he will never get ahead of number 9, even if the latter is dressed in the most modest of worker's overalls. The omnibus does not scrutinise individuals: it takes into account only numbers. It does not accept any privilege and recognises only one right, equal for all, preserved from any violation by general monitoring, a protective guardian of equity that cannot be defied for the benefit of one without affecting all.)

The omnibus logic, as Raymond sees it, is based on reason and numerical order and thus serves as a model for a just social order.

Other commentators were more prescriptive, reminding readers that equality was the fundamental underlying principle of conduct on board a public conveyance. For example, in her 1829 *Manuel complet de la bonne compagnie,* Elisabeth Félicie Byle-Mouillard cautions omnibus passengers against taking advantage of their rank: 'On serait également mal vu de profiter de sa qualité et de supériorité que donne le rang pour prendre toutes ses aises. Il faut au contraire avoir grand soin de ne gêner qui que ce soit, et montrer beaucoup d'honnêteté pour ses compagnons de voyage.'[19] (It would be unacceptable to take advantage of one's superior rank and to act as one pleases. On the contrary, one must not bother anyone and show courtesy to fellow passengers.)

The prolific popular writer Paul de Kock also expresses optimism about the social function of the omnibus: 'Comme toutes les classes s'y mêlent, comme les rangs y sont confondus! ... Si l'égalité doit régner un jour sur terre, c'est dans les Omnibus qu'elle aura pris naissance!' (How all classes are mixed together, how the ranks are combined! ... If one day equality should reign on earth, it's on the Omnibus that it will have been born!) In describing the omnibus interior, he highlights the social diversity of the passengers: a lovely young lady, a worker wearing a *casquette*, a government clerk, a drunkard, a dandy sporting fashionable yellow gloves, a corpulent country woman with baskets overflowing with food, a *grisette*, a respectable older gentleman and, finally, an old marquise, who had lost her fortune in the Revolution. Yet, de Kock suggests, the omnibus space promotes what he calls a 'co-fraternity' among these diverse types of people: 'Et bien! Malgré ses différences de rangs, de fortune, d'éducation et de costume, la voiture à six sous établit entre les voyageurs une espèce de confraternité qui se traduit ordinairement en échanges de petits services et de politesses.'[20] (Despite differences in rank, fortune, education and dress, the *voiture à six sous*[21] establishes a kind of fraternity among the passengers, one that manifests itself through small gestures of kindness and courteousness.)

Social diversity and the purported role the omnibus played in fostering social equality continued to fascinate writers well beyond the early years of the omnibus service. In 1863, thirty-five years after its launch, writer Charles Soullier still marvelled at the class heterogeneity of the vehicle and its potential for symbolising equality. In an introductory poem to his volume on omnibus history and practical information, he wrote:

> Les états et les rangs s'y mêlent confondus,
> Là le gros commerçant coudoie un prolétaire;
> Le froc sacerdotal touche au frac militaire;
> On voit s'y réunir, en toute liberté,
> Les filles de Vénus aux sœurs de charité.
> L'on y trouve pressés, entassés pêle-mêle,
> La bure et le velours, la serge et la dentelle.[22]

> (The professions and ranks are mixed there all together
> The stout shopkeeper is next to a worker
> The priest's frock mingles with military uniform;
> You see here united in all liberty
> Daughters of Venus and sisters of charity
> There you find homespun wool next to velvet
> Twill and lace, all thrown together in a jumble.)

It is readily apparent that social class is conveyed metonymically through the types of fabric that various passengers are wearing – that the diversity of fabric represents a diversity of social positions. Soullier extols the omnibus as the embodiment of equality: if in the past, only the chosen ones had access to carriages ('Jadis les seigneurs seuls cheminaient en carrosses'), now everyone has the right to ride. This right, in Soullier's view, is emblematic of his century's move toward privileging merit over birth:

> Une voiture à tous! Voilà du communisme
> Pratiqué sans l'emphase et prêché sans cynisme!
> [...]
> Mais aujourd'hui, le siècle a annulé les races;
> Il partage entre tous les faveurs et les grâces.
> L'homme est ce qu'il devient, et non pas comme il nait;
> L'on marche côte à côte et l'on se reconnait.

> (A vehicle for all! What communism!
> Practised without fuss and preached without cynicism!
> [...]
> But today, the century cancelled race distinctions;
> It shares among all its favours and graces.
> The man is what he becomes and not how he is born;
> All walk side by side in mutual recognition.)

All these texts consider the omnibus as a utopian space of class equality, a place where difference in rank and fortune is subsumed under the equalising power of a modern conveyance governed by an order rooted in fairness and merit, rather than privilege. The omnibus instructs urban dwellers in this new social order and enforces it.

If the omnibus represented a hope for a more equal society and social transformation, it also embodied republican ideology through the image of the vehicle as a literal building block for revolutionary barricades. Numerous texts – from popular omnibus literature to Victor Hugo's *Les Misérables* – evoke this image of the omnibus as an actual instrument of revolution. For example, Gourdon writes: 'Le peuple aime l'omnibus… La première barricade a été faite avec un omnibus. Ce fut sur un omnibus qu'on planta le premier drapeau rouge, la veille du 6 juin 1832'[23] (The people adore the omnibus. The first barricade was built using an omnibus. It was on top of an omnibus that a red flag was planted the night before 6 June 1832). Maxime Du Camp, in 'Les voitures publiques', reminds us that omnibuses were heavily used to build barricades during the revolution of 1848: 'L'année 1848 a coûté cher à la Compagnie qui s'en souvient encore avec une certaine amertume'[24] (The year 1848 turned out to be costly for the Companie (Generale des Omnibus), which remembers it with bitterness). And Edmond Texier recalls the 'bruises' incurred by omnibuses during insurrections when 'il est si vite renversé et transformé en barricade!'[25] (it is quickly tipped over and transformed into a barricade!).

The striking image of an overturned omnibus, its spire crowned with a red flag, appears most famously in Victor Hugo's 1862 *Les Misérables*, testifying to its power in the nineteenth-century imagination. One of the central episodes in the novel is the construction and defence of a barricade during the insurrection of June 1832, spurred by the death and the funeral of a liberal general and former revolutionary hero Lamarque: 'Les chevaux dételés s'en allaient au hasard par la rue Montedour, et l'omnibus, couché sur le flanc completait le barrage de la rue… La flèche de l'omnibus était dressée droite et maintenue avec les cordes, et un drapeau rouge, fixé sur cette flèche, flottait sur la barricade'[26] (The detached horses were wondering off down the rue Montedour, and the omnibus, lying on its side, completed the barricade… The omnibus spire pointed straight up and was adorned with a red flag floating over the barricade). The events of 1832 expressed the revival of republicanism under the July Monarchy and the aspirations and discontents of the working class and the lower-middle classes. It is, then, not a matter of chance that the omnibus, the epitome of the republican value of *égalité*, completed the barricade, whose defenders were fighting 'for all'. In a highly symbolic detail, the overturned omnibus originates at the Place de la Bastille, reinforcing its lineage from 1789.[27] Hugo heralds the omnibus as part of the revolutionary heritage,

Circulation and visibility

thus pairing revolution and urban modernity. From panoramic texts by Gourdon, Delord and Texier to Hugo's monumental masterpiece, the omnibus emerges as the utopian emblem of a new society that embodies republican values and the democratic potential of the French Revolution.[28]

Equality not delivered

Despite the plethora of texts extolling the equalising qualities of the omnibus, many social observers were keenly aware of the serious shortcomings of this conveyance as a space that erases social boundaries. Historical evidence suggests that most members of the working class could not afford its modest price, and even members of the middle class sometimes found it unaffordable. Balzac, for example, in his poorest moments, complained bitterly to his sister that an omnibus ride was out of reach for him ('Un port de lettre, un omnibus me sont une horrible dépense et je ne sors pas pour ne pas user d'habits.'[29] (Sending a letter or an omnibus ride are a huge expense, and I don't even go out so as to not use up my clothes.)). Moreover, a regulatory provision gave conductors the freedom to exclude anyone whose attire seemed objectionable or who otherwise threatened to disturb order.[30] Many writers and artists criticised the omnibus service for promising equality but not delivering it: far from being inclusive, the argument went, the omnibus was instead an emblem of social exclusion.

The suspicion about the vehicle's practices appears early on in omnibus literature. For example, in his 1828 poem *Réflexions d'un patriarche sur les voitures dites omnibus!*, Félix Nogaret, an early critic of the service, laments that the poor and the poorly dressed are not admitted:

> Quant à la classe malheureuse
> Qui n'a pas de si beaux habits,
> La manœuvre, la ravaudeuse,
> Ces gens-là ne sont point admis
> (As for the unfortunate class
> That does not have beautiful clothes,
> A labourer or a mender,
> Those are not admitted on board).

The omnibus companies, Nogaret contends, are only interested in making a profit, rather than ensuring the well-being of the public or serving a greater good ('Empilez, empilez; les sous font des écus'[31] (Go on stacking your coins)). The service does not live up to the name's promise: 'Bon! Mais votre Omnibus est, vous dis-je, un mensonge; C'est un mot sur lequel il faut passer l'éponge' (Well! I am telling you: your Omnibus is nothing but a lie; it's a word we should all forget about).

Indeed, for several other commentators the omnibus became a visible symbol of *in*equality, the very embodiment of social exclusion. Madame de Flesselles's didactic city guide for young people visiting Paris, *Les jeunes voyageurs dans Paris* (1829), echoes Nogaret's reproach and even refers to his poem.[32] This text features a conversation between a father and his teenage son, who is curious about the unusual-looking vehicles. The father explains the meaning of the name, and the dialogue is worth quoting in full for it captures well the vehicle's perceived shortcomings:

PAPA: C'est comme qui dirait: la voiture *à tous*; c'est l'équipage de tout le monde: le pauvre comme le riche y sont admis au nombre environ vingt personnes à la fois, moyennant cinq sous par tête, et transportés d'un point central à un autre que la voiture ne saurait dépasser; ou elle doit se rendre sans se détourner de sa route.

LE FILS: Ainsi, papa, on peut se trouver là-dedans avec un chiffonnier, un mendiant? –

PAPA: Oui, si le chiffonnier ou le mendiant ont mis leurs habits des dimanches; mais sous les livrées de la misère, ils n'y seront point reçus.

LE FILS: –Alors il me semble que le nom d'*Omnibus* n'est pas rempli, car *tous* ne dit pas seulement les gens proprement vêtus.

PAPA: –Ton raisonnement est juste et tiens, il me rappelle une brochure que je lisais hier au salon littéraire. Dans ce badinage gracieux, le patriarche de la littérature, M. Félix Nogaret, également connu des hommes de lettres sous le nom de L'Aristenete français, adresse précisément aux *Omnibus* le même reproche.[33]

(DAD: It is, as they say, a vehicle *for all*; a conveyance for everyone: the rich and the poor are admitted there equally, about twenty people at once, for only 5 *sous* per head, and transported from one place to another. The vehicle goes to its destination without deviating from its route.

SON: So, papa, you can find a rag picker and a beggar there?

DAD: Yes, if the rag picker and the beggar put on their Sunday best; but if they are wearing their suit of misery, they will not be admitted.

SON: So, it seems that the name 'Omnibus' is not justified, because *all* does not mean only people who are well dressed.

DAD: Your reasoning is correct. It reminds me of a booklet I read yesterday in a reading salon. In this graceful banter, the literary patriarch, Monsieur Félix Nogaret, known among men of letters as the French Aristaenetus, reproaches the Omnibus for the same thing.)

In a classic move, truth comes from the mouth of a child: Madame de Flesselles brings attention to the unjust contradictions and the false promise inherent in the omnibus project as the boy points out the inconsistency in calling the vehicle 'for all' but excluding passengers based on their attire. If the overarching pedagogical mission of *Les jeunes voyageurs* is to instil good morals and a sense of ethical responsibility in young people, the injustices imposed on the omnibus passengers despite its egalitarian promise underscore society's hypocrisy and exclusionary practices.

Like Madame de Flesselles, Louis Huart, in his 1834 essay 'Les voitures publiques', deploys the omnibus as shorthand for a critique of inequality. He begins by associating the omnibus with the utopian socialism of Saint Simon, a philosophy that flourished in the 1820s and endorsed the idea of democratic equality, noting that that the omnibus service and the philosophy were created at about the same time. Yet the narrator's irony is inescapable, as he recalls the demise of Saint-Simonian philosophy, thus implying that the democratic potential of the omnibus, if not the vehicle itself, will be equally short-lived: 'Les apôtres ont vu s'écrouler bien vite tous leurs beaux rêves, tandis que l'omnibus continue à faire son chemin dans le monde'[34] (The apostles saw all their beautiful dreams crumble fast, whereas the omnibus continues on its merry way). Like the utopian vision of society it once embodied, that of the omnibus as a social equaliser will give way to commercial interests.[35]

Huart insists that the omnibus is decidedly not meant 'for all', but, rather, that it serves to reinforce existing social divides. He constructs a kind of hierarchy of Parisian vehicles in which each mode of transport is associated with a differently classed neighbourhood, here personified:

> Le noble faubourg St. Germain a ses équipages aux panneaux armoriés; la Chaussée-d'Antin monte dans ses calèches et dans ses coupés attelés de chevaux fringans [sic]; le commerçant qui fait sa fortune se contente du cabriolet en attendant mieux; les bourgeois et les petits propriétaires prennent les fiacres, et enfin les petits rentiers, les étudiants et les grisettes se blottissent dans les omnibus.[36]

> (The noble *faubourg St. Germain* has its carriages emblazoned with coats of arms; the Chaussée-d'Antin goes in its coupés pulled by elegant horses; the shopkeeper busy making his fortune resigns himself to a cabriolet, for lack of a better option; the bourgeois and the small business owners take a hackney cab while the small *rentiers*, students and *grisettes* crowd inside omnibuses.)

Huart places the omnibus – and, by extension, its passengers – at the very bottom of the social ladder of vehicles, reserving it for *rentiers*, students and *grisettes*. In doing so, he contests the democratic utopian ideals that some writers attached to this vehicle, seeing it instead as a continuation and perhaps even an expansion of old hierarchies. By using the verb 'se blottir' ('to crowd'), Huart reminds his reader that the omnibus was the transport for the masses, rather than 'for all'. Ultimately, he sees the omnibus as an incarnation and a visual symbol of old hierarchical structures, rather than an embodiment of progress. Like Madame Flesselles, he highlights the hypocrisy of the purportedly democratic omnibus project.

This critique is also at work in an image by Daumier published during the revolutionary year of 1848, in which an older working-class woman is refused entry because of her dog (Figure 3.2). The caption reveals a curious interplay of class tensions among members of the same class: 'Désolé, citoyenne, mais on ne reçoit pas de chien. –Aristocrate, va!' (Apologies, citizen, but we don't

Figure 3.2 Honoré Daumier, 'Désolé, citoyenne, mais on ne reçoit pas de chien. –Aristocrate, va!'. 1848.

take dogs! – Go on, aristocrat!) The conductor addresses the rejected passenger as 'citizen', a term made popular during the Revolution of 1789, and referencing urban modernity's potential for social equality, symbolised by the omnibus. Yet the woman takes it personally as an insult to her class position, the underlying suggestion being that the woman and the dog have equal social standing, since neither is permitted to board. She calls the conductor an 'aristocrat', mocking his attempt at upward mobility via the omnibus. The conductor is, of course, not an aristocrat – he is merely one member of the working class putting down another, who happens to occupy a position one step lower on the social ladder than his own.

Taken together, these texts and images highlight how contemporary observers deployed the omnibus not as a symbol of equality embedded in its name but as its opposite, a vehicle that brings to the fore bourgeois hypocrisy, makes visible social divisions and calls out society's inability to achieve progress. Yet other texts take up the idea of inclusiveness and treat it ironically. As we shall see, nineteenth-century vaudeville proved a perfect vehicle for satirising the idea of the omnibus as a class equaliser and a site of class performance.

A journey to nowhere: vaudeville and the performance of class

In 'Un voyage en omnibus', Ernest Fouinet proclaims that the interactions among passengers are a form of entertainment far superior to theatre:

> L'omnibus, c'est la vie, le monde, le public, l'homme; c'est tout: le latin le dit. Ah! Que ne peut-on, au lieu de ces immobiles planchers où des hommes presque immobiles, quant à l'âme, viennent chanter l'opéra et déclamer l'alexandrin, que ne peut-on nous donner des représentations d'omnibus! Profonde comédie, drame au puissant intérêt, malicieux vaudeville, bouffonnerie à faire pouffer Héraclite ou Chodruc-Duclos, on y verrait tout cela mieux qu'aux Français, au Gymnase, aux Variétés.[37]

> (The omnibus is life, it is the world, it is the public, it is the man – it is all of this – the Latin sums it up well. Ah! Why, instead of the stale performances on static stages where inert actors drone on their old-fashioned alexandrines, why can't we have omnibus performances instead? Hilarious comedy, profound drama, vicious vaudeville, you can see it all on an omnibus so much better than in any theatre – be it Théâtre des Français, Théâtre du Gymnase or Théâtre de Variétés.)

Fouinet's assertion is undoubtedly tongue-in-cheek, and yet he rightly captures the intrinsic theatricality of the public transport experience in drawing an explicit parallel between the social world of the omnibus and that of the popular theatre. On the one hand, the omnibus passengers enjoyed the moving spectacle of the modern city in all its multiplicity. Most importantly, however, the interior of the omnibus doubled as a roving theatrical stage where passengers are at once spectacle and spectators:

> O théâtre ambulant, comédie roulante, tu n'as pas besoin de souffleurs, la nature en sert à tes acteurs! Ils n'ont point de fard, de déguisement: ils sont spectateurs les uns des autres, ils jouent leurs rôles en se voyant jouer, toujours comme dans le monde, et tous ils paient trente centimes pour amuser le public et pour s'amuser. Quelle meilleure école dramatique que l'omnibus?[38]

> (Oh you, the roving theatre, the rolling comedy! You do not need the prompter – nature does this for your actors! They don't need makeup or costumes. They are spectators of one another; they perform just as they watch themselves perform – and all this for only 30 centimes. Can there be a better drama school than an omnibus?)

If the omnibus interior and its diverse passenger body lent themselves particularly well to theatrical situations, actual theatrical productions, conversely, took up the omnibus as a favoured topic and setting. Vaudeville was particularly well suited to the kind of social commentary and satire that pervaded all forms of omnibus literature; and with its focus on everyday situations and its dependence on slapstick humour, dramatic irony, stock characters and formulaic plot turns (such as mistaken identity, *quid pro quo*, chance encounters, reversal of fortunes or a threatened marriage plan), it was particularly well suited to working out tensions about class mixing on the omnibus. While urban literature stages class performance within the virtual space of the page, we find social class literally performed on the vaudeville stage: vaudeville reflected the everyday concerns of the middlebrow public, concerns that invariably revolved around jockeying for position in an unstable class hierarchy, for which the omnibus provided a perfect setting.[39]

Consider *J'attends un omnibus* (1849), a vaudeville play that capitalises on the inherent theatricality of the omnibus experience and setting in order to stage – and ultimately resolve – tensions associated with class mixing. It offers an ironic take on performing class identity, using the omnibus both as a setting and a device to engage with questions of social mobility.

Like many vaudeville plays, *J'attends un omnibus* features a complicated marriage plot. The play is set inside an omnibus station, where passengers wait to board an omnibus or to transfer between different lines; a 'cachet', a ticket dispensed by a conductor, was necessary for the transfer. Stage directions call for abundant realistic details in reproducing a setting presumably familiar to the majority of the play-goers: 'Porte au fond donnant sur la voie publique. Large vitrage de chaque côté. Banquettes pour les voyageurs. Cadres d'annonces sur les mûrs. –A droite, vers le fond, le bureau du contrôleur entouré d'un grillage'[40] (A door in the back opening to the street. Large windows on both sides. Benches for passengers. Announcement posters on the walls. On the right, in the back, the conductor's desk separated by a railing). The setting, with its walls plastered with posters, its seating for the waiting passengers and its door at the back, is a mirror image of the theatre, where members of the audience, like the omnibus passengers, are thrown together by the luck of the draw. They are, in a sense, looking at themselves.

The first lines of the dialogue emphasise the diverse background and social standing of the passengers: one passenger asks for a ticket for 'le faubourg Saint-Germain', inhabited by high aristocracy. Another passenger is on his way to Batignolles, a newly developing part of town on the outskirts of Paris popular among the bourgeois merchant class. Finally, a female passenger is heading for 'la rue Notre-Dame de Lorette', an area linked to prostitution.[41] The social heterogeneity of the omnibus is thus masterfully sketched in the first few lines of the play by associating the travellers with their destinations. The play presumes that the audience is familiar with the social topography of Paris; and, later on, when the audience learns that the mistress of the protagonist, Tiburce, lives on rue Bréda, also located in the neighbourhood of Notre-Dame de Lorette, it would not have missed the connotations of improper behaviour and loose morals.[42]

The omnibus station provided an ideal setting for vaudeville because it also served as a plot device: in *J'attends un omnibus*, the space brings together and allows for spontaneous comings and goings, unexpected encounters and social interactions among a wide array of characters, who, it turns out, are all connected to each other: two provincial ladies, Mme Barège and her niece Athénais, out shopping for the young woman's trousseau; Tiburce, Athénais's fiancé, who is on his way to salvage his savings from a corrupt banker; Francfort, a stereotypically comical German shoemaker, who is Tiburce's creditor; Stanislas Bouillabaisse, who happens to be both Athénais's guardian and Tiburce's rival with his mistress Amanda; and Cigarette, Tiburce's former mistress and mother of their illegitimate daughter, who is now Bouillabaisse's wife. Here the vaudeville exploits and literalises the idea of 'correspondence', meaning literally 'omnibus transfer' but here signifying a web of complex relationships and connections among the characters.

The plot revolves around Tiburce's attempts to recover his money from Gorinflot, his banker, who is about to flee with his clients' funds, and at the same time to conceal his wayward past (and present) from his fiancée and her aunt, who insists that Athénais be Tiburce's first love: 'Il faut à ma nièce un Coeur tout neuf, qui n'a jamais été habité'[43] (My niece must have a heart that's all new, one that has never been possessed before). His marriage to Athénais, which, thanks to her handsome dowry, will secure his financial future, is predicated on his success in these two pursuits. Athénais, for her part, is looking forward to moving to Paris from her native provincial Pithiviers ('Il est bien plus agréable d'habiter la capitale'[44] (It is so much more pleasant to live in the capital)). For both characters, the marriage will lead to a different form of upward mobility and social advancement.

Mobility, or lack thereof, is at the heart of the play: Tiburce, who is in a hurry, keeps missing his omnibus. While other characters come and go, ferried by various omnibuses to their destinations, Tiburce spends the entire play trapped in the station: his upwardly mobile aspirations notwithstanding, he is literally going nowhere. The irony of this situation does not escape him as he exclaims, 'Que de choses on apprend en voyageant... Mais, à propos de cela... c'est que je ne voyage pas du tout'[45] (You learn so much by travelling... But about this... it's just that I haven't travelled anywhere). Paradoxically, Tiburce manages to settle both his financial and his amorous affairs without ever leaving the omnibus station, as other characters act as his proxy by securing his money (Francfort) and neutralising his jealous mistress (Bouillabaisse), thus ensuring him both an advantageous marriage and social advancement.

The main objects of satire are the play's two central male characters, both of whom are clearly recognisable types. At first, Tiburce and Bouillabaisse appear to be polar opposites in terms of their social standing: Tiburce is ostensibly a scholar, a 'professeur de langues vivantes et de littérature morte' (professor of living languages and dead literatures). He is intellectual but poor. Meanwhile, his foil Bouillabaisse is a wealthy *fabricant du noir animal*, an industrialist in the bone-char business, whose ridiculous name points to his propensity for physical pleasures and consumption.[46] The play seemingly opposes men of different social spheres, of cultural and financial capital. Tiburce engages in intellectual but not very lucrative pursuits, while Bouillabaisse has built a fortune from a lowly trade. Yet the play debunks the opposition of the 'intellectual' and the 'material' by showing that the two men are eminently interchangeable. Tiburce, despite his intellectual pretensions, appears neither particularly intelligent nor wise. Throughout the play, dramatic irony is used to emphasise his lack of understanding of the unfolding events; as spectators, we often see him failing to recognise connections among characters. Moreover, as a professor of 'langues vivantes', Tiburce presumably possesses a mastery of his own native language, yet he repeatedly fails to understand what others say. When Cigarette informs him that her husband is 'cossu' (wealthy), he immediately chastises her for what he assumes is improper use of language, assuming she meant 'cocu', or cuckolded: 'Cossu!... pourquoi cette cédille? C'est une faute d'orthographe Cigarette... Vous avez une prononciation défectueuse, ma chère amie' (You're making a spelling error, Cigarette. Your pronunciation is defective, my dear friend). He not only denigrates Cigarette by making assumptions about her virtue and by presuming that her language is faulty, but he displays his own ignorance by misunderstanding 'cossu'.

Circulation and visibility

Having dismantled Tiburce's supposed intelligence, *J'attends un omnibus* proceeds to undercut the social distinctions between Tiburce and Bouillabaisse through complex marriage and adultery plots. As different as the two men may seem, they sleep with and are involved with the same women: Bouillabaisse, it turns out, is the lover of Tiburce's current mistress, the husband of his former mistress, and his fiancée's guardian. Sharing women as well as the omnibus (and the omnibus station) neutralises their ostensible differences. The play thus points to a confusion of class distinctions, a phenomenon of which the omnibus is a symbol. The vaudeville concludes with a formulaic happy ending: Tiburce and Athénais are united, Bouillabaisse and Cigarette are reconciled and social order is restored.

Similar to the plot of *J'attends un omnibus*, that of *Mon voisin d'omnibus* (1846) exposes and mocks obsession with social mobility and class tensions. This vaudeville play features a central male character who is diminished and on the brink of financial ruin but saved through an advantageous marriage. *Mon voisin d'omnibus* explicitly taps into class issues and different forms of upward mobility characteristic of the first half of the nineteenth century. Although this play is set in a 'salon bourgeois', we learn that the plot is launched on – and thanks to – an omnibus. The protagonist, Charles de Varennes, is so deeply in debt that he is literally chased by his creditors and a bailiff, who is about to arrest him. To avoid the bailiff, he jumps on a passing omnibus, only to discover that he does not even have the requisite fare of 30 centimes:

Je dis au conducteur que je demeurais rue Lafitte 42, que je m'appelais Charles de Varennes, lorsque mon voisin, sur la banquette, un monsieur d'une physionomie originale et ayant le dos assez remarquablement vouté .. parut frappé de mon nom, me demanda la permission de payer pour moi, et cela, avec une si gracieuse et si joviale insistance que je ne pus refuser.[47]

(I was telling the conductor that I live on rue Lafitte 42, that my name is Charles de Varennes, when my seatmate, a gentleman with an interesting face and an extremely bent back, appeared impressed by my name and asked if he could pay my fare, and he did this so graciously and with such jolly insistence that I just couldn't refuse.)

Charles, who claims to be the illegitimate child of an aristocratic father, presumes that Clérisseau, the omnibus neighbour of the title, is smitten by his aristocratic name and that he assists him out of pure deference to his presumed higher social status. Clérisseau becomes Charles' benefactor, arranging an advantageous marriage for him with Hortense, daughter of a merchant, paying off his debts, and helping him conceal his past sexual indiscretions. At the end of the play, we learn that far from being an admirer of Charles's pedigree, Clérisseau is, in fact, his creditor; securing a respectable wife with a good dowry was the surest way for him to be paid. If he were struck by de Varennes' name on the omnibus, it was because he recognised it as that of his debtor.

The play makes visible and at the same time satirises the upwardly mobile class aspirations of the bourgeoisie, the declining aristocracy's financial woes and the wiles to which the latter resorts to improve its financial standing (even if the authenticity of de Varennes' aristocratic origins is questioned). Godibert (Hortense's merchant father) is willing to give away his daughter solely because of the aristocratic particle in de Varennes' name; and Charles himself sees this marriage to Hortense merely as a way to secure his shaky financial situation. As Mary Gluck rightly points out, vaudeville 'was unambiguously identified with the newly enriched and increasingly respectable commercial middle classes',[48] the very classes that constituted a majority of omnibus passengers. Although *Mon voisin d'omnibus* concludes with the formulaic happy ending and marriage, it is Clérisseau, the shrewd and prudent omnibus passenger, who emerges as the clear winner – and as an author figure who crafts the play's plot. *Mon voisin d'omnibus* thus invites the audience to recognise themselves in the play's characters, to gently laugh at their own social practices – and yet, in the end, to feel justified in upwardly mobile social ambitions.

These plays served as a privileged space in which to work through class tensions symbolised by the omnibus, a space where aspirations of social mobility are lightly mocked and thoroughly vindicated. The vaudeville experience provided the audience with a comforting mirror of its own social world. But if these plays bring class tensions to a satisfactory resolution, other works present the potential inclusiveness of the omnibus as threatening and disruptive. Rather than a space where tensions are resolved, the omnibus is figured as a stage where class conflicts come to the fore.

Class conflict 'for all'

In an 1856 letter to Louise Colet, Gustave Flaubert provocatively suggests that it was the invention of the omnibus that lead to the demise of the bourgeoisie: 'Depuis l'invention des omnibus la bourgeoisie est morte; oui, elle s'est assise là, sur la banquette populaire, et elle y reste, toute pareille maintenant à la canaille, d'âme, d'aspect et même d'habit: (voir le chic des grosses étoffes, la création du paletot, les costumes de canotiers, les blouses bleues pour la chasse).'[49] (Since the invention of the omnibus the bourgeoisie is dead; yes, the bourgeoisie sat on a bench next to commoners, and it remains there, all similar now to the riffraff, both in their souls, in their appearance and even in their clothing (just look at the 'chic' rough fabric, *paletot*, sailor suits, or workers' blue overalls some now wear to hunting parties).) In Flaubert's view, the inevitable physical proximity of omnibus passengers belonging to different social classes fostered destructive uniformity, an ultimate erasure of boundaries between social groups and the disappearance of distinction (here manifested through its most visible marker, clothing) that had long been the hallmark of the upper classes.[50]

Flaubert was not alone in voicing his dismay about the enforced intimacy that came with sharing the cramped space of an omnibus. Visual and literary representations of the omnibus interior frequently staged scenes of class tensions that either reflected or mocked the anxiety about the potential mixing. This unwelcome proximity of different social classes threatened the stability of social structures based on the strict separation of space according to class and suggested the breakdown of existing social hierarchies. The erasure of physical boundaries between bourgeois and working-class passengers was associated with the 'contamination' and contagion – both physical and moral – to which sharing such close quarters could lead. In the rest of this chapter, I explore how the genre of lithography laid bare and ridiculed bourgeois anxieties about class mixing, and then turn to a short story by Guy de Maupassant that offers a different, more sombre, vision of this phenomenon.

Visualising class

The uneasy coexistence of different classes was writ large in visual representations of the omnibus, and especially in lithography, the urban, middlebrow audience for which also constituted the majority of omnibus riders. Lithography was the medium of choice for many of the omnibus images I consider in this book. Invented at the end of the eighteenth century as a cheap and easy way to disseminate Revolutionary caricatures, lithographs, unlike the older media of etching and engraving, could be reproduced in the thousands at a low cost. Not considered a form of high art, lithography was often disdained by the art establishment. According to art historian Patricia Mainardi, it 'represented modernity, creeping industrialization, and opposition politics, while etching and engraving signaled tradition, the high standards of artisanal craftsmanship, and respectable upper-crust taste'.[51] Moreover, Mainardi shows that lithography quickly became a favoured medium for representing modern life 'because of the ease with which it could be executed… and its ability to depict the ephemeral and shifting scenes of a rapidly changing society'.[52] As such, lithography was an ideal form for depicting the omnibus, a modern urban phenomenon. Well-established masters like Grandville and Daumier, as well as numerous lesser-known and often anonymous artists, capitalised on the popularity of the omnibus as a vehicle for social satire and commentary and on lithography's association with oppositional politics and social critique in order to expose and mock bourgeois anxieties about class mixing, encapsulated by the omnibus.[53]

Visual representations of class tensions on the omnibus appeared almost at the same time as the omnibus itself. Consider, for example, an 1829 lithograph by Ratier in which the artist placed travellers of widely varied social classes within the confined space of the vehicle as a way to tackle both social mobility and class privilege in post-Revolutionary French society, characterised by instability and flux (Plate 4). A cross-section of an omnibus, the image makes the vehicle's social diversity visible through the passengers' clothing and body language. On the far left, a young woman, whose apron and bonnet suggest her working-class status, is seated uncomfortably next to an officer or a gendarme holding his hat. The interaction between the conductor, who is standing, and the nearly-seated officer highlights how the omnibus setting upsets traditional social relationships: inside the vehicle, it is the conductor, who collects the fare and assigns seats, who is clearly in charge.

At the centre of the image, a foppish young gentleman sports a fashionable cream-coloured *redingote*, whose tails he carefully holds in his hands so as not to crease them; his bright-yellow stylish *cravate* and matching yellow gloves, reminiscent of the yellow gloves so coveted by Balzac's hero, Eugène de Rastignac, mark him as a dandy and indicate that he belongs to a higher social sphere than his fellow passengers – or perhaps, like Rastignac, his clothes and posture are symbols of his social aspirations. Contrary to the precepts of the contemporary conduct manuals cited earlier, the gentleman asserts his social and sartorial superiority by extending his elbows and knees into his fellow passengers' space without any regard for his seatmates, as he crushes a petit-bourgeois man to his left and a woman in a humble grey dress to his right, likely a *grisette*.[54] Other passengers – the man in a worker's blue cap, and a woman in a modest green dress but fashionable shoes, holding her child next to her – add to the social diversity of the image. The woman appears to be speaking – but to whom? her seatmate? no one in particular? – thus invading everyone's auditory space and violating rules of proper conduct.

Finally, the corpulent and solidly bourgeois couple rigidly seated on the right end of the bench looks on in disapproval as the conductor orders them to make room for the officer. The woman's lavish purple shawl, her gigantic purse, and the man's umbrella all indicate that they are well off. This couple embodies ideals of bourgeois propriety and moral rectitude, and their displeasure with their fellow passengers is visible. This image is just one of many that exploited the idea of class mixing embedded in the name 'omnibus' to reveal the social complexities and tensions of the vehicle's public but paradoxically intimate space (see also Figure 3.3).

Other artists tackled class tensions on public conveyances more explicitly. In Grandville's lithograph from *Les Métamorphoses du jour*, a well-dressed bourgeois bird couple enquires in horror whether the obviously low-class monkey and mouse couple behind them are boarding as well (Plate 5). The birds' faces express disgust and disdain, not only because the other passengers belong to a lower class but because they are a 'mixed-species' couple, thus

Circulation and visibility

Figure 3.3 Gobert, 'Intérieur d'un équipage de la petite propriété. Ah dieu! que ces Omnibus sont mal composés! ne m'en parlez pas!'. 1829.

stirring the spectre of miscegenation. The birds convey their fear of exposure to the lower classes, here literally figured as different species. The conductor's reply ('Omnibus!!! Madame!') implies that the sharing of the space is in the nature – and the very name – of the vehicle, and that the bird's indignation is misplaced: monkeys and birds *must* travel together.

In another example, Daumier's 'Madeleine–Bastille' depicts two elegant young women and a gentleman, who look on disapprovingly as an extremely corpulent lower-class woman boards the omnibus (Figure 3.4). The corpulent woman, who invades a good deal of space in the vehicle as well as most of the foreground of the image, literally eclipses some of the middle-class passengers and squeezes others out of the way. The man in a hat on the left of the image appears practically crushed by the woman's heavy hips. Her massiveness embodies the masses, and the reaction of her fellow passengers points to the underlying class threat that she represents. Notably, although the young ladies look contemptuous of the woman and of the way she invades the common space of the omnibus, that is exactly what their own ample skirts do. The title of the lithograph, 'Madeleine–Bastille', refers to the itinerary of one of the main omnibus lines and alludes to the two different social worlds to which the passengers belong: Madeleine is an elegant and affluent part of town, while Bastille is a working-class neighbourhood, evocative of the revolutionary spirit.

Class, gender and locomotion

Figure 3.4 Honoré Daumier, 'Madeleine-Bastille. Un zeste, un rien… et l'omnibus se trouve complet'. 1862.

Another Daumier image, 'Intérieur d'un Omnibus', presents a close-up of a young woman squeezed between an obviously drunk gentleman indecorously asleep next to her, and a rough-looking butcher clad in an apron (Figure 3.5). Hands on his hips, the butcher aggressively asserts his claim on the omnibus space without regard for the young woman. Although she most likely belongs to the working class as well, we can call her class belonging 'aspirational', perhaps a few steps above her seatmates based on her clothes and her fashionable umbrella, or parasol. The drunkard appears to be down on his luck: his clothes display vestiges of elegance, evoking downward mobility.

These lithographs visually staged performance of class identity in the discursive space of the page. Addressed to – and circulated among – a middlebrow

Circulation and visibility

Figure 3.5 Honoré Daumier, 'Intérieur d'un omnibus. Entre un homme ivre et un charcutier'. 1839.

audience, they portray the omnibus as a battleground where the lower and middle classes confront the need to continuously renegotiate their social space, reflecting the changing structures of a society in flux.

'Un musée des grotesques': Maupassant's 'La Dot' and a journey through smells

While lithographs from the middle decades of the nineteenth century offer a satirical take on class mixing aboard the omnibus, a late-nineteenth-century short story by Maupassant, 'La Dot' (1884), presents a very different, darker vision of what the omnibus meant in terms of class. In this story, the omnibus functions as a site of bourgeois anxiety and discomfort, a space that symbolises the heroine's dramatic downfall. Although by the late nineteenth century public conveyances had long been a common feature of everyday life, and their heterogeneous composition a commonplace, Maupassant's tale shows that they continued to serve as a powerful emblem of class tensions.

'La Dot' tells the story of Jeanne, a newly-wed young woman from the provinces who comes to Paris with her husband to deposit her dowry with a notary, whose practice the husband ostensibly intends to buy. Upon arriving in Paris, Jeanne is scandalised by her husband's decision to take an omnibus rather than a *fiacre*. After he scolds her for being a spendthrift, Jeanne cautiously acquiesces. While she takes a seat inside the vehicle, her husband goes up to the *impériale* on the pretext that he wishes to smoke. After a long and arduous journey through unfamiliar and frightening city streets, Jeanne discovers that her husband has disappeared, along with her dowry, never to be seen again. At the end of the story, when the conductor informs the station manager that there is a woman abandoned by her husband ('C'est une dame que son époux a lâché en route' (It's a lady whose husband dumped her along the way)), the other man's response is emblematic of the alienation and indifference characteristic of the big city: 'Bon, ce n'est rien, occupez-vous de votre service. Et il tourna les talons.'[55] (Well, it's nothing, mind your own business. And he turned away.)

The main body of the story describes Jeanne's nightmarish and anxiety-ridden experience of the omnibus ride. Her intense anguish during the journey is the story's focal point. The omnibus becomes a vehicle of destiny beyond Jeanne's control, carrying her off to an uncertain and ominous future. As her husband pushes her toward the vehicle, 'le conducteur, qui l'avait saisie par le bras pour l'aider à escalader le marchepied, la précipita dans la voiture, et elle tomba, effarée, sur une banquette, regardant avec stupeur par la vitre de derrière, les pieds de son mari qui grimpait sur l'impériale. Et elle demeura immobile entre un gros monsieur qui sentait la pipe et une vieille femme qui sentait le chien'[56] (the conductor, who had seized her by the arm to help her up the step, pushed her inside, and she fell into a seat, bewildered, looking through the back window at the feet of her husband as he climbed up to the upper deck. And she sat there, motionless, between a fat man who smelled of cheap tobacco and an old woman who smelled of dog). Jeanne is but a feeble victim at the mercy of destiny, personified by the omnibus conductor.

From this point on, the narrative is focalised through Jeanne's sensory perception. If for Edouard Gourdon, writing in 1842, the omnibus, with its multiplicity of human types, was an exciting microcosm of society, and if other mid-century observers presented the omnibus interior with bemusement and curiosity, Maupassant depicts it as an assemblage of terrifying and grotesque caricatures:

> Tous les autres voyageurs, alignés et muets, - un garçon épicier, une ouvrière, un sergent d'infanterie, un monsieur à lunette d'or coiffé d'un chapeau de soie aux bords énormes et relevés comme des gouttières, des dames à l'air important et grincheux, qui semblait dire par leur attitude: 'Nous sommes ici, mais nous valons mieux que ça,' deux bonnes sœurs, une fille en cheveux et un croque-mort, – avaient l'air d'une collection de caricatures, d'un musée des grotesques, d'une série

de charges de la face humaine, semblables à ces rangés de pantins comiques qu'on abat, dans les foires, avec des balles.⁵⁷

(All the other passengers were lined up in silence – a grocer's boy, a female worker, a soldier, a gentleman with gold-rimmed spectacles and a big silk hat, two ladies with a self-satisfied and crabbed look, which seemed to say: 'We are riding in this thing, but we are worth better than that,' two sisters of charity and an undertaker. They looked like a collection of caricatures, a museum of grotesque figures, a series of cut-outs with human faces, similar to the target dummies you knock over to win prizes at fairs.)

What is striking in this description of omnibus passengers is their profound dehumanisation. Silent and akin to static images, these anonymous characters are reduced to caricatures, or practice targets; they seem to embody the alienation of the modern city. Rather than describing Jeanne's hellish ride through Paris in visual terms, Maupassant conveys it through a series of oppressive olfactory experiences, generated by her working-class fellow passengers, each emitting smells associated with their trade or social position:

Les bonnes sœurs firent signe d'arrêter, puis elles sortirent l'une devant l'autre, répandant une odeur fade de vieille jupe. On repartit, puis on s'arrêta de nouveau. Et une cuisinière monta, rouge, essoufflée. Elle s'assit et posa sur ses genoux son panier aux provisions. Une forte senteur d'eau de vaisselle se répandit dans l'omnibus. [...] Le croque – mort s'en alla et fut remplacé par un cocher qui fleurait l'écurie. La fille en cheveux eut pour successeur un commissionnaire dont les pieds exhalaient le parfum de ses courses.⁵⁸

(The sisters motioned to the conductor to stop, and they got off one after the other, leaving in their wake the pungent smell of camphor. The omnibus started up and soon stopped again. And in got a cook, red-faced and out of breath. She sat down and placed her basket of provisions on her lap. A strong odour of dishwater filled the vehicle. The undertaker went out and was replaced by a coachman smelling of the stable. The young girl was succeeded by a messenger, whose feet bore the odour of his errands.)

What emerges from this passage is the idea of contagion through smells within the confined space of the omnibus.⁵⁹ Since the smells permeating the omnibus interior indiscriminately envelop and contaminate all passengers, regardless of class or rank, the slippage among these classes appears unavoidable. This journey told through odours conveys Jeanne's mounting anxiety and desperation and perhaps prefigures her tragic destiny: we are left to wonder what lot could be reserved for a young provincial woman abandoned penniless in the midst of the metropolis.

Maupassant's story brings into sharp relief the representational power of the omnibus as a class signifier. Although class mixing in public spaces – aboard the omnibus, in parks, boulevards, cafés and department stores, which were staples of the urban landscape – was most certainly a reality of city life in 1884, in the cultural imagination it was the omnibus that remained a symbol of menacing class diversity, a literary device to convey bourgeois anxiety about shifting social structures.

The omnibus served as a flashpoint of class aspirations and anxieties in nineteenth-century France, where social mobility was perceived as a promise by some social observers and as a dangerous challenge by others. The omnibus was discursively constructed in literature and visual culture as a key urban site where class identity was continuously negotiated and contested, and where central questions of equality, social mobility and class distinction agitating the nineteenth century were mediated. Just as the vehicle's physical space made lower classes visible to their bourgeois fellow passengers in unprecedented ways, popular literature replicated this visibility within the discursive space of the page, making the lower classes doubly present through representation and circulation. By populating newspapers, works of urban observation, city guide-books and other genres with images of class mixing, popular literature and visual culture amplified both the anxieties and aspirations of their prime target audience.

If Maupassant's 'La Dot' showcases the symbolic power of the omnibus to represent class tensions, it also points to another set of anxieties that were pervasive in omnibus literature throughout the nineteenth century: the profound disquiet on the part of male bourgeois observers about the presence of women in the public space. It is to these concerns that the next chapter turns.

Notes

1. Uzanne, 'Omnibus de Paris', 483.
   'Omnibus travel unites all classes without distinction or division. Of all the Parisian sites where people gather, the omnibus offers the most perfect image of democracy and polite fraternity. Workers, shopkeepers, people of independent means, scientists, poets, financiers, actors and actresses, servants and masters, musicians and singers, members of the Academy and cigarette-butt pickers all rub shoulders with one another every day for a few brief moments, in the open air on the upper deck, among the crowds on the platform, or upon the seats inside.'
2. Nicholas Papayanis, *Horse-Drawn Cabs*, p. 57.
3. Maxime Du Camp, *Paris, ses organes, ses fonctions et sa vie dans la seconde moitié du XIXe siècle*, vol. I (Paris, Hachette, 1869–75), p. 200. Quoted in Papayanis, *Horse-Drawn Cabs*, p. 58.
4. Papayanis, *Horse-Drawn Cabs*, pp. 58–9. See also Maxime Du Camp, 'Les voitures publiques', 342.

Circulation and visibility

5   For a history of the *carrosse à cinq sous*, see Introduction.
6   See 'Les histoires et chronologies melées des transports parisiens (1828–1997)', in Zuber *et al.*, *Guide des sources de l'histoire des transports publics urbains à Paris*, pp. 37–8.
7   David H. Pinkney, *Napoleon III and the Rebuilding of Paris* (Princeton, NJ: Princeton University Press, 1958), p. 167.
8   Papayanis, *Horse-Drawn Cabs*, pp. 61–3.
9   Thompson, 'Telling spatial stories', 527.
10 Thompson, 'Telling spatial stories', 537.
11 As I pointed out in the Introduction, sociologist Georg Simmel was the first to indicate that public transport created for the first time a setting where urban dwellers were exposed to each other's gaze for prolonged periods of time.
12 Gourdon, *Physiologie de l'omnibus*, p. 95.
13 Delord *et al.*, *Paris-en-omnibus*, pp. 11–12.
14 Friès, 'Le Conducteur d'omnibus', p. 102.
15 Edmond Texier, 'Les voitures à Paris', in *Tableau de Paris*, vol. 2 (Paris: Paulin et le Chevalier, 1852–53), p. 315.
16 'Quelques remarques sur les omnibus', *Le Magasin pittoresque* (1843), 103.
17 'Quelques remarques sur les omnibus', 103.
18 Raymond, 'L'omnibus', 351–2.
19 Elisabeth Félicie Byle-Mouillard, *Manuel complet de la bonne compagnie, ou guide de la politesse, des égards, du bon ton et de la bienséance*, 5th edn (Paris: F. Ancelle, 1829), p. xxx.
20 Paul de Kock, 'Etudes de mœurs. Les pensionnats à voiture', *Musée des familles* (1 January 1841).
21 The omnibus was often referred to as *voiture à six sous* – a six-penny carriage.
22 Soullier, *Les omnibus de Paris*, pp. 3–4.
23 Gourdon, *Physiologie de l'omnibus*, pp. 105–6.
24 Du Camp, 'Les voitures publiques', 351. Du Camp provides a vivid account of how the omnibuses were used during insurrections: 'L'omnibus qui pouvait, sain et sauf, regagner son dépôt, avait été favorisé du ciel; à tous les coins de rues, les insurgés le guettaient; on se jetait à la tête des chevaux, on les arrêtait, on faisait descendre les voyageurs, on laissait au cocher le temps de dételer; puis la voiture, en deux coup d'épaule, était jetée bas, les roues en l'air; on l'assurait de quelques pavés, on la flanquait de deux ou trois tonneaux remplis de sable; au sommet du timon redressé comme un mât, on arborait un drapeau, et la barricade était faite. L'omnibus devenait ainsi un instrument de désordre ou de victoire, selon les péripéties de la journée' (The omnibus that was able to return to the depot in one piece had been blessed by heavens. At every corner, the insurgents were lying in wait. They would pounce on the horses and stop them; they would make all passengers get off; they would leave the coachman just enough time to unhitch the horses. Then, with a kick of the shoulder, the vehicle would be thrown on its back, wheels in the air. The omnibus was set on the street, complete with two or three barrels of sand; at the top of the beam, straightened up like a mast of a ship, a flag would be planted, and the barricade was ready. Thus, the omnibus became an instrument of the upheaval or of victory, depending on the events of the day), pp. 350–1.

25 'On a remarqué qu'en temps de révolution, l'omnibus faisait comme bon nombre de citoyens, honorables d'ailleurs, et surtout comme ceux-là qui font le plus de bruit après la victoire. Ils se hâtent de regagner leurs asiles ignorés, leurs lointaines remises, cachées dans les rues les plus obscures des banlieues. Ce n'est pas sans raisons : un omnibus n'a qu'à perdre à l'émeute, il est si vite renversé et transformé en barricade ! A ce rôle, il ne peut que gagner des renforcements et de funestes horizons; la bataille ne lui est d'aucun profit, et il se retire toujours avec quelque fracture, quelque lésion considérable.' (During revolutions, the omnibus behaved the same way as a good number of honourable citizens, and especially like those who make the most noise after a victory. They hasten to return to their far-away depots, hidden away on an obscure suburban street. And this is not without reason: the omnibus always loses during an insurrection, because it is quickly turned over and made into a barricade! In that role, it can only gain from reinforcements and sinister horizons. It does not gain anything from the battle, and it always leaves with a fracture or a considerable wound.) Texier, 'Les voitures à Paris', pp. 315–16.

26 Victor Hugo, *Les Misérables* (Paris: Garnier 1963), pp. 335–8.

27 On Hugo and the barricade, see David Charles, 'Le trognon et l'omnibus: faire de sa misère sa barricade', in Alain Corbin and Jean-Marie Mayeur (eds), *La Barricade* (Paris: Publications de la Sorbonne, 1997), pp. 137–49.

28 We also find the topos of an overturned omnibus in Flaubert's *L'éducation sentimentale*, in a scene describing the detritus of a barricade during the 1848 revolution: 'L'insurrection avait laissé dans ce quartier-là des traces formidables. Le sol des rues se trouvait, d'un bout à l'autre, inégalement bosselé. Sur les barricades en ruine, il restait des omnibus, des tuyaux de gaz, des roues de charrettes; de petites flaques noires, en de certains endroits, devaient être du sang.' (The insurrection had left formidable traces on the neighbourhood. From one end to another, the ground on the streets was unevenly bumpy. On a destroyed barricade, there remained omnibuses, gas pipes, cart wheels. Red spots here and there must have been blood stains.) Here Flaubert draws on the existing repertoire of images that were ingrained in the cultural imagination. Gustave Flaubert, *L'éducation sentimentale* (Paris: Les Belles Lettres, 1942), p. 169.

29 Honoré de Balzac, *Correspondance* (1832), R. Pierrot (ed.), vol. 1 (Paris: Garnier, 1960–66), p. 380.

30 Papayanis, *Horse-Drawn Cabs*, p. 64.

31 Félix Nogaret, *Réflexions d'un patriarche sur les voitures dites omnibus!* (Paris: Leclerc, 1828).

32 Nogaret's slim volume was well known and frequently quoted by authors writing about the omnibus. For example, Jules Clarétie cites him in his article 'Les omnibus parisiens', in *Les annales politiques et littéraires*, 1200 (24 June 1906).

33 Madame de Flesselles, *Les jeunes voyageurs dans Paris* (Paris: Locard et Davi, 1829), pp. 233–4.

34 Huart, 'Les voitures publiques', p. 177.

35 As Nicholas Papayanis shows, the launch and development of the omnibus service was indeed motivated not by a belief in equality or common good but by commercial interests in the context of nascent capitalism. Papayanis, *Horse-Drawn Cabs*, pp. 162–71.

36 Huart, 'Les voitures publiques', p. 164.
37 Fouinet, 'Un voyage en omnibus', p. 61.
38 Fouinet, 'Un voyage en omnibus', p. 61.
39 For a discussion of the connection between vaudeville and omnibus, see Chapter 1.
40 J. Gabriel and P. Vermond, *J'attends un omnibus* (Bruxelles: J-A Lelong, 1849), p. 3.
41 For an illuminating discussion of the figure of the *lorette*, see Thompson, *The Virtuous Marketplace*.
42 Xavier Aubryet, in 'La Chaussée d'Antin', from *Paris-guide par les principaux écrivains et artistes de la France*, tells the story of rue Bréda's name, which belonged originally to a respectable entrepreneur: 'En 1825, Breda (sic) n'évoquait à l'esprit que l'idée d'un spéculateur de terrains; vingt ans après et encore aujourd'hui, Bréda fait sourire les gens mariés et froncer le sourcil aux belles-mères. Ce nom vertueux et légitime sent le péché mignon et le fruit défendu, il est incorruptible et il est corrupteur!' (In 1825, Breda evoked only the idea of land speculation. Twenty years later, and still to this day, Breda makes married men smirk and mothers-in-law frown. This virtuous and legitimate name smells of sweet vice and forbidden fruit: it is incorruptible, and it is corrupting!) He then laments that the neighbourhood is trying in vain to correct its reputation: 'Seulement, le préjugé tient bon, et il faudra peut-être des siècles de chasteté pour effacer l'effet de quelques années trop légères' (Only the prejudice sticks, and we'll need centuries of chastity to erase the effects of a few years of frivolity). *Paris-guide par les principaux écrivains et artistes de la France* (Paris: Edition de la Découverte, 1983), p. 98.
43 Gabriel and Vermond, *J'attends un omnibus*, p. 9.
44 Gabriel and Vermond, *J'attends un omnibus*, p. 5.
45 Gabriel and Vermond, *J'attends un omnibus*, p. 31.
46 Bone char is a by-product of animal bones.
47 Gustave Albitte and Louis Dugard, *Mon voisin d'omnibus*, in *La France dramatique au dix-neuvième siécle* (Paris: Tresse, 1841), p. 2.
48 Gluck, *Popular Bohemia*, p. 48.
49 Gustave Flaubert, *Correspondance, 1856* (Paris: L. Conard, 1926–54), p. 21.
50 Flaubert was not the only writer to express dismay over the *paletot*, a loose overcoat introduced in the nineteenth century. According to Anne Green, for many writers, the *paletot* became a symbol of bourgeois mediocrity and dull uniformity. For example, Eugene Chapus (pseudonymously 'Vicomte de Marennes') was outraged by the erasure of class distinctions and the way they were expressed through dress; in his *Manuel de l'hommes et de femmes*, he reserved his strongest vitriol for the *paletot*: 'Class distinctions, professional values and character hardly exist. And so what did we do? We adopted the *paletot*, which is not made to fit anyone, and which doesn't suit anyone (…) The order went out to tailors; practicality, ease, comfort, vulgarity, anonymity; and the *paletot* was created. They tossed us the *paletot*, that absolute annihilation of dress, the ultimate egalitarian garment, a veritable uniform of the phalanstery', pp. 68–9, quoted in Anne Green, *Changing France: Literature and Material Culture in the Second Empire* (London: Anthem Press, 2013), p. 123.
51 Patricia Mainardi, *Husbands, Wives, and Lovers: Marriage and Its Discontents in Nineteenth-Century France* (New Haven, CT: Yale University Press, 2003), p. 77.

52 Patricia Mainardi, *Another World: Nineteenth-Century Illustrated Print Culture* (New Haven, CT: Yale University Press, 2017), p. 14. The book discusses the invention and cultural significance of nineteenth-century print media.
53 On lithography as a medium for oppositional politics, see Richard Terdiman, *Discourse/Counter-Discourse: The Theory and Practice of Symbolic Resistance in Nineteenth-Century France* (Ithaca, NY: Cornell University Press, 1985), pp. 151–2.
54 This image represents what we might call today 'manspreading'. The Oxford Dictionary, which recently added the word, defines it as 'when a man sits with his legs wide apart on public transport, encroaching on other seats'. In 2014, the New York City Metropolitan Transportation Authority unveiled a new public advertisement campaign aimed at curbing the behaviour, after it gained notoriety through a campaign in feminist social media.
55 Guy de Maupassant, *Contes et Nouvelles*, Albert-Marie Schmidt and Gérard Delaisement (ed.) (Paris: Albin Michel, 1957), p. 564.
56 Maupassent, *Contes et Nouvelles*, pp. 561–2.
57 Maupassant, *Contes et Nouvelles*, p. 562.
58 Maupassant, *Contes et Nouvelles*, p. 562.
59 On urban smellscapes, see Victoria Hanshaw, *Urban Smellscapes: Understanding and Designing City Smell Environments* (London: Routledge, 2014).

4

Moral geographies: women and public transport

> Mais tante, je n'ai besoin de personne. Je suis venue toute seule.
> -Seule! A pied? En voiture?
> -Non, tante, dans Panthéon-Courcelles.
> -Mon Dieu, mon Dieu, que Claude est coupable....[1]
>
> Colette, *Claudine à Paris*

When 17-year-old Claudine, the eponymous protagonist of Colette's 1901 novel, informs her prim and proper Aunt Cœur that she arrived at her house not only unaccompanied but also by way of the Panthéon–Courcelles omnibus, her aunt is profoundly scandalised. Why, we may wonder, did Aunt Cœur find it so inappropriate for a young woman from a respectable family to ride on an omnibus alone in 1901? After all, by that time the omnibus had been a feature of everyday city life for decades. And from numerous references in literary and visual culture, as well as newspaper accounts and conduct manuals, we know that women of all classes, including respectable *bourgeoises*, used the omnibus to move about the city.

The omnibus was by law available to men and women of all classes from the time when it was first launched; in the 1830s and 1840s, it was indeed one of the few public places where, at least in theory, respectable women could find themselves sitting next to men without risking their reputation. Moreover, nineteenth-century conduct manuals included sections on proper behaviour for both sexes aboard the omnibus, thus suggesting that this practice was normalised fairly early. For example, a manual published in 1829, the year following the launch of the omnibus, appealed to both 'gentlemen' and 'ladies' to conduct themselves according to principles of French chivalry. Gentlemen were asked to cede their seat to a lady should she find herself in a less comfortable one: 'La galanterie française demande qu'un cavalier offre poliment la sienne (la place) à une dame qui en aurait une moins commode; car il paraîtrait inconvenant qu'un homme se trouvât assis dans le fond,

133

tandis que celle-ci siégerait sur les banquettes du devant.' (French gallantry requires that a gentleman offers his seat to a lady who has a less comfortable one; it would be inappropriate for a man to occupy a seat in the back while a lady has a seat in front.) Ladies were admonished not to be overly exacting or hold particular expectations of male passengers: 'Les dames de leur côté ne doivent pas se montrer trop exigeantes, ni trop mettre à l'épreuve la complaisance des hommes.' (Ladies, for their part, should neither be too demanding nor test too much the gentlemen's readiness to oblige.)[2] And in the 1860s, Emmeline Raymond, a prominent voice in shaping urban bourgeois femininity, penned an article in *La Mode illustrée* in which she not only discussed different female types found aboard, but also dispensed advice to her female readers about proper behaviour during the omnibus journey:

> Comme l'on ne connaît pas ses compagnes et ses compagnons de route, comme on n'en est pas connu, il faut éviter toute conversation et réduire le dialogue autant que possible si on tentait de l'engager. Il ne faut point oublier, en effet, d'une part, que les apparences peuvent être trompeuses, et, d'une autre, qu'une certaine dose d'empressement peut être mal interprétée.[3]

> (Since you're not acquainted with your fellow passengers and they are not acquainted with you, you must avoid all conversation and limit interaction as much as possible, if you must have it at all. You must not forget that, on the one hand, appearances may be deceiving, and, on the other, a certain eagerness on your part may be misinterpreted.)

Perhaps even more importantly than the specifics of her advice, the article is based on Raymond's personal experience, thus indicating that taking public transport was an entirely proper and common thing to do for a woman of good moral standing. If this paragon of bourgeois propriety and feminine virtue could ride an omnibus alone, then any respectable woman could too, without risking her reputation.

And yet Aunt Cœur's reaction of shock and disbelief is emblematic of how the omnibus was viewed in the nineteenth-century French cultural imagination: as a place associated with improper female conduct and with different forms of sexual transgression. Many cultural documents present this vehicle as a space of dubious repute, where respectable girls like Claudine could become 'contaminated' by the inappropriate behaviour of other, less virtuous women passengers, or, worse, be taken for a woman of loose morals. In fact, by the last quarter of the nineteenth century, despite the fact that many women of different classes used public transport on a daily basis – whether to go to work, shopping or visiting – we find a well-established gendered mythology of the omnibus as a 'vehicle of vice', one that linked it with sexually transgressive female behaviour, moral decay and loss of respectability.

To be sure, the omnibus was hardly the only vehicle associated with illicit female sexuality in nineteenth-century culture, as readers of *Madame Bovary* can attest. In Flaubert's 1857 novel, Emma Bovary consummates her adulterous affair with Léon inside a *fiacre*. In this famous scene, the description of the frenetic peregrinations of the *fiacre* through the streets of Rouen metaphorically conveys the lovemaking taking place inside the vehicle. When Emma hesitates for a moment before getting into the *fiacre*, Léon's justification is that 'ça se fait à Paris'[4] (it's done in Paris), meaning that this behaviour was taken as a norm in the capital.[5] In this scene, Flaubert draws on a well-established literary and visual topos dating back to the 1830s and 1840s that links the *fiacre* to adultery: this vehicle provided convenient anonymity and privacy for adulterous trysts.[6]

Of course, no work of literature or visual culture claimed that the omnibus was a site of actual sexual encounters. And yet various forms of improper behaviour on the part of women were a leitmotif in omnibus literature and visual representations by men. One early example is an 1829 lithograph depicting the interior of an omnibus with a number of passengers packed in close together (Plate 6). The central figures are a well-appointed young woman and her unattractive, boorish-looking petit-bourgeois husband, with their little boy leaning on both his parents' knees, linking them visually. To the left of the young woman, an elegant gentleman, whose top hat and fashionable attire indicate that he belongs to a higher social class, surreptitiously holds her hand. The gentleman's other hand is holding up two fingers, as if to indicate that he is paying for two seats, presumably his own and the woman's. At the same time, this gesture was a universal symbol for 'cocu' (cuckold), here clearly referring to the husband, who appears to be oblivious to his wife's dalliance. The caption cautions, 'Maris honnêtes garde à vous!'[7] ('Honest husbands, beware!'). This image is representative of how the liminal space of the omnibus interior – both public and private, anonymous and intimate – was perceived and imagined in the nineteenth century. In their insistent depiction of diverse iterations of sexualised femininity, from wet nurse to prostitute, both well-known and popular texts and images reveal the complexity of cultural attitudes toward women's power of locomotion, an ambivalence about the blurring of boundaries between private and public realms, and anxieties about women taking over public space.

The omnibus was not the only urban space that was imbued with gendered moral meaning in the nineteenth-century cultural imagination: boulevards, restaurants, theatres and, beginning in the 1850s, department stores and parks were also evaluated in relation to women's respectability. What was unique about the omnibus was that, regardless of their sex or class, passengers were gathered together in a kind of enforced proximity. Although the conveyance was by definition public, it was also cramped and intimate, evocative of a private, domestic space. As most visual representations show, passengers were seated close to one another, their bodies often touching, and they had to literally face each other for the duration of the ride. Moreover, the ephemeral, transient nature of omnibus encounters was imagined as conducive to fleeting sexual pursuits. It is thus not surprising that the vehicle was construed at once as a space of moral dangers for respectable women and as a site of erotic opportunities for men. The narrow interior encapsulated particularly well tensions and ambiguities surrounding the presence of women in public space. Priscilla Ferguson's notion of a 'moral geography' that connects urban mobility and transgression, a term she introduces to analyse Zola's *La Curée*, helps us understand how omnibus literature addressed women's participation in modern urban life.[8] In the context of this literature, 'moral geography' describes how cultural production of the time conceived of the omnibus as a space of female sexual transgression, even if women's presence on public transport was endorsed in practice.

Scholarly debates about the place of women in public spaces in the nineteenth century inform my discussion of the omnibus and gender. Cultural critics and sociologists of the city such as Walter Benjamin, Georg Simmel and Marshall Berman presented the story of modernity as that of the public space from which middle-class women were excluded. Confined to the domestic sphere, women did not participate in spaces of modernity that were public and belonged to men. Feminist scholars writing in the 1980s (in particular, sociologist of visual culture Janet Wolff and art historian Griselda Pollock) challenged this narrative by pointing out the failures of this literature to account for women's experiences of modernity. Pollock argued for the inclusion of domestic, private spaces as a valid experience of the modern.[9] But it is only in the past two decades that scholars across disciplines in the humanities, including literary scholars Sharon Marcus and Catherine Nesci, art historians Marni Kessler, Lynda Nead and contributors to the volume *The Invisible Flâneuse?*, among others, have considerably nuanced this approach, questioning the hegemony of the public–private dichotomy and the ideology of separate spheres.[10] These scholars have convincingly shown that, although women were unquestionably excluded from many aspects of political and cultural life, the story of female presence in the city and the ways it was imagined by writers and artists is much more complex than proponents of the separate-spheres paradigm had initially proposed. While these debates have largely been settled, they provide an important context for my discussion here, as I draw on recent rethinking of what it meant to be a woman in a nineteenth-century metropolis.[11] Stories and images involving Parisian omnibuses contribute to a better understanding of how the culture of this period grappled with gendered perception of public urban space.

In examining textual and visual representations of the omnibus alongside contemporary historical and journalistic accounts, we find ample evidence that working-class and middle-class women constituted a large proportion of actual omnibus passengers throughout the nineteenth century. Women took advantage of the possibilities for urban mobility and participation in public life offered by public transport, and I venture to assert that the majority of them were neither prostitutes, nor adulteresses, nor women otherwise transgressing sexual or social norms. Yet there emerges a mythology that consistently pairs women omnibus passengers with different types of sexual misbehaviour. Because the omnibus allowed for unprecedented proximity and mixing, it offered male writers and artists a convenient framework to treat salacious topics and to work out their fantasies about women in the public space. Even if in reality it was not improper for respectable women to take the omnibus, it was often imagined as such in omnibus literature. In other words, representational practices departed from actual everyday practices.[12]

This mythology linking the omnibus and sexual promiscuity informs two well-known late-nineteenth-century works: Zola's novel *La Curée* (1872) and Maupassant's short story 'Le père' (1883), which deploy the omnibus as a metaphor for female sexual transgression and moral failure. These two texts draw on patterns of representation that were well established by the second half of the nineteenth century. The next part of this chapter turns to the excavation of this gendered mythology through an analysis of popular literature and images that symbolically united public transport and transgressive female sexuality.

'Vehicle of vice' in Zola and Maupassant

In Zola's urban novel *La Curée* and in Maupassant's 'Le père', the omnibus makes a brief but crucial appearance as what may be called a 'vehicle of vice': it is closely associated with sexually transgressive female behaviour. An ambivalent setting, where boundaries between private and public are troubled, the omnibus engenders sexual disorder on a micro level and ultimately threatens established social structures. Central to *La Curée* and 'Le père' are ways in which social and moral meanings are mapped on to the physical and spatial organisation of the newly reconstructed Paris. These meanings are constructed through a series of oppositions of different urban spaces: the omnibus and a restaurant's private room in *La Curée*, the omnibus and the park in 'Le père'. In these two texts, the omnibus emerges as a sexually charged space through which anxiety about social disorder is articulated.

La Curée is a spatial novel. It tells the story of the early years of Haussmann's radical remaking of Paris and paints a portrait of the profoundly corrupt and degenerate society that is forged in the process. *La Curée* is organised around a number of emblematic urban spaces that generate the novel's meaning. The story moves seamlessly from Aristide Saccard's extravagant mansion, the brand-new ornate façade of which conceals the ephemeral nature of the protagonist's paper fortune, to the sombre Hotel Béraud (his wife Renée's parental home), which embodies traditional bourgeois values and morality, and from the salons and ballrooms of the novel's courtesans to the city's recently created public spaces, such as boulevards, cafés, restaurants and parks. Famous sequences of carriage-traffic jams in the Bois de Boulogne provide the novel's bookends. In Zola's Paris, space is never neutral.[13] Although Zola meticulously reproduces the topographical reality of the recently Haussmannised Paris, famously compiling a detailed dossier on every aspect of the city that makes its way into his novel, what emerges most powerfully is not merely a recognisable realist setting but a system of moral geography, essential to the novel's overall social critique of the corrupt and degenerate Second Empire. As we shall see, the omnibus occupies a key place in this moral geography.

A central scene in *La Curée* depicts Renée and her stepson Maxime consummating their adulterous and quasi-incestuous love affair, an affair that, in Zola's novelistic universe, encapsulates the moral failures of the Second Empire. The scene literally takes place in the *cabinet particulier*[14] (private room) of the fashionable Café Riche but is metaphorically dominated by the omnibus. While the omnibus is only marginally present in this scene (none of the action takes place in the vehicle), it is invested with enormous symbolic value, emblematic of the sexual and moral corruption that the novel portrays. In *La Curée*, the *cabinet particulier* and the omnibus are foils for one another: they highlight the association of these spaces with illicit sexuality in the city's moral economy.

When Renée accepts Maxime's invitation to dine at a restaurant (after an incognito appearance at a courtesan's ball), what attracts her is precisely the risqué nature of such a venue for a proper high-society lady – she takes pleasure in her stepson's idea 'de lui faire goûter au fruit défendu'[15] (letting her taste forbidden fruit). What she does not yet realise is that she herself is the fruit to be consumed. Indeed, the heroine, suffering from intense boredom in her comfortable bourgeois world, delights in finding herself in a vaguely disreputable place: 'elle jouissaient profondément de ce mobilier équivoque, qu'elle sentait autour d'elle... de ce divan qui la choquait par sa largeur'[16] (she derived profound enjoyment from the suggestive furniture around her... from the divan, whose width shocked her). The setting includes a dusty mirror, in which Renée imagines courtesans adjusting their false chignons, and aphrodisiac oysters, which she consumes for dinner. Illicit sexuality is thus coded in the space itself, because the *cabinet particulier*, in the sociolect of the nineteenth century, signified sexual transgression.[17]

The extensive description of the view from the window, focalised through Renée's perspective, builds up anticipation of the erotic dénouement. Renée's eyes follow customers drinking in cafés, couples strolling along the boulevard, prostitutes seeking clients. From her vantage point, high above the crowd and (ostensibly) sheltered inside a luxury restaurant, hers is a master gaze, safely separated from the boulevard below, teeming with various forms of vice. Yet the boulevard, with its vague connotation of both literal and figurative filth, ends up bursting into the *cabinet particulier*, effectively removing both spatial and moral boundaries between private and public, proper and perverse. The vehicle of this invasion is none other than the omnibus:

> De cinq à cinq minutes, l'omnibus des Batignolles passait, avec ses lanternes rouges et sa caisse jaune, tournant le coin de la rue Le Péletier, ébranlant la maison de son fracas; et elle voyait les hommes de l'impériale, des visages fatigués qui se levaient et les regardaient, elle et Maxime, du regard curieux des affamés mettant l'œil à une serrure.
>
> (Every five minutes, the Batignolles omnibus passed by, with its red lamps and yellow sides, turning the corner of rue Le Péletier, shaking the building as it went, and she saw the men on the upper deck look up at them with their tired faces, with the expectant look of famished people peering through a keyhole.)[18]

The omnibus assaults the senses of those inside the restaurant with its jarring colours – the ominous red of the lantern, the yellow of the cash register – and clamour ('fracas') that produces violent shaking. What is more, this passage performs a clear reversal with regard to the idea of spectacle: while throughout the scene Renée was observing the spectacle of urban life on the boulevard, now it is Renée and Maxime who become the spectacle for the riders of the *impériale*.

In his perceptive reading, Christopher Prendergast interprets this passage in terms of class tensions. For him, the term 'affamés' is taken as the literal hunger of the have-nots who peek through the window of a luxury restaurant.[19] Their curiosity about the abundance from which they are permanently excluded is insatiable. But the term 'affamés' can also be read as sexual hunger. The men riding on the *impériale* look into the *cabinet particulier* as if through the keyhole of a bedroom (or a brothel), amplifying the sexual charge of the scene. The male passengers are cast as voyeurs who exercise a kind of power over the young woman objectified by their sullying invasive stares. The illusion of mastery over the boulevard upon which she was looking vanishes when the two lovers become objects of the men's covetous gaze. Just as the boundaries between inside and outside, spectacle and spectator collapse, so does the difference between a proper lady and a prostitute.

If the lustful passengers on the *impériale* peeping into the room prefigure the scene of the sexual act, then it comes as no surprise that the encounter itself takes place under the literal and figurative omnibus shadow. As Renée and Maxime make love on the sofa prominently occupying the *cabinet*, a passing omnibus with its deafening roar seems once again to invade the room: 'Dans le grand silence du cabinet, où le gaz semblait flamber plus haut, elle sentit le sol trembler et entendit le fracas de l'omnibus des Batignolles qui devait tourner le coin du boulevard. Et tout fut dit.' (In the profound silence of the room, where the gas seems to flare up higher, she felt the ground tremble and heard the clatter of the Batignolles omnibus turning the corner of the boulevard. The talking was over.)[20] While the transgressive sexual act itself is described elliptically ('tout fut dit'), it is represented symbolically through the omnibus: the clatter ('fracas') and the throbbing ('trembler') of the ground describe what is happening between the two characters.[21] What Zola achieves here is a recasting of the orderly spaces of the recently Haussmannised Paris into spaces of moral disorder, so that his novel creates an alternative Parisian topography in the service of his critique of the Second Empire's degenerate society.[22] In redrawing the map of Paris, he relies on cultural associations between the omnibus and transgressive female sexuality (here in the form of adultery and incest) that had been established in the French cultural imagination almost from the moment the omnibus was launched.

Similarly to Zola, Maupassant draws on the link between the omnibus and sexual transgression in 'Le père', but here the vehicle is associated with a woman's loss of innocence and respectability. The story tells a tale of a love affair between an office clerk, François Tessier, and a shop girl, Louise, who meet on an omnibus. Learning of his mistress's pregnancy a few months into the affair, Tessier abandons her. Ten years later he encounters her by chance in the Parc Monceau. Upon seeing his son for the first time, he is consumed by paternal love and belated regrets.

The story takes us through a series of spaces that organise the plot. Each space acquires its symbolic significance through its juxtaposition with the others. The story begins inside an omnibus, where the couple meets, then briefly moves to the countryside where their affair is consummated. The second part of the story takes us first to the respectable bourgeois space of the Parc Monceau and finally to the 'salon bourgeois' in the apartment Louise now shares with her husband, 'un honnête homme de mœurs graves' (a respectable man with serious manners).

In this story, the omnibus functions as an erotically charged space that engenders the (illicit) relationship between the two protagonists. Tessier's feelings for the young woman arise from the daily repetition of the omnibus commute: 'Chaque matin il voyageait jusqu'au centre de Paris, en face d'une jeune fille dont il devient amoureux'[23] (Every morning he travelled to the centre of Paris sitting face-to-face with a young girl with whom he fell in love). The attraction between the two characters emerges in the enclosed and intimate space of an omnibus, dominated by anonymity and chance. This attraction is fostered by the vehicle's seating arrangement of two rows facing one another: 'Il la regardait obstinément, malgré lui. Gênée par cette contemplation, elle rougit. Il s'en aperçut et voulut détourner les yeux; mais il les ramenait à tout moment sur elle, quoiqu'il s'efforçât de les fixer ailleurs.'[24] (He was looking at her obstinately, despite himself. Unsettled by his stares, she blushed. He noticed and wanted to look away. But he kept casting his eyes upon her, even though he was trying to fix them elsewhere.) It is as if the set-up of the omnibus interior compels the two solitary characters to engage in this chance intimacy, bringing them together almost despite themselves. Here we see the complex dynamic of the omnibus setting, blurring the boundaries between public and private, as the two characters develop a private rapport in the middle of this public space. But their intimacy is paradoxically accompanied by anonymity: the two characters, in fact, do not know each other's names. And since this third-person narrative is focalised through Tessier's eyes, we as readers only know the young woman as 'elle'. Only when Tessier and the young woman travel to the countryside together, does he finally ask her: 'Comment vous appelez-vous?'[25] (What is your name?)

The text draws our attention to the short duration of the omnibus trip and the fleeting and ephemeral nature of the daily encounters: 'Une sorte d'intimité rapide s'établit entre eux, une intimité d'une demi-heure par jour'[26] (A kind of quick intimacy was established between them, an intimacy of half an hour a day). This 'intimité rapide' both befits and replicates the anonymity and speed of the modern city. Unlike the light-hearted songs depicting love encounters on the omnibus that I discuss in Chapter 2, Maupassant's story draws our attention to the alienating and dehumanising aspect of public transport, which serves here as a *mise en abyme* for urban alienation and anomie. Although it is a different modern vehicle – a train – that later takes Louise to the countryside – the actual site where she loses her virginity – it is the omnibus that symbolically represents her passage from innocence to 'faute' (fault), for it is there that the erotic attraction takes hold. The transience of their daily omnibus meetings foreshadows the ephemeral nature of the relationship itself. For Tessier, the half-hour on the omnibus becomes the highlight of his monotonous existence: 'Et c'était là, certes, la plus charmante demi-heure de sa vie à lui'[27] (It was the most charming half an hour of his life). Perhaps, however, the charm of the encounter is precisely its brevity: three months into the affair, 'il commençait à se lasser d'elle' (he was beginning to tire of her). Having learned of Louise's pregnancy, 'il n'eut plus qu'une idée en tête: rompre à tout prix'[28] (he only had one thought in mind: to break up at all costs). He soon abandons her by moving to a new apartment, thus avoiding the daily omnibus commute that brought them together in the first place.

The space of the initial illicit attraction that eventually leads to a breakdown of social order – the birth of an illegitimate child – is contrasted with another highly symbolic space that dominates the second part of the story: the orderly space of the Parc Monceau. Parallel to the beginning of the story, the park is the site of a second chance encounter between Tessier and Louise, who is now accompanied by their child. The park, however, could not be more different from the omnibus.[29] Essential to Napoleon III's conception of the new city, parks were intended as spaces of regulated leisure and bourgeois sociability, a staging ground for a public display of family life and proper bourgeois femininity.³⁰ A space of propriety, Parc Monceau imposed, in the words of art historian Greg Thomas, 'visual and social order to the city and its classes' and provided the bourgeoisie with a prescribed way to spend their leisure time.³¹ Its well laid out paths and lawns embodied bourgeois respectability and dominant moral values.³² It is in this context that Tessier and Louise meet again. Louise's demeanour, that of the proper married bourgeois lady she has now become, contrasts sharply with how she is described at the beginning of the story. When we first see her, she runs after the omnibus 'd'un petit air pressé'³³ (with a hurried little look) and is out of breath when she finally gets on board. Now, in the park, everything about her – her clothes, her way of walking – reinforces the image of respectability: 'Elle avait un air sérieux de dame, une toilette simple, une allure assurée et digne'³⁴ (She had a serious look of a lady, a simple dress, a confident and dignified way of walking). If, like the omnibus, the park is a space where chance encounters are possible, it is, by contrast, one where such a meeting is avoidable. This time, Louise flees at the sight of her former lover: as a bastion of bourgeois respectability, Parc Monceau imposes certain modes of behaviour and does not condone inappropriate contact. The park both reflects the moral values it professes to represent and enforces them upon visitors to its well-organised space. Louise has travelled a long way from the erotic titillations of the dangerously intimate public space of the omnibus. The juxtaposition with the park underscores the association of the omnibus with illicit sexuality: in Maupassant's text, the omnibus embodies sexual and social disorder engendered by the modern metropolis.

As the two works by Zola and Maupassant show, by the late nineteenth century the omnibus was coded as a vehicle of sexual transgression and was associated with illicit female sexuality. While these two writers may not have been familiar with the particular popular texts and images teeming with wet nurses baring their breasts or prostitutes soliciting clients that I analyse in the pages that follow, in sketching the gendered moral geography that structures their work, they implicitly drew on cultural associations between the omnibus and the commerce of sex.

Buses, breasts and babies

On the surface, the figure of the wet nurse that appears in several works of omnibus literature seems to be used mostly for comic effect: she is the source of slapstick humour.³⁵ But I would argue that this figure expresses a fascination with female sexuality and anxiety about its overt manifestation in public space, and provides fodder for male writers and artists to depict topics that were otherwise off limits.³⁶ Sequences involving the wet nurse unfold in a surprisingly similar way in different texts; typically, she is the source of chaos that ensues aboard the vehicle. For instance, in 'Un voyage en omnibus' Ernest

Fouinet describes 'une grosse et grasse nourrice' (a fat and corpulent wet nurse) frenetically chasing after an omnibus while holding an infant. The redundancy of 'grosse et grasse' brings into relief the emphasis on the body as well as the disruptive effect this character's presence has on other passengers.[37] When the wet nurse finally climbs on board, she is a dishevelled mess: 'Essoufflée, pantelante, pourpre, elle allait tomber avec son enfant quand on l'aperçut: elle monta colère et hors d'haleine, et son enfant bondissait au flux et reflux de son large sein palpitant qu'il cherchait, en vagissant, à saisir de ses petites mains potelées.'[38] (Out of breath, panting, all red, she was about to collapse with her baby when she was noticed; she got on board, furious and out of breath, and her bawling baby bounced up and down trying to grasp her large breast with his little pudgy hands.) This vividly depicted scene is meant to make the reader laugh, yet it is also troubling, for the wet nurse here is both abject and disorderly, occupying too much space, disrupting the peace.

We encounter an even more troubling wet nurse figure in Gourdon's *Physiologie de l'omnibus*:

> Une nourrice, grosse et gaillarde provinciale, étale à tous les yeux sa gorge brune et fortement accusée; mais le marmot ne tette pas: sans cesse en émoi par le cahotement de la voiture, sa tête ne peut s'attacher au sein. La nourrice fouette le marmot qui crie, le petit monsieur se plaint au conducteur qui ne l'écoute pas et compte son argent.[39]

> (A fat and saucy wet nurse from the provinces spreads her dark-coloured and well-rounded bosom for everyone to see; but the little brat does not nurse: his head constantly bopping up and down from the vehicle's movement, he fails to latch on. The wet nurse spanks the brat who howls; the little monsieur complains to the conductor who doesn't listen and counts money instead.)

Here again we see both class and gender at play. As a 'provinciale', the wet nurse is coded as lacking in knowledge of proper conduct in the city. Described as 'saucy', she seems more interested in displaying her large bosom for the viewing pleasure of her fellow passengers than in taking care of her charge. Like her counterpart in Fouinet's text, this wet nurse is depicted as a grotesque caricature, an object of the narrator's contempt. Through an exaggerated display of her body she causes chaos and confusion. Curiously, in both Gourdon and Fouinet's texts, the wet nurse also fails at her main job – nursing the baby – because the omnibus is depicted as an inappropriate place for this activity. The two texts ostensibly present this as a practical problem of movement and locomotion, rather than one of respectability. Yet we can't help but wonder: does the implicit condemnation of the wet nurse in these texts also reveal a deeper fascination with – and anxiety about – the female body on display in public?

We find many of the same themes and imagery elaborated upon in more detail in a late-nineteenth-century short story by Emile Dartès, 'Madeleine-Bastille' (1894). A bourgeois mother, a baby, and a wet nurse board a Parisian omnibus, and their interactions provide the primary source of narrative interest. The two women present a study in contrasts. The mother, in her forties, is bony, dried-up and unattractive-looking ('maigre, jaune, longue comme un jour sans pain'[40] (thin, yellow, long like a day without bread)). She is doubly de-feminised: first, as a bad mother who does not nurse her child and, second, as sexually unappealing. The voluptuous wet nurse, Françoise, is her exact opposite: 'une superbe nounou rouge, joufflue, satisfaite, portant sur ses bras un énorme nourrisson qui se débat comme un cabri et crie comme un poulet qu'on écorche'[41] (a superb wet nurse, chubby and content, carrying in her arms an enormous baby who kicks like a mountain goat and shrieks like a chicken that's being skinned). Here we find the by that time familiar descriptive vocabulary ('joufflue', 'rouge'), and her generic name appears to suggest that she can be any woman.

When the baby begins to cry, the mother loudly orders Françoise to give him the breast in the middle of the moving vehicle: 'Celle-ci, d'un mouvement brusque, fait sauter les boutons de son corsage et met à nu un magnifique sein, blanc comme la neige, et gonflé de lait. De sa main droite elle en empoigne le bout épais et l'enfonce dans la bouche du môme qui s'arrête enfin de brailler pour boire gloutonnement.'[42] (With a quick movement, she unbuttons her blouse and exposes a magnificent breast, white as snow and engorged with milk. With her right hand, she grabs her thick nipple and shoves it into the mouth of the baby, who finally stops screaming and begins to nurse greedily.) Although there were no laws prohibiting breastfeeding in public, the scene clearly depicts it as improper. But what is striking about this passage and several following ones is that it lavishly dwells on the wet nurse's exposed white breasts, at once eroticising her and portraying her as grotesque.

The impropriety of the scene is highlighted through a humorous displacement: while Françoise nurses the baby, her mistress sternly admonishes her for violating rules of proper behaviour on public transport. But what the mother criticises is not breastfeeding in public or exposing her breasts; rather, it is the fact that the wet nurse engages in conversation with other riders, a violation of the code of proper conduct on public transport. In particular, the mother is upset that Françoise converses with a middle-aged man, who introduces himself as a mayor of a village and is described as 'un paillard' (a bawdy chap). The text emphasises the erotic effect that the wet nurse's exposed bosom produces on male passengers. For example, 'les seins rebondis de la nourrice émoustillaient fortement'[43] (the round breasts of the wet nurse greatly aroused) the provincial 'paillard'. Similarly, an old man nodding off in the corner 'se ragaillardissait un peu. Ses petits yeux s'éclairaient et reprenaient l'imperceptible lueur de vivacité à la vue de l'imposant néné que la nourrice étalait avec une innocente franchise

Moral geographies

devant tout le monde'[44] (perked up. His small eyes lit up and became alert at the sight of the imposing boob that the wet nurse was spreading in front of everyone with a frank innocence). The scene descends into further chaos as the baby begins to scream and kick the wet nurse, who is then unable to button her dress, leaving her bosom exposed to her fellow passengers' gaze: 'Elle ne peut même reboutonner son corsage qui, largement ouvert, laisse voir sa luxuriante poitrine si attirante pour l'œil chargé de convoitise de ce gros rougeaud de M. le maire.'[45] (She can't even button her blouse, which, mostly open, exposes her luxurious breast, so attractive to the desiring eye of the red-faced Monsieur the mayor.) This sequence appears not only to describe the desire that Françoise's bosom elicits in her fellow male passengers but to stimulate a similar desire in the reader. The episode is accompanied by two illustrations that visually reiterate and reinforce the text's obsession with the wet nurse's bare breast. The first image zooms in on Françoise nursing a large, overdressed child (Figure 4.1). Her breast is disproportionally enormous and oddly shaped, its stark whiteness contrasting with her dark clothing. This exaggerated breast dominates the image

Figure 4.1 Emile Dartès, *Contes en omnibus*. Illustration, 'Madeleine–Bastille'. 1894.

Class, gender and locomotion

just as it dominates the narrative. The wet nurse's face is turned away from the child, as if to emphasise her indifference toward her charge.

In the second illustration, we see the wet nurse from a slightly different angle, her breast still exposed, as she now engages in conversation with the lustful provincial mayor (Figure 4.2). This second image does not add anything new to the portrait of Françoise. Rather, its inclusion seems to be due to an obsessive desire to re-present (to present again) the wet nurse's breast, sexualised through the desirous eyes of the male passenger (the 'paillard') and those of the viewer outside the image.

While it is easy to presume that the writers I examine here milk the figure of the wet nurse solely for its obvious comic effect, I would argue that these representations reflect an anxiety about female sexuality that is particularly acute in the public space of the omnibus. Lisa Algazi Marcus reminds us that in the nineteenth century, breastfeeding was closely associated with sexual pleasure that took place outside of male control, and that, for many authors, especially toward the end of the century, 'the representation of the act of breast-feeding [was] both revolting and alluring'.[46] This dynamic is evident in the three texts I have examined: the wet nurse is depicted as incongruous, repulsive, grotesquely excessive and inappropriate. Yet at the same time, all three texts seem to take particular pleasure in painting the portrait of the wet nurse. Beyond being a vehicle of satire, this figure embodies male anxieties about women's bodies taking over public space.

Although not a wet nurse, a figure closely allied with her is 'la femme qui accouche' (the woman who gives birth), which appears in the 1854 *Paris-en-omnibus* by Delord, Frémy and Texier. As I discussed in Chapter 1, this book's many chapters vary greatly in both genre and register. This particular

Figure 4.2 Emile Dartès, *Contes en omnibus*. Illustration, 'Madeleine–Bastille'. 1894.

chapter was clearly written in a satirical mode. Claiming that 'la femme qui accouche' is a common type, one that readers must have encountered themselves, the passage presents the following male fantasy of childbirth aboard public transport:

> Ne vous est-il jamais arrivé, en allant en omnibus de la rue Notre-Dame-de-Lorette à l'Odéon, d'entendre tout à coup un Ah! Mon Dieu! retentir à l'un des coins du véhicule? Ce cri vient d'être poussé par une femme; on arrête, on s'empresse autour d'elle, on regarde à ses pieds, on y trouve, devinez quoi? Un enfant, un superbe enfant, gros, gras, dodu, le plus né viable de tous les enfants.
>
> La femme qui accouche en omnibus est un type, vous la reconnaîtriez entre mille, rien qu'à sa physionomie. Elle a quelque chose de tranquille, de paisible, de calme, d'heureux, qui fait dire: cette femme est capable d'accoucher partout, même en omnibus.... La femme qui accouche en omnibus appartient à toutes les classes de la société; il y en a des riches, il y en a des pauvres, il y en a du peuple et de l'aristocratie, du commerce et de la finance. Il n'y a que les femmes du notariat qui n'accouchent jamais en omnibus. La mère et l'enfant se portent toujours bien après un accouchement en omnibus. Quand une femme accouche en omnibus elle peut revenir facilement chez elle en fiacre.⁴⁷

> (Hasn't it happened to you that while riding the omnibus from Notre-Dame-de-Lorette to Odéon, you heard a sudden Ah! My God! emanating from the corner? These screams come from a woman. The vehicle stops, everyone rushes over to her; then, guess what they see at her feet? A baby, a superb, round, fat baby, the sturdiest of all babies ever born. The woman who gives birth on the omnibus is a type; you will recognise her among all others, just by looking at her face. There is something calm, peaceful, content about her that prompts you to say: this woman is able to give birth anywhere, even on the omnibus. The woman giving birth on the omnibus belongs to all classes of society. She can be rich or poor, she can be working-class or an aristocrat, she could be from the world of commerce or that of finance. Only the wives of notaries do not ever give birth aboard an omnibus. Mother and child do very well after childbirth on an omnibus. When a woman gives birth on an omnibus, she can easily return home in a hackney cab.)

On the face of it, this passage seems to be pure satire, as evidenced by the sheer absurdity of its assertions (the baby is born in a matter of minutes, the mother utters nothing more than 'Ah! Mon Dieu!' while in labour, both mother and child are always in perfect health and omnibus childbirth happens to women of all classes), yet there is something quite troubling in this passage. This outlandish tale may be a way to broach a topic that is usually off limits, a way to peek into – or imagine – a female space from which men are normally excluded. Although the passage humorously claims that women giving birth on the omnibus can hail from all social classes, it doesn't fail to mention that this line originates at the rue Notre-Dame-de-Lorette, a neighbourhood associated with prostitution, thus suggesting a link between public women and public transport. And, indeed, women engaged in sexual commerce abound in cultural representations of the omnibus.

Public transport for a public woman

One of the first texts about the omnibus, the satirical *Les omnibus. Premier voyage de Cadet la Blague de la place de la Madeleine à la Bastille et retour* (1828) opens with a poem that explicitly articulates male fantasies about female passengers that characterise nineteenth-century omnibus literature. Addressed to male readers seeking sexual adventures – the 'vous' of the poem – this text places the erotic potential of this mode of transport front and centre:

> Vous qui courez après les aventures,
> Ne regardez point ceci comm' des rébus;
> Pour en trouver prenez donc ces voitures,
> Que dans Paris on nomm' des *Omnibus*.
>
> (Those of you who seek adventure,
> It's not so hard
> To find one, just take one of those carriages
> That in Paris are called *Omnibus*.)

In the second stanza, the poem offers a panorama of female types aboard omnibus:

> On y rencontre des fill', des femm,' des veuves
> De ces maris qu' leur épous' rim'en *us*,
> Et des beautés qui veul' passer pour neuves,
> Quoique'elles soient au nomb' des *Omnibus*
>
> (There you meet ladies, young and old,
> Whose husbands bear the name of cuckold,
> And beauties who want to pass for fresh ones
> Although they are among the *Omnibus*).

By playfully linking 'omnibus' with 'us' (meaning 'cocus': cuckold), the poem implies that female passengers (whether girls, wives or widows) who take the omnibus are *a priori* morally compromised and prone to sexual promiscuity, adultery and prostitution. In the last two lines, the poem makes an explicit connection between the vehicle and prostitution, playing on the meaning of the word 'omnibus' to suggest that female passengers were women destined 'for all'.[48]

Moral geographies

Having established an equivalence between the vehicle and the prostitute, the third stanza tells us that this public transport provides prostitutes ('un essaim de Vénus') with an ideal place to solicit clients when their business among pedestrians on the boulevards is lacking. The poet overhears the women wishing that they could 'try their luck' on the omnibus:

Sur le boulevard quand le chaland leur manque,
Vous entendez un essaim de Vénus,
Dir' si j'savais gagner un billet de banque,
J'irais tenter fortun' dans l's *Omnibus*

(When clients are hard to find on the boulevard
You will hear the swarm of Venuses
Say if I knew how to earn a buck,
I'd try my luck on the *Omnibus*).

This early text establishes themes of female impropriety in general, but also introduces the fiction of the omnibus as a place for prostitutes to seek out clients. As we shall see, this fiction permeates popular culture, as numerous other documents imagine the omnibus as a playing field for women of loose morals. As with 'la femme qui accouche', rather than being a reliable reflection of actual everyday practices, these documents offer a window into male fantasies according to which the omnibus was a place of dubious female behaviour. There are no records indicating that in reality Parisian prostitutes used the omnibus to solicit clients, just as it would be impossible to ascertain whether adulterous trysts ever occurred because men and women found themselves in close proximity to one another. But in mapping out their 'moral geographies', nineteenth-century male authors and visual artists coded this vehicle as a site where women are likely to engage in sexually transgressive behaviour.[49]

Let us consider an anonymous print from an 1859 satirical series, *Paris Grotesque*, which depicts a character named Madame Crinoliska aboard a crowded omnibus. (Figure 4.3). Madame Crinoliska invades the space of the omnibus, overwhelming her fellow passengers with the lacy layers of her large, luxurious skirt.[50] Her entire outfit – a tiered skirt, a bonnet with a wide-flowing ribbon and enormous bow, a fur-trimmed shawl nonchalantly draped over her shoulders, as well as scandalously visible legs and a crinoline cage – suggests ostentation, lack of propriety and conspicuous consumption. While Madame Crinoliska's skirt consumes most of the space of the image, she herself is also an object to be consumed – by her fellow passengers, by the crinoline and, of course, by the viewer.[51] On display for the benefit of other passengers, she is depicted literally making a spectacle of herself ('faisant son entrée') as if she were stepping on to a theatre stage. A woman literally identified with her

Figure 4.3 'Madame Crinoliska faisant son entrée dans un omnibus'. *Paris Grotesque*, 1859.

skirt – and displaced by it – Madame Crinoliska embodies the excesses associated with women who wear crinolines.

According to Lynda Nead, images satirising the crinoline craze appeared as soon as the fashion itself, spanning media including photography, prints and illustrated books.[52] From the beginning, attacks against the crinoline vogue took on distinctly gendered tones. Nead offers several reasons for this. First, crinolines were a health hazard: they frequently caught fire and killed their wearers, including Madame Crinoliska, who, in another image from the series, is consumed by the flames she sets off by igniting the hearts of her admirers.[53] But the main reason for crinoline contempt was their girth. Women in crinolines simply took up too much space, in the opinion of many – and, as Nead explains, 'men felt crowded out of social life' and sometimes eclipsed altogether.[54] As we see in this image, several respectable-looking male passengers, including a priest and three bourgeois men, are virtually engulfed by the voluminous ruffles of the skirt and pushed into the edges of the image. Crinolines and crinoline wearers represented excess, and their exaggerated physical presence flew in the face of rules of propriety and proper behaviour and threatened men through their sheer scale. According to Nead, 'rather than being kept in their place, women, it seemed, were getting out of place in their crinolines'.[55] The omnibus interior helped highlight this aspect of crinoline fashion.

Beyond anxiety about the scale of crinoline skirts and women exceeding the boundaries of their bodies in public spaces, what underlies this particular image is a concern that a woman of loose morals such as Madame Crinoliska was sharing a bench with respectable passengers. Since there were no legal restrictions on who was allowed on board, the omnibus presented a particular conundrum for the bourgeois moral order. How does one distinguish a loose woman from a respectable one at the time when their sartorial differences were increasingly blurred? Scholars such as Susan Hiner and Marni Kessler have convincingly demonstrated that with the advent of mass-produced clothing and accessories it was becoming difficult to differentiate between a respectable woman and a courtesan out in public.[56] In *Physiologie de l'omnibus*, Edouard Gourdon bemoans the difficulty of establishing female passengers' moral and social standing based on attire: 'La robe de satin, le cachemire, et le chapeau de la femme comme il faut sortent souvent des magasins où la Lorette va s'approvisionner; l'une et l'autre ont souvent la même tailleuse et le même bijoutier'[57] (The satin dress, the cashmere shawl, and the hat of a proper woman often come from the same shop where the *Lorette* does her shopping. The two often share a seamstress and a jeweller). As Hiner shows in her analysis of the role of fashion accessories in creating social distinction, the ambiguity of dress codes in determining a woman's social class and respectability was seen as a threat to social hierarchies.[58] In the case of Madame Crinoliska, it is not the crinoline itself that identifies her as a *cocotte*, since they were worn by respectable women as well. Nor was it the fact that she travelled unaccompanied. Rather, what marks Madame Crinoliska is the outrageous way she carries herself, scandalously displaying a good deal of her dainty legs and even a bit of the cage, flaunting her sartorial excesses and spreading her skirts everywhere, a visual metaphor for venal contagion.[59]

And this brings us back to Aunt Coeur and her indignation at Claudine's omnibus adventure. Was Aunt Coeur's main concern that her niece might find herself next to a prostitute and thus be exposed to her disorderly and contaminating presence? Or was it that Claudine could have been mistaken for a courtesan? It was believed that merely witnessing unbecoming conduct could lead an honest woman into the temptation of engaging in similar behaviour herself. As Hollis Clayson reminds us,

> The honest woman must [therefore] never even see the prostitute. Prostitution had to be hidden from the dominated honest woman at any price, because... it carried a force harmful to the masculine order. The lapsing of the honest woman into the immoral woman – even if such yielding never penetrated her actions and remained merely a shift in consciousness – would erode the patriarchal system of domination.[60]

Certainly, there were other city spaces where a respectable woman could encounter a prostitute, especially as it became more acceptable for the former to circulate in cafés, parks, boulevards and department stores. But those encounters would be fleeting and thus of little consequence. The omnibus was different in that passengers could be exposed to a prolonged face-to-face contact with a prostitute. Respectable ladies risked moral contagion from sharing close quarters with a public woman.

The figure of a potential prostitute aboard the omnibus should be considered in the context of a widespread and thoroughly documented cultural obsession with prostitution that spans the nineteenth century.[61] The 1830s, the early years of the omnibus service, coincided with a period during which prostitution grew exponentially in Paris. According to Jann Matlock, 'Prostitution became a central issue – if not the central issue – by the early years of the July Monarchy.'[62] The number of unregistered prostitutes grew from 9,000 in 1820 to 22,000 in 1831. It is not surprising that it was around the same time that the most comprehensive and defining work on regulating prostitution in nineteenth-century France was produced: Alexandre Parent-Duchâtelet's *De la prostitution dans la ville de Paris* (first published in 1836). The study, based on extensive research and statistical data, served as a justification for strict police practices regulating the sex trade and the prostitute's body. Parent-Duchâtelet's book, as well as other writings on prostitution, reflected bourgeois anxieties about both women's sexuality and class. The increased number of prostitutes in 1830s Paris resulted from an influx of working-class, female job-seekers, who were often unable to find employment or were so underpaid that they could not make a living.[63] Social fears about class and female sexuality in the urban context, articulated during the July Monarchy and continuing through the Second Empire and beyond, often focused on working-class women. But they had far-reaching implications for bourgeois women as well. As Rachel Fuchs and Victoria Thompson note, 'To the middle classes, prostitutes symbolised working-class women's rampant sexuality and all that was wrong with urban women's work. Middle-class policy makers failed to acknowledge that women might engage in sex work as a temporary measure when there was no other work.'[64] Works about prostitutes represented them as disruptive of the established social order and associated with working-class depravity, providing a rationale for why they should be regulated and why their presence in the public space had to be circumscribed. It is no wonder that against this backdrop, the omnibus, a space open to all without restrictions, was seen as a likely site for prostitutes to seek out clients or model sexually transgressive behaviour for proper women. As such, it provoked anxiety among bourgeois observers.

An 1865 lithograph (based on a painting by Morlon) illustrates an attempt to restrict omnibus entry to a woman of easy virtue. A woman in flashy dress seeks to board an omnibus on a rainy day (Figure 4.4). While there is clearly a practical explanation for why she is lifting her full skirts – to avoid getting them wet – her gesture, exposing most of her petticoat, goes beyond the imperative of bad weather. Like Madame Crinoliska, this woman also shows a quite a bit of her ankle. The caption, 'Une poule mouillée', literally 'a wet

Figure 4.4 'Une poule mouillée'. 1865. Based on a painting by Morlon.

hen', plays on the colloquial definition of the word 'poule', meaning 'slut'.[65] Meanwhile, the uniform-clad conductor blocks her way, lifting his finger toward the sign that says *complet* (full). This gesture could simply mean that there are no more seats on the omnibus. Yet there is something stylised in the way he holds his hand, suggesting that perhaps this is also a gesture of moral opprobrium. I read the conductor's pose as that of a gatekeeper, whose job is not just to collect the fare but also to keep women such as this one at bay, outside in the rain, blocking her way with his own uniformed body. His uniform confers a certain moral authority upon him. Meanwhile, the melon-hatted man inside appears either to sneer at the woman, delighting in her misfortune, or to flirt with her.

A different take on prostitutes on public transport is found in *Paris-en-omnibus*, a work that focuses not so much on morality as on commercial interests shared by omnibuses and prostitutes. This text stages the omnibus as an ideal place for men to find erotic adventures (the chapter is titled 'Si on a de bonnes fortunes en omnibus' (When one gets lucky on an omnibus)). Here we find a mise-en-scène involving a prostitute and a male passenger she works to seduce. The chapter is written in the second-person plural, thus implicating the presumptive male reader. The loose woman on the omnibus is described as a recognisable urban type ('tout le monde l'a rencontrée': everyone has met her), and her appearance and behaviour follow a seemingly predetermined script:

> Elle est mise avec assez de coquetterie et d'élégance, et elle occupe ordinairement la place du coin, près de l'estrade du conducteur. Elle est âgée de 25 à 35 ans. Si elle n'est pas de la première jeunesse, elle a de beaux restes. Si votre toilette indique une certaine aisance, si vous avez l'air d'un homme poli et discret, ses yeux, si vous la regardez, ne fuiront pas les vôtres. Elle tient son voile baissé; mais il est assez transparent pour laisser voir le jeu de la physionomie.[66]

> (She is dressed rather coquettishly and elegantly, and she usually sits in the corner, next to the conductor. She is between 25 and 35 years old. Although she is no spring chicken, she looks good for her age. If your clothes suggest solid financial footing, if you look like a man who is polite and discreet, she will not turn away when you look at her. Her veil is lowered, but it is sufficiently transparent to reveal her facial expression.)

This woman, who we will soon learn is a prostitute, is difficult to distinguish from a proper woman. She is well dressed, and, unlike Madame Crinoliska, is not ostentatious or inappropriate. In fact, she is a wearing a veil, ordinarily a sign of respectability and higher social class.[67] Marni Kessler explains that although any woman could wear a veil, the manner in which it was worn was key in determining the woman's class and respectability.[68] Here, although the woman's face is veiled, it is transparent enough to reveal her facial expression. The narrator suggests that by wearing a veil, the woman attempts to pass for respectable: 'Elle se donne tantôt pour la femme d'un petit employé, tantôt pour une maîtresse de piano, le plus souvent pour une provinciale à Paris pour un grand procès'[69] (She sometimes pretends to be the wife of a clerk, sometimes a piano teacher, most frequently a woman from the provinces who came to Paris for a big trial).

The rest of the story is written in the style of a user's guide addressed to the male reader and adventure seeker, instructing him how to go about approaching the courtesan. The process of seduction in an omnibus setting appears to be codified into a set of well-rehearsed rules:

> Après les premiers regards, poussez hardiment votre pied; il est probable que le sien répondra à l'appel. Ceci fait, attendez qu'elle dise au cocher d'arrêter, et qu'elle descende en ayant soin de laisser voir un bas bien tiré sur une jambe bien tournée. Descendez à votre tour et suivez-la. Si vous l'abordez, elle fera semblant de s'effaroucher tout d'abord. Insistez, elle vous répondra, et il y a cent à parier contre un qu'au bout de 5 minutes de conversation, elle vous accordera l'autorisation, ardemment sollicitée, de vous recevoir chez elle pour entendre une communication importante que vous avez à lui faire.[70]

> (After the first glances are exchanged, daringly press your leg against hers; it is likely that she will respond favourably to the call. Once that's done, wait for her to tell the driver to stop and for her to get off; as she does so, she makes sure to show her tight stockings and her well-rounded legs. Get off as well and follow her. If you approach her, she will at first pretend to be offended. Be persistent, and chances are that after a five-minute discussion she will grant you an eagerly solicited permission to visit her at her home in order to hear an important message you would like to deliver.)

After the rendezvous takes place and the lucky adventure seeker takes his leave of the woman, the narrator suggests that if he spends a few minutes lingering in the neighbourhood, he can watch her embark on her next omnibus escapade:

> Placez-vous maintenant au coin de la rue; cinq minutes s'écouleront à peine, et vous verrez votre conquête s'arrêter sur le seuil de la maison et faire signe au premier omnibus qui passe. Elle recommencera ce petit commerce cinq ou six fois dans la journée, le plus souvent qu'elle pourra.[71]

> (Now stand at the corner of the street. Barely five minutes later, you will see your conquest emerge from the entrance and flag the first omnibus that passes by. She will engage in this sort of commerce five or six times a day, as often as she can.)

The author thus creates a clear parallel between the ephemeral, fleeting experience of an omnibus ride and the equally short-lived nature of a sexual encounter with a prostitute. They are of a piece – part of the big metropolis emerging at the time, reflecting and complementing one another.

Moreover, the conductor does not seem to be concerned with morality but rather with the company's commercial interests, to which the commerce of sex contributes: 'Les conducteurs connaissent tous cette femme: "C'est une bonne *pratique*" disent-ils quelquefois en souriant. Je suis parfaitement de leur avis'[72] (The conductors all know this woman. 'It's a good *habit*' they say sometimes, smiling. I am entirely in agreement with them). In the emerging modern economy, prostitution and the omnibus business were mutually beneficial: both participated in systems of circulation – of vehicles, bodies and money – that were at the heart of urban modernity, and *Paris-en-omnibus* brings to the fore their shared economic dependence. But these systems also included writers of popular literature, such as the collective authors of *Paris-en-omnibus*: they capitalised on both the omnibus and the prostitute for their writerly business, appropriating these two phenomena of urban life as objects of literary production. Writers had much to gain from stories of prostitution aboard omnibuses: these stories were titillating and promised to sell well. The emerging modern commercial system of circulation of which prostitution and public transport were a part thus also included works of popular literature.[73]

Gendered ambivalence in Delondre's *En omnibus*

The courtesan in *Paris-en-omnibus* could easily pass for a respectable woman because of her clothes and demeanour. As a result, she could elicit ambivalence, both anxiety-provoking and titillating, in nineteenth-century male observers. This ambivalence stands at the centre of the 1880 painting 'En omnibus' by Maurice Delondre (Plate 7). The painting depicts the interior of an omnibus occupied by six passengers, two men and four women. A seventh, faintly outlined figure of a woman flagging the omnibus with her umbrella outside on the boulevard is barely visible in the far background. Although the omnibus is not crowded, the low curved roof adorned with colourful advertisements and the angle from which we are viewing the scene create the impression of a constricted space.

As in many depictions of the omnibus interior, the scene appears intimate. In the foreground, a kitchen maid or a cook is clutching a basket bursting with brightly coloured vegetables or flowers. Seated beside her is an elegantly dressed young woman, and to the young woman's left a gentleman holding a newspaper. Finally, in the background, a gaunt-looking working-class woman is hugging a small child, her head turned away from the viewer.

On the opposite side, there are two figures in profile: a bourgeois man in a top hat whose body is obscured by a young woman seated to his right. This young woman, modestly dressed, appears to be absorbed by something in her hands. She may perhaps be putting away her change. A hat box on the seat next to her suggests she may be coming home from shopping or that she may be a *modiste* (a hat maker) or a *trottin* (a shop girl) delivering a hat to a client. The kitchen maid, the *modiste* and the gaunt mother are depicted with attributes that allow us to infer their profession, social standing and the reason for their omnibus journey.

This painting captures the socio-economic diversity of the passengers, which, as we saw in the previous chapter, is a preoccupation of many urban observers. But it is the scene's gendered dimension that interests me here. What especially draws attention is the tension between the gentleman in the top hat and the fashionably attired young woman seated side by side on the right side of the painting. While pretending to read his newspaper, the man surreptitiously stares at the woman; he seems, in fact, more interested in 'reading' his seatmate. How are we to interpret the man's scrutinising gaze? Is she an object of erotic interest or of moralising curiosity? Could he be wondering if she is a woman of easy virtue disguised as a proper lady? Is his look one of misgiving and disapproval or desire?

But the young woman herself is the most enigmatic among the painting's figures. In contrast with the other female passengers, it is difficult to surmise either her social status or the purpose of her unaccompanied outing on the omnibus. Her attire – the subtle flowers adorning her skirt, the ornate black hat, the pink bow at her neck that draws the eye, her stylish accessories, such as the black leather gloves and umbrella – speaks to her elegance and taste. She does not seem overly flirtatious or inappropriate. She does not engage with the man looking at her; rather, she looks straight in front of her, following rules of proper conduct. And yet her faint smile suggests that she may be well aware of the man's curiosity and attention. Is she enjoying the attention? This female figure is profoundly ambiguous: she resists knowledge or classification, and it is her unknowability that creates the tension permeating this painting.

Delondre's *En omnibus* may offer a key to nineteenth-century representations of women passengers in the male-authored documents I have considered here. The ambiguity of the central female figure invites speculations and conjectures and serves as a projection screen for the fantasies and anxieties that agitated nineteenth-century male observers. The cipher-like appearance and comportment of female passengers – so close and yet so remote – were both troubling and titillating. In grappling with gendered perceptions of urban space, writers and artists fashioned a mythology of the omnibus as a 'vehicle of vice', imagining it as brimming with prostitutes, wet nurses baring their breasts

Class, gender and locomotion

and other transgressive female characters, producing images that were perhaps appealing to the public but remote from the reality of everyday experience.

Coda: beyond the frame

In 1889, British poet Amy Levy published 'Ballad of an omnibus', a poem celebrating women's freedom of urban locomotion in late nineteenth-century London:

> I mark, untroubled by desire,
> Lucullus, phaeton and its freight
> The scene whereof I cannot tire,
> The human tale of love and hate
> The city pageant, early and late
> Unfolds itself, rolls by, to be
> A pleasure deep and delicate
> An omnibus suffices me[74]

This joyful celebration of the omnibus as a medium for a woman's carefree urban exploration stands in sharp contrast with the male-authored salacious tales and images of sexual transgression examined in this chapter. Although there does not appear to be a textual counterpart to Levy's poem in the French context, a comparable spirit can be found in *En Omnibus* (1891), a remarkable colour print by Mary Cassatt (Plate 8).[75]

The print depicts three interlocking figures – a mother, a nanny and a small child – travelling on the omnibus through Paris. The city is faintly visible in the background, its slender bridges crossing the Seine. The women are seated close together on an omnibus bench. The image speaks volumes about key questions of class, gender, modern motherhood, domesticity, urban life and gendered public spaces. A well-dressed middle-class mother and her nanny are visually linked to one another, both by how the baby is positioned between them and by the way their skirts blend together, distinguished only by a faint shade of colour. The nanny is composed and proper, a far cry from the dishevelled wet nurses we have seen in other works, and the baby, dressed in a frilly outfit, appears to be well behaved and accustomed to city outings such as the one depicted here. While the nanny is engaged with the baby, the mother looks out of the window, seemingly absorbed by something beyond the picture's frame. It is this absorption that is for me the focus of the image.

In her seminal study on Mary Cassatt, Griselda Pollock interprets this image as a 'tiny incident of class'.[76] For Pollock, it is the relationship between two women of different classes that is at the centre of this image. She argues that Cassatt explores 'rich possibilities of this simple juxtaposition of modern, classed femininities in public space'.[77] While I don't disagree with Pollock that class relations play an important role here, I want to argue instead that what is at the centre of this image is the way the middle-class mother relates to the public urban space of the omnibus. It is the relationship between the woman and the city, here represented by the omnibus, that draws our attention.

In a preliminary drawing, Cassatt included a top-hatted male figure seated to the women's right, along with a standing lady.[78] It is telling that in the final version of the print, Cassatt excluded this figure, depicting instead the omnibus as a feminine space of introspection. This indeterminacy and the ambivalence of the mother's gaze, her absorption with what is beyond the frame, are the crux of this image. Where is the mother directing her gaze? Is she curious about another passenger we cannot see? Captivated by the view outside the window? Enchanted by the spectacle of modern life? Is she simply lost in her thoughts in a quiet moment of reflection?

Read against the context of the gendered omnibus mythology, *En omnibus* presents a stark counterpoint to the numerous nineteenth-century male-authored representations of women on public transport as sexually transgressive and inappropriate. Cassatt is not interested in the omnibus as a site of sexual tensions or erotic pursuits. Indeed, this image likely represents a more typical female experience of public transport – as it actually was, rather than as it was imagined. In this representation of the omnibus interior, female subjectivity is staged in relation to a city space that is decidedly *not* eroticised. By compositionally linking this image to her domestic scenes, Cassatt may be suggesting that this public space is just one among many where women can safely perform their femininity. The image does not offer an explanation or justification for why these women are on an omnibus journey – they may be going to the park, shopping or visiting. Or perhaps, like Amy Levy, they are simply taking an omnibus ride to enjoy the city pageant – to experience the city in all its urban splendor, 'a pleasure deep and delicate' – on their own terms.

Notes

1. 'But aunt, I don't need anyone. I came by myself. –By yourself! Did you come by foot? In a cab? –No, aunt, I took the Panthéon-Courcelles omnibus. –Oh my God, my God, it's all Claude's fault.' Colette, *Claudine à l'école* (Paris: Albin Michel, 1976), p. 80.
2. Elisabeth Félicie Byle-Mouillard, *Manuel complet de la bonne compagnie ou guide de la politesse, des égards, du bon ton et de la bienséance*, 5th edn (Paris: F. Ancelle, 1829), p. 30.
3. Raymond, 'L'omnibus', 351–2.
4. Gustave Flaubert, *Madame Bovary* (Paris: Gallimard, 2004), p. 288.
5. Michael Riffaterre explains that the *fiacre* was recognised 'as a metonym of wifely treason. ... It is a prop borrowed from the adulteress system: honesty in a wife presupposes she has no secrets from her husband. Infidelity calls for secrecy and

requires a cabman who does not know her'. Michael Riffaterre, 'Flaubert's presuppositions', in Naomi Schor and Henry F. Majewski (eds), *Flaubert and Postmodernism* (Lincoln, NE: University of Nebraska Press, 1984), p. 186. In his analysis, Riffaterre relies on Hippolyte Lucas's 'La femme adultère' from *Les Français peints par eux-mêmes* (1842).
6   An earlier well-known literary example of the *fiacre* as metonym of adultery is found in Balzac's novella *Ferragus* (1833). And an ironic rewriting of the *fiacre* episode in Flaubert appears in Rachilde's 1884 novel *Monsieur Venus*, where the protagonist, Raoule de Vénérande, pleasures herself inside a carriage while returning alone from a meeting with Jacques Silvert. See Rachilde, *Monsieur Vénus. Roman matérialiste* (New York: MLA, 2004), pp. 18-19.
7   This theme is echoed in Gourdon's *Physiologie de l'omnibus*, where he proclaims, 'L'Omnibus est la providence des amans [sic] et l'enfer des maris' (The Omnibus is a godsend for lovers and hell for husbands), p. 20.
8   Ferguson, *Paris as Revolution*, p. 134.
9   Janet Wolff, 'The invisible flâneuse: women and the literature of modernity', *Theory, Culture, and Society*, 2:3 (1985), 37–46; Griselda Pollock, 'Modernity and spaces of femininity', in *Vision and Difference*.
10 These works include (but are not limited to) the following: Aruna D'Souza and Tom McDonough (eds), *The Invisible Flâneuse? Gender, Public Space, and Visual Culture in Nineteenth-Century Paris* (Manchester: Manchester University Press, 2006); Marcus, *Apartment Stories*; Lynda Nead, *The Victorian Babylon: People, Streets and Images in Nineteenth-Century London* (New Haven, CT: Yale University Press, 2000); Nesci, *Le flâneur et les flâneuses*; Marni Kessler, *Sheer Presence: The Veil in Manet's Paris* (Minneapolis, MN: University of Minnesota Press, 2006).
11 These debates were revisited in two recent books: Temma Balducci, *Gender, Space, and the Gaze in Post-Haussmann Visual Culture* (New York: Routledge, 2017) and Temma Balducci and Heather Belnap Jensen (eds), *Women, Femininity and Public Space in European Visual Culture, 1789–1914* (Farnham: Ashgate, 2014).
12 Lynda Nead confirms this in the context of nineteenth-century London. One of her examples is a lithograph representing a clergyman approaching a respectable woman on a busy London street. Assuming that the woman is a streetwalker, the clergymen hands her a Bible in hopes to save her. The woman assures him that she is merely waiting for a bus. Nead rightly reads this lithograph not just as confirmation of preconceived notions about unaccompanied women in public spaces, but, more importantly, as evidence that respectable middle-class women could and did indeed walk in the city on their own. *The Victorian Babylon*, p. 64.
13 In her study of the novel, Susan Harrow writes that 'the treatment of space in *La Curée* is ambitious and complex, and far exceeds the objective of textbook Naturalism of placing a character in a given milieu'. Susan Harrow, *Emile Zola*, La Curée (Glasgow: University of Glasgow French and German Publications, 1998), p. 86. On various aspects of the treatment of space in the novel, see the following studies: David Baguley (ed.), *'La Curée' de Zola, ou 'La vie à outrance': Actes du colloque du 10 janvier 1987* (Paris: SEDES, 1987); Florence de Chalonge, 'Espaces, regards et perspectives: la promenade au Bois de Boulogne dans *La Curée* d'Emile

Zola', *Littérature*, 65 (1987), 58–69; Larry Duffy, *Le Grand Transit Moderne: Mobility, Modernity and French Naturalist Fiction* (Amsterdam: Rodopi, 2005); Brian Nelson, *Zola and the Bourgeoisie: A Study of Themes and Techniques in* Les Rougon-Macquart (London: Macmillan, 1983); Ferguson, *Paris as Revolution*; Prendergast, *Paris and the Nineteenth Century*; Jessica Tanner, 'Speculative Paris: Zola's repossession of Paris', *L'Esprit Créateur*, 55:3 (2015), 114–26. On the theoretical reconsideration of spatial urban practices, see Michel de Certeau, *The Practice of Everyday Life*, trans. Steven Rendall (Berkeley, CA: University of California Press, 1984).

14 Restaurants emerged in the eighteenth century and flourished in the nineteenth as premier sites of bourgeois leisure. The restaurant provided the middle class with a regulated space to spend free time, to consume in an orderly fashion and to both enjoy and participate in the spectacle of modern life. In addition to the main dining room, where the bourgeoisie could display proper behaviour and taste, many restaurants offered small private rooms, or *cabinets particuliers*. A *cabinet particulier* exemplifies how the restaurant blurs the boundaries between public and private. If the restaurant's main dining hall was a distinctly public space, the *cabinet particulier* was a 'public boudoir', as Rebecca Spang concludes: '*cabinets particuliers* notoriously concealed as much as its main dining room made visible' (*The Invention of the Restaurant: Paris and Modern Gastronomic Culture* (Cambridge, MA: Harvard University Press, 2001), p. 19). Associated with illicit sexuality and political intrigue, the *cabinets particuliers* were deemed deeply suspicious. According to Rachel Rich, 'In Paris, if one can believe contemporary remarks, those whose object was good food ate in the main room, while those with other goals ate in the *cabinets*.' Rachel Rich, *Bourgeois Consumption: Food, Space and Identity in London and Paris, 1850–1914* (Manchester: Manchester University Press, 2011), p. 138.

15 Emile Zola, *La Curée* (Paris: Gallimard, 1981), p. 175; Emile Zola, *The Kill*, trans. Brian Nelson (Oxford: Oxford University Press, 2004), p. 124.

16 Zola, *La Curée*, p. 177; *The Kill*, p. 125.

17 In this and other novels, Zola reiterates that just as the woman consumer is emerging as a new modern force, her power is undermined as she herself becomes the object consumed. This motif of a woman as an object of consumption is particularly prevalent in *La Curée* and *Au Bonheur des Dames*.

18 Zola, *La Curée*, p. 179; *The Kill*, p. 127.

19 Prendergast, *Paris and the Nineteenth Century*, p. 44.

20 Zola, *La Curée*, p. 185; *The Kill*, p. 132.

21 We find an echo of this moment in Rachilde's 1884 *Monsieur Vénus* in one of the scenes of lovemaking between Raoule and Jacques: 'Le bruit des omnibus et des voitures passant dans la rue s'affaiblissait à travers le double vitrage; on ne percevait plus qu'un grondement sourd pareil au grondement d'un train express' (p. 87). Unlike in *La Curée*, here the lovemaking is described in detail, and the rumbling of the omnibus merely replicates what is articulated explicitly. Yet it appears that Rachilde may be ironically alluding to Zola's novel through the figure of the omnibus that accompanies transgressive lovemaking.

22 See Masha Belenky, 'Disordered topographies in Zola's *La Curée*', *Romance Notes*, 53:1 (2013), 27–36.

23 Maupassant, *Contes et Nouvelles*, Forestier (ed.), p. 1071.
24 Maupassant, *Contes et Nouvelles*, Forestier (ed.), p. 1071.
25 Maupassant, *Contes et Nouvelles*, Forestier (ed.), p. 1074.
26 Maupassant, *Contes et Nouvelles*, Forestier (ed.), p. 1072.
27 Maupassant, *Contes et Nouvelles*, Forestier (ed.), p. 1072.
28 Maupassant, *Contes et Nouvelles*, Forestier (ed.), p. 1076.
29 On the political significance of Napoleon III's parks, Christopher Prendergast writes: 'The park, as the grafting of soothing Nature on to the turbulence of the City, was a means of proposing and organizing an illusion of social tranquility.' *Paris and the Nineteenth Century,* p. 167. On literary representations of parks and gardens in Paris during the Second Empire, see José Santos, 'Réalité et imaginaire des parcs et des jardins dans la deuxième moitié du XIXe siècle', *Nineteenth-Century French Studies* 31:3–4 (2003), 278–96. Santos argues that parks were miniature versions of the state: 'Le jardin serait-il alors l'aboutissement suprême de l'état? Celui de s'infiltrer jusqu'aux portes de l'inconscient du peuple, d'inscrire dans la conscience les lois étatiques du comportement (ne marcher que dans les allées, etc)', pp. 280–1.
30 On the creation and rehabilitation of Parisian parks during the Second Empire, see Pinkney, *Napoleon III and the Rebuilding of Paris*.
31 Greg Thomas, 'Women in public in the parks of Paris', in D'Souza and McDonough (eds), *The Invisible Flâneuse?*, p. 35.
32 Many paintings from the second half of the nineteenth century depict parks as spaces of bourgeois family leisure. Claude Monet, for example, painted Parc Monceau five times between 1876 and 1878. His 1878 *Parc Monceau* depicts a group of women, most likely nannies, seated in the shade and occupied by sewing or needlework, with well-dressed children at their feet, while ladies with parasols are visible in the background. A lone gentleman, whose averted gaze poses no threat, is seated to the right of the nannies. With its many references to domesticity and family life, this painting reinforces the view of the park as a space of bourgeois respectability.
33 Maupassant, *Contes et Nouvelles*, Forestier (ed.), p. 1071.
34 Maupassant, *Contes et Nouvelles*, Forestier (ed.), p. 1077.
35 According to George D. Sussman, the wet nurse was a stock figure in nineteenth-century visual culture. See 'The wet nurse in Daumier's *Third-Class Carriage*', *Metropolitan Museum Journal*, 53 (2018), 83–95.
36 The wet-nurse figure also conveyed anxieties about class: as a representative of the lower classes, she often stood in contrast to respectable bourgeois women. In this chapter, however, I focus primarily on the gendered aspect of this figure's representation.
37 Mocking overweight passengers is another topos of the omnibus repertoire (see Chapter 3).
38 Fouinet, 'Un voyage en omnibus', p. 65.
39 Gourdon, *Physiologie de l'omnibus*, p. 80.
40 Dartès, *Contes en omnibus*, p. 106.
41 Dartès, *Contes en omnibus*, pp. 106–7.

42 Dartès, *Contes en omnibus*, pp. 110–11.
43 Dartès, *Contes en omnibus*, p.114.
44 Dartès, *Contes en omnibus*, p.112.
45 Dartès, *Contes en omnibus*, p.119.
46 Lisa Algazi Marcus, 'The corruption of breastmilk in Alexandre Hepp's *Le lait d'une autre*', *Romance Studies*, 32:1 (January 2014), 13.
47 Delord *et al.*, *Paris-en-omnibus*, pp. 73–4.
48 In fact, the word 'omnibus' eventually takes on an idiomatic meaning of 'prostitute'. The 1903 *Dictionnaire étymologique de mille et une expressions propres à l'idiome français fondé sur des faits linguistiques et des documents exclusivement nationaux* gives the following definition: 'Omnibus – prostituée: femme à tous.' Adrien Timmermans (ed.) (Paris: Didier, 1903), p. 293. It is not clear precisely when the word acquired this meaning.
49 Nicolas Papayanis briefly discusses social attitudes toward unaccompanied women riding an omnibus, pointing out that they were often treated with suspicion. See *Horse-Drawn Cabs*, p. 66.
50 The series satirises the fashion of wearing enormous hoop skirts that began in the mid-1850s and lasted into the 1860s. During the early 1850s, skirts grew wider and increasingly ornate. The turning point in crinoline fashion came in 1856 with the invention of the cage crinoline, made of steel ribs. Instead of wearing layers upon layers of cumbersome petticoats, fabric could be draped upon the cage for a more natural and bouncy look. Crinolines continued to grow in size, reaching their apex in 1860, until gradually shrinking back to a more modest scale by the middle of the 1860s. As Anne Green points out, 'By 1860 the crinoline had puffed out to its widest circumference, before gradually deflating and becoming more oval over the following decade.' See *Changing France*, p. 117.
51 Anne Green notes that during the Second Empire 'a remarkable number of texts of the period feature a moment when a man is engulfed by a woman's voluminous skirts as if eclipsed by her presence' (*Changing France,* p. 132). Green writes that these scenes 'tap into archetypal male anxieties about being engulfed by a predatory woman,' p. 133.
52 Lynda Nead, 'The layering of pleasure: fashionable dress and visual culture in the mid-nineteenth century', *Nineteenth-Century Contexts: An Interdisciplinary Journal*, 35:5 (2013), 496–7.
53 See Alison Matthews David, *Fashion Victims: The Dangers of Dress Past and Present* (New York: Bloomsbury, 2015), p. 165.
54 Nead, 'The layering of pleasure', p. 499.
55 Nead, 'The layering of pleasure', p. 450.
56 Hiner, *Accessories to Modernity*; Marni Kessler, *Sheer Presence*.
57 Gourdon, *Physiologie de l'omnibus*, p. 42.
58 Hiner, *Accessories to Modernity*.
59 There has been some scholarly disagreement about the meaning of lifting the skirt and revealing ankle in nineteenth-century iconography. It has been an accepted opinion among scholars that representations of women showing their legs coded

them as improper. Recently Temma Balducci (in *Gender, Space, and the Gaze,* pp. 40–2) and others suggested that this gesture was not necessarily erotically charged but could result from the reality of walking in the city. In this image, Madame Crinoliska shows her legs even though there is no practical reason for doing so, as she is already seated. I would argue that her exposed ankles signal her loose morals.

60 Hollis Clayson, *Painted Love: Prostitution in French Art of the Impressionist Era* (New Haven, CT: Yale University Press, 1991), p. 15.

61 The present discussion draws on extensive scholarship on prostitution in nineteenth-century France by historians, art historians and literary scholars, and in particular the following works: Charles Bernheimer, *Figures of Ill Repute: Representing Prostitution in Nineteenth-Century France* (Durham, NC: Duke University Press, 1997); Hollis Clayson, *Painted Love*; Alain Corbin, *Women for Hire: Prostitution and Sexuality in France after 1850*, trans. Alan Sheridan (Cambridge, MA: Harvard University Press, 1996); Jann Matlock, *Scenes of Seduction: Prostitution, Hysteria, and Reading Difference in Nineteenth-Century France* (New York: Columbia University Press, 1994). See also Jessica Tanner's forthcoming book, *Mapping Prostitution: Sex, Space and the Novel in Nineteenth-Century Paris* (Chicago, IL: Northwestern University Press, forthcoming).

62 Matlock, *Scenes of Seduction*, p. 22.

63 Literary examples of this phenomenon abound, but the best-known one is perhaps Fantine in Victor Hugo's *Les Misérables*.

64 Rachel G. Fuchs and Victoria Thompson, *Women in Nineteenth-Century Europe* (New York: Palgrave, 2005), p. 69.

65 'Poule mouillée' also means 'coward'.

66 Delord *et al.*, *Paris-en-omnibus*, p. 88.

67 Kessler, *Sheer Presence*, pp. 7–8.

68 Kessler, *Sheer Presence*, p. 7.

69 Delord *et al.*, *Paris-en-omnibus*, p. 89.

70 Delord *et al.*, *Paris-en-omnibus*, pp. 88–9.

71 Delord *et al.*, *Paris-en-omnibus*, p. 90.

72 Delord *et al.*, *Paris-en-omnibus*, p. 90.

73 For an in-depth analysis of the metaphor of popular literature as a prostitute in the nineteenth century, see Eléonore Reverzy, *Portrait de l'artiste en fille de joie. La Littérature publique* (Paris: CNRS Édition, 2016).

74 Amy Levy, 'Ballad of an omnibus', Representative Poetry Online, https://rpo.library.utoronto.ca/poems/ballade-omnibus, accessed 24 September 2018.

75 Although Cassatt was, of course, American, rather than French, she lived and worked in France most of her adult life and participated in French artistic circles.

76 Griselda Pollock, *Mary Cassatt: Painter of Modern Women* (London: Thames and Hudson, 1998), p. 169.

77 Pollock, *Mary Cassatt*, p. 169.

78 See Nancy Mowll Mathews and Barbara Stern Shapiro, *Mary Cassatt: The Color Prints* (New York: Harry N. Abrams, 1989), p. 115.

Epilogue: final stop

When the omnibus was first introduced on to the streets of Paris, it irrevocably changed everyday life, the lived urban environment and the nature of human relationships among Parisians. But the biggest impact of this new form of transport was on the literary and cultural imagination. In literature and popular visual culture, authors and artists mused on the effects of the omnibus upon the city, its inhabitants and society as a whole. Deploying it as a narrative form, they sought to capture a broad scope of human experiences contained within the confines of the vehicle. A laboratory of social relations, the omnibus offered an ideal space for social observation and storytelling. In just a few short years, the omnibus became a topos of popular literature and visual culture – both in the literal sense of a *place* and as a commonplace of this corpus. Yet what distinguishes this topos of urban travel is that its true concern is rarely travel at all. As I have argued in this book, when nineteenth-century documents talk about the omnibus, it is about much more than a journey from one part of the city to another. Instead, the omnibus became a way to broach an astonishingly wide range of issues: social mobility, urban alienation, anxiety about class mixing, discomfort and fascination with women in public spaces, the fragmentation and rapidity of modern life and the breakdown of boundaries between the public and the private. In other words, the nineteenth-century omnibus became what we can call a 'super-topos',[1] a concept and a form that because of its very 'omni-ness' – its all-encompassing nature – enabled writers and artists to grapple with multiple facets of modernity.

What emerges most powerfully from these representations is the ambivalence of the omnibus as an emblem of urban modernity. Was it a symbol of progress? Or a painful reminder that the pace of city life accelerated to the point of dehumanising urban dwellers? A metaphor for social equality? Or a visible symbol of class oppression? A site of imagined female transgressions? Or a schoolroom of proper manners? All these conflicting meanings were encompassed within and projected upon the space of the omnibus. To study

Engine of modernity

nineteenth-century representations of the omnibus is to confront its paradoxes. I will conclude with two competing visions of the omnibus from the late nineteenth century: one shared by Fortuné du Boisgobey, a prolific and popular author of detective fiction, and Emile Zola, both of whom imagined the vehicle as a symbol of destructive modernity, and one from Octave Uzanne, who offered a portrait of the omnibus as a relic of a genteel past imbued with nostalgia.

Fortuné du Boisgobey's popular crime novel of 1881 titled *Le Crime de l'omnibus* begins with a brutal murder. On a cold winter night in Paris, a young and beautiful woman is mysteriously killed while riding on a crowded midnight omnibus heading to the Place Pigalle. Remarkably, other passengers do not become aware of the young woman's death until the omnibus reaches its final destination and the novel's protagonist, Paul Freneuse, along with the conductor are faced with her lifeless corpse. The rest of this fast-paced novel's rather improbable plot, with its many twists and turns, revolves around solving the mystery of this murder. The assassin, it turns out, was another passenger, a woman whose face is hidden behind a thick veil ('une épaisse voilette lui cachait le visage').[2] The murder itself is facilitated by the configuration of the omnibus seating: placing herself next to her future victim, the murderess takes advantage of a bump in the road that causes passengers to fall against each other, to prick the young woman's arm with a poisoned needle. The victim dies instantly, while unsuspecting fellow passengers around her go about their business, assuming that the young woman is simply asleep, as are many other riders of the nocturnal omnibus. Du Boisgobey's novel amplifies the dangers of urban life and the anxieties associated with it: the anonymity of public transportation as well as a kind of enforced proximity to strangers make this crime possible, even easy. Above all, it highlights a sense of profound alienation, the ultimate evil of modern urban life: one can die in the midst of a crowd without anyone noticing. Here the omnibus serves as an accessory to murder – both because its physical setting makes it possible and because it fosters an environment devoid of personal connection. Du Boisgobey could have disposed of his heroine without having recourse to a complicated and implausible plot line, yet he casts the omnibus as complicit in her murder because it embodied the dangers of modernity.

This idea finds its fullest realisation in Emile Zola's 1883 novel *Au Bonheur des Dames*. The omnibus is depicted as an instrument of physical mutilation and death, and as a symbol of a ruthless modern world. Set in the early days of the Second Empire, Zola's novel recounts the birth of the first department store in Paris and the dramatic and often traumatic shift from traditional forms of commerce to the capitalist consumer economy. The rise and the spectacular success of the fictional department store, *Au Bonheur des Dames*, brings about the ruin of small traditional shops in the neighbourhood, which is literally and figuratively demolished to make room for the ever expanding *grand magasin*, the main agent of modern commerce – and the omnibus serves as a stand-in for the 'creative destruction' this commerce engenders.

First, we learn that M. Lhomme, the head cashier, has lost his right arm in an omnibus accident. This foreshadows a dramatic episode later in the novel, when Robineau, a small shopkeeper whose silk-fabric shop was run out of business by *Au Bonheur des Dames*, throws himself under the wheels of a speeding omnibus. Unable to compete with the big department store, Robineau is one of many shopkeepers whose physical demise or injury figuratively represents the death of traditional commerce. Zola's text explicitly equates the two 'modern machines' – the department store and the omnibus – as embodying the exhilaration and the dangers of the new. When the injured Robineau is brought home, he explains to his wife how, overwhelmed by the idea of his impending bankruptcy, he resorted to suicide: 'Je descendais la rue de la Michodière, j'ai cru que les gens du *Bonheur* se fichaient de moi, cette grande gueuse de maison m' écrasait... alors, quand l'omnibus a tourné, j'ai songé à Lhomme et à son bras, je me suis jeté dessous...'[3] (I was going down rue de la Michodière; I thought that the *Bonheur* people were laughing at me, that tramp of a store was crushing me... so when an omnibus turned the corner, I thought of Lhomme and his arm, and I threw myself under...). The word 'écrasait' here applies not to the omnibus that literally crushes Robineau's legs but to *Au Bonheur des Dames*, which suffocates his business, deprives him of his livelihood and destroys his dignity. The omnibus and the department store are clearly conflated into one image of the dangerous modern world that destroys everything and everybody that gets in its way as it triumphantly rushes toward progress. In his *Dossier préparatoire* for the novel, Zola famously declared that he wished 'dans *Au Bonheur des Dames* faire le poème de l'activité moderne' (in *Au Bonheur des Dames*, to write a poem to modern activity), and the novel has been heralded as one of his most optimistic works. Yet we see the text's ambivalence vis-à-vis this very *activité moderne*, or modernity itself, because of its alienating effect and the ease with which it obliterates the weak who cannot keep up with its pace. And this ambivalence is embodied in the department store's dangerous double: the omnibus.

A very different vision of the cultural valence of the omnibus emerges from Octave Uzanne's 1900 article 'Omnibus de Paris'. For Uzanne, the omnibus represents nostalgia:

> Les omnibus parisiens... sont très arriérés, vieux jeu, très *papa* sinon très *grand-papa*; toutefois, ailleurs, on circule, on est emporté comme un billet roulé dans un pneumatique, mais on ne voyage pas. Il n'y a que dans ces vieux fourgons, que le monopole de la municipalité maintient à Paris, que nous pouvons aimablement gaspiller notre temps, tisser les idylles, des romans, des églogues, flâner sans souci, nous sentir vivre enfin.[4]

> (Parisian omnibuses... are very backwards, old game, very *daddy*, even *granddaddy*, yet, on other modes of transport, you are carried off like a piece of paper in a pneumatic tube, but you don't actually travel. It's only in these old wagons that the municipal monopoly maintains in Paris that we can leisurely waste our time, spin idylls, novels and eclogues, stroll worry-free – in short, feel alive.)

Contrasting the outmoded omnibus with the technologically advanced system of pneumatic tubes, which were used to deliver letters within Paris from 1866 until 1984, Uzanne explains that other modes of transport dehumanise travellers, who are blown from place to place like mere pieces of paper (perhaps this is a reference to the newly inaugurated Metropolitain). Instead, the slow pace of the omnibus allows you to deeply engage with the city, and above all it inspires creative endeavours. Uzanne's choice of words here (*idylles*, *églogues* and, of course, *flâner*) explicitly evokes associations of omnibus travel with writing and more broadly the idea of the city as literary inspiration. A relic of the past, yet so much part of the present, the omnibus thus offers Uzanne a perfect view of tradition and modernity and the intricate ways the two notions are intertwined.

Zola, du Boisgobey and Uzanne perfectly capture, each in their own way, the diverse facets of the nineteenth century that the Parisian omnibus represented and that I have explored in this book: a material change in the fabric of the city, new forms of sociability, social and economic mobility, alienation and flux. But it is above all the cultural work it performed that made the omnibus a powerful engine of modernity.

Notes

1 I thank Christopher Prendergast for suggesting this term to me (Symposium on Literary History and Topology, May 2018, University of Copenhagen).
2 Fortuné du Boisgobey, *Le Crime de l'omnibus* (Paris: Encrage, 2005), p. 10.
3 Emile Zola, *Au Bonheur des Dames* (Paris: Flammarion, 1999), p. 448.
4 Uzanne, 'Omnibus de Paris', p. 494.

Bibliography

Albitte, Gustave and Dugard, Louis, *Mon voisin d'omnibus*, in *La France dramatique au dix-neuvième siècle* (Paris: Tresse, 1841).
Algazi Marcus, Lisa, 'The corruption of breastmilk in Alexandre Hepp's *Le lait d'une autre*', *Romance Studies*, 32:1 (2014), 3–15.
Alkan, Charles-Valentin, *Les Omnibus. Variations dédiées aux Dames Blanches*. Variation for piano in C major (Paris: M. Schlesinger, 1828).
Allen, James Smith, *Popular French Romanticism: Authors, Readers, and Books in the 19th Century* (Syracuse, NY: Syracuse University Press, 1981).
Almanach des Omnibus, des Dames blanches et autres voitures nouvellement établies (Paris: Lenormant fils, 1829).
Amann, Elizabeth, 'Reading (on) the tram: Benito Péres Galdós's "La novella en el tranvía"', *Orbis Litterarium*, 69:3 (2014), 193–214.
Amann, Elizabeth, 'The devil in the omnibus: from *le Charivari* to *Blackwood's Magazine*', *Nineteenth-Century Contexts*, 39:1 (2017), 1–13.
Aubryet, Xavier, 'La Chaussée d'Antin', in *Paris-guide par les principaux écrivains et artistes de la France* (Paris: Edition de la Découverte, 1983).
Auriac, Eugène d', *Histoire anecdotique de l'industrie française* (Paris: E. Dentu, 1861).
Baguley, David (ed.), *'La Curée' de Zola, ou 'la vie à outrance': Actes du colloque du 10 janvier 1987* (Paris: SEDES, 1987).
Balducci, Temma, *Gender, Space, and the Gaze in Post-Haussmann Visual Culture* (New York: Routledge, 2017).
Balducci, Temma and Jensen, Heather Belnap (eds), *Women, Femininity and Public Space in European Visual Culture, 1789–1914* (Farnham: Ashgate, 2014).
Balzac, Honoré de, 'Histoire et physiologie des Boulevards de Paris. De la Madeleine à la Bastille', in *Le Diable à Paris*, 2 vols (Paris: Hetzel, 1845–46, II (1846)).
Balzac, Honoré de, *La Comédie humaine*, vol. 5 (Paris: Gallimard, 1977).
Balzac, Honoré de, *Ferragus*, in *Histoire des treize* (Paris: Garnier-Flammarion, 1988).
Bastard, George, *Paris qui roule* (Paris: Georges Chamerot, 1889).
Baudelaire, Charles, *Œuvres complètes* (Paris: Gallimard, 1938).
Baudelaire, Charles, *The Parisian Prowler*, trans. Edward Kaplan (Athens, GA: University of Georgia Press, 1989).

Beaumont, Matthew and Freeman, Michael (eds), *The Railway and Modernity. Time, Space, and the Machine Ensemble* (Oxford: Peter Lang, 2007).

Belenky, Masha, 'From transit to transitoire: omnibus and modernity', *Nineteenth-Century French Studies*, 35:1/2 (2007), 84–96.

Belenky, Masha, 'Transitory tales: writing the omnibus in nineteenth-century Paris', *Dix-Neuf: Journal of the Society of Dix-Neuviémistes*, 16:3 (2012), https://www.tandfonline.com/doi/full/10.1179/1478731811Z.0000000005.

Belenky, Masha, 'Disordered topographies in Zola's *La Curée*', *Romance Notes* 53:1 (2013), 27–36.

Bell, David, *Real Time: Accelerating Narrative from Balzac to Zola* (Chicago, IL: University of Illinois Press, 2004).

Bellu, René, *Les Autobus parisiens des origines à nos jours* (Paris: Delville, 1979).

Benjamin, Walter, *The Arcades Project*, trans. Howard Eiland and Kevin McLaughlin (Cambridge, MA: Harvard University Press, 1999).

Berman, Marshall, *All That Is Solid Melts into Air: The Experience of Modernity* (New York: Penguin, 1988).

Bernard, Léo de, 'Les Wagons de Paris', *Naguère et Jadis* (March 1964).

Bernheimer, Charles, *Figures of Ill Repute: Representing Prostitution in Nineteenth-Century France* (Durham, NC: Duke University Press, 1997).

Boisgobey, Fortuné de, *Le Crime de l'omnibus* (Paris: Encage, 2005).

Boutin, Aimée (ed.), 'The flâneur and the senses', *Dix-Neuf: Journal of the Society of Dix-Neuviémistes*, 16:2 (2012).

Boutin, Aimée, *City of Noise: Sound and Nineteenth-Century Paris* (Urbana, IL: University of Illinois Press, 2015).

Bowie, Karen (ed.), *La Modernité avant Haussmann: formes de l'espace urbain à Paris 1801–1853* (Paris: Editions Recherches, 2000).

Byle-Mouillard, Elisabeth Félicie, *Manuel complet de la bonne compagnie or guide de la politesse, des égards, du bon ton et de la bienséance*, 5th edn (Paris: F. Ancelle, 1829).

Calmettes, Pierre, 'En Omnibus', *Le Monde Moderne* (1906), 242–6.

Carter, Ian, *Railways and Culture in Britain: The Epitome of Modernity* (Manchester: Manchester University Press, 2001).

Certeau, Michel de, *The Practice of Everyday Life*, trans. Steven Rendall (Berkeley, CA: University of California Press, 1984).

Chalogne, Florence de, 'Espaces, regards et perspectives: la promenade au Bois de Boulogne dans *La Curée* d'Emile Zola', *Littérature*, 65 (1987), 58–69.

Charles, David, 'Le trognon et l'omnibus: faire de sa misère sa barricade', in Alain Corbin and Jean-Marie Mayeur (eds), *La Barricade* (Paris: Publications de la Sorbonne, 1997).

Childs, Elizabeth C., *Daumier and Exoticism: Satirizing the French and the Foreign* (New York: Peter Lang, 2004).

Clarétie, Jules, 'Les omnibus parisiens', *Les annales politiques et littéraires*, 1200 (24 June 1906).

Clayson, Hollis, *Painted Love: Prostitution in French Art of the Impressionist Era* (New Haven, CT: Yale University Press, 1991).

Cohen, Margaret, 'Panoramic literature and the invention of everyday genres', in Leo Charney and Vanessa Schwartz (eds), *Cinema and the Invention of Modern Life* (Berkeley, CA: University of California Press, 1996).

Bibliography

Cohen, Richard I., 'The "Wandering Jew" from medieval legend to modern metaphor', in Barbara Kirshenblatt-Gimblett and Jonathan Karp (eds), *The Art of Being Jewish in Modern Times* (Philadelphia, PA: University of Pennsylvania Press, 2008).
Colette, *Claudine à l'école* (Paris: Albin Michel, 1976).
Coppée, François, 'Croquis parisiens: l'omnibus', *Les annales politiques et littéraires* (7 September 1902).
Coppée, François, 'Physionomies parisiennes: le conducteur de l'omnibus', *Les annales politiques et littéraires*, 1200 (24 June 1906).
Corbin, Alain, *Women for Hire: Prostitution and Sexuality in France after 1850*, trans. Alan Sheridan (Cambridge, MA: Harvard University Press, 1996).
Darasse, P., 'Un coup de foudre en omnibus', *Comédies pour salons et théâtre*, 2nd edn (Paris: impr. de la Publicité générale, 1889).
Dartès, Emile, *Contes en omnibus* (Paris: Flammarion, 1894).
Davidson, Denise, *France after the Revolution: Urban Life, Gender, and the New Social Order* (Cambridge, MA: Harvard University Press, 2007).
Dejean, Joan, *How Paris Became Paris: The Invention of the Modern City* (New York and London: Bloomsbury, 2014).
Delord, Taxile, Arnould Frémy and Edmond Texier, *Paris-en-omnibus* (Paris: Libraire d'Alphonse Taride, 1854).
D'Souza, Aruna and McDonough, Tom (eds), *The Invisible Flâneuse? Gender, Public Space, and Visual Culture in Nineteenth-Century Paris* (Manchester: Manchester University Press, 2006).
Du Camp, Maxime, 'Les voitures publiques dans la ville de Paris: les Fiacres et les Omnibus', *Revue de deux mondes*, 62 (1867), 318–52.
Du Camp, Maxime, *Paris, ses organes, ses fonctions et sa vie dans la seconde moitié du XIXe siècle*, 6 vols (Paris: Hachette, 1869–75).
Ducoux, 'Les voitures publiques de Paris', *Paris-guide par les principaux écrivains et artistes de la France*, vol. 2 (Paris: A. Lacroix et Verboeckhoven, 1867).
Dufay, Pierre, 'Le Triomphe et le bicentenaire des omnibus', *Mercure de France* (1 February 1928), 628–40.
Duffy, Larry, *Le Grand Transit Moderne: Mobility, Modernity, and French Naturalist Fiction* (Amsterdam: Rodopi, 2005).
Dupeuty, Charles, De Courcy, Frédéric and Lassagne, Espérance, *Les omnibus, ou la revue en voiture* (Paris: J.-N. Barba, 1828).
Faÿ-Sallois, Fanny, *Les Nourrices à Paris au XIXe siècle* (Paris: Payot, 1980).
Felski, Rita, *The Gender of Modernity* (Cambridge, MA: Harvard University Press, 1995).
Ferguson, Priscilla Parkhurst, 'The flâneur on and off the streets of Paris', in Keith Tester (ed.), *The Flâneur* (London: Routledge, 1994).
Ferguson, Priscilla Parkhurst, *Paris as Revolution: Writing the Nineteenth-Century City* (Berkeley, CA: University of California Press, 1994).
Flaubert, Gustave, *Correspondance, 1856* (Paris: L. Conard, 1926–54).
Flaubert, Gustave, *L'éducation sentimentale* (Paris: Les Belles Lettres, 1942).
Flaubert, Gustave, *Madame Bovary* (Paris: Gallimard, 2004).
Flesselles, Comptesse de, *Les jeunes voyageurs dans Paris* (Paris: Locard et Davi, 1829).
Forbes, Amy Wiese, *The Satiric Decade: Satire and the Rise of Republicanism in France, 1830–1840* (Lanham, MD: Lexington Books, 2010).

Fouinet, Ernest, 'Un voyage en omnibus de la barrière du Thrône à la barrière de l'Etiole', in *Paris, ou le livre des cent-et-un*, vol. 2 (Paris: C. Ladvocat, 1831).

Fournel, Victor, *Ce qu'on voit dans les rues de Paris* (Paris: Delahays, 1858).

Fournier, Edouard, *Paris démoli* (Paris: E. Dentu, 1883).

Friès, Charles, 'Le Conducteur d'omnibus', in *Les Français peints par eux-mêmes: encyclopédie morale du dix-neuvième siècle* (Paris: Curmer, 1840–42).

Fuchs, Rachel G. and Thompson, Victoria E, *Women in Nineteenth-Century Europe* (New York: Palgrave, 2005).

Gabriel, J. and Vermond, P., *J'attends un omnibus* (Bruxelles: J-A Lelong, 1849).

Gaillard, Marc, *Histoire des transports parisiens: de Blaise Pascal à nos jours* (Le Coteau: Horvath, 1987).

Gaillard, Marc, *Du Madeleine-Bastille à Météor: histoire des transports parisiens* (Amiens: Martelle, 1991).

Gautier, Théophile, Dumas, Alexandre and de Musset, Paul, *Paris et les Parisiens au XIXe siècle* (Paris: Morizot, 1856).

Gavarni, Paul, 'Une aventure d'omnibus', *Le Charivari* (26 August 1840).

Gavin, A. and Humphries, A. (eds), *Transport in British Fiction: Technologies of Movement, 1840–1940* (London: Palgrave, 2015).

Girardin, Delphine de, *Chroniques parisiennes*, Jean-Louis Vissière (ed.) (Paris: Des femmes, 1986).

Gluck, Mary, *Popular Bohemia: Modernism and Urban Culture in Nineteenth-Century Paris* (Cambridge, MA: Harvard University Press, 2008).

Goncourt, Edmond de and Goncourt, Jules de, *Journal*, 1 (1851–63), A. Ricatte (ed.) (Paris: Flammarion, 1959).

Gourdon, Edouard, *Physiologie de l'omnibus* (Paris: Terry, 1842).

Gozlan, Léon, *Le Triomphe des Omnibus* (Paris: Abroise Dupont, 1828).

Green, Anne, *Changing France: Literature and Material Culture in the Second Empire* (London: Anthem Press, 2011).

Griveau, Lucien, 'En omnibus', *Journal des démoiselles*, 51:2 (1883), 48–50.

Guerrand, Roger-Henri, *Mœurs citadines. Histoire de la culture urbaine, XIX–XXe siècles* (Paris: Edima, 1992).

Hahn, H. Hazel, *Scenes of Parisian Modernity: Culture and Consumption in Nineteenth-Century Paris* (New York: Palgrave Macmillan, 2009).

Harrow, Susan, *Emile Zola,* La Curée (Glasgow: University of Glasgow French and German Publications, 1998).

Harvey, David, *Paris, Capital of Modernity* (New York: Routledge, 2003).

Hénard, Robert, 'En omnibus', *Le Magasin Pittoresque* (January 1898), 346–9.

Higonnet, Patrice, *Paris: Capital of the World* (Cambridge, MA: Harvard University Press, 2002).

Hiner, Susan, *Accessories to Modernity: Fashion and the Feminine in Nineteenth-Century France* (Philadelphia, PA: University of Pennsylvania Press, 2010).

Huart, Louis, 'Les voitures publiques', in *Nouveau tableau de Paris au XIXe siècle*, vol. 4 (Paris: Madame Charles-Béchet, 1834).

Huart, Louis, *Physiologie du flaneur* (Paris: Aubert, 1841).

Hugo, Victor, *Les Misérables* (Paris: Garnier, 1963).

Janin, Jules, *L'omnibus complet* (Paris: J. Juteau, 1866).
Kalifa, Dominique, *La Culture en masse en France, 1860–1930* (Paris: La Découverte, 2001).
Kalifa, Dominique (ed.), *La Civilisation du journal. L'histoire culturelle et littéraire de la presse au XIXe siècle* (Paris: Nouveau Monde, 2011).
Kessler, Marni, *Sheer Presence: The Veil in Manet's Paris* (Minneapolis, MN: University of Minnesota Press, 2006).
Kock, Paul de, 'Etudes de mœurs. Les pensionnats à voiture', *Musée des familles* (1 January 1841).
Lasserre, *Paris en omnibus, itinéraire pittoresque, historique et industriel. Ligne H, de l'Odéon à Clichy* (Paris: A. Parent, 1867).
Lauster, Martina, *Sketches of the Nineteenth Century: European Journalism and Its Physiologies, 1830–50* (Basingstoke: Palgrave Macmillan, 2007).
Lavollée, Charles, *Les Omnibus à Paris et à Londres* (Paris: Renou & Maulde, 1868).
Levy, Amy, 'Ballad of an omnibus', Representative Poetry Online, https://rpo.library.utoronto.ca/poems/ballade-omnibus, accessed 24 September 2018.
Loeillot, Karl, *Les Nouvelles voitures publiques de Paris* (Paris: Gihaut Frères, 1832).
Lyon-Caen, Judith, 'Saisir, décrire, déchiffrer: les mises en texte du social sous la monarchie de Juillet', *Revue Historique*, 306:2 (2004), 301–30.
Lyons, Martyn, *A History of Reading and Writing in the Western World* (New York: Palgrave, 2010).
Mainardi, Patricia, *Husbands, Wives, and Lovers: Marriage and Its Discontents in Nineteenth-Century France* (New Haven, CT: Yale University Press, 2003).
Mainardi, Patricia, *Another World: Nineteenth-Century Illustrated Print Culture* (New Haven, CT: Yale University Press, 2017).
Marcus, Sharon, *Apartment Stories: City and Home in Nineteenth-Century Paris and London* (Berkeley, CA: University of California Press, 1999).
Marcus, Sharon, 'Transparence de l'appartement parisien entre 1820 et 1848', in Karen Bowie (ed.), *La Modernité avant Haussmann: formes de l'espace urbain à Paris 1801–1853* (Paris: Editions Recherches, 2000).
Martin-Fugier, Anne, *La Vie élégante, ou, la formation de Tout-Paris 1815–1848* (Paris: Fayard, 1990).
Matlock, Jann, *Scenes of Seduction: Prostitution, Hysteria, and Reading Difference in Nineteenth-Century France* (New York: Columbia University Press, 1994).
Matthews David, Alison, *Fashion Victims: The Dangers of Dress Past and Present* (New York: Bloomsbury, 2015).
Maupassant, Guy de, 'Le père Mongilet', *Gil Blas* (24 February 1885).
Maupassant, Guy de, *Contes et Nouvelles*, Albert-Marie Schmidt and Gérard Delaisement (eds) (Paris: Albin Michel, 1957).
Maupassant, Guy de, *Contes et Nouvelles*, Louis Forestier (ed.) (Paris: Gallimard, 1974).
Maza, Sarah, *The Myth of the French Bourgeoisie* (Cambridge, MA: Harvard University Press, 2003).
Meiner, Carsten, *Le carrosse littéraire et l'invention du hasard* (Paris: Presses Universitaires de France, 2008).
Mowll Mathews, Nancy, and Shapiro, Barbara Stern, *Mary Cassatt: The Color Prints* (New York: Harry N. Abrams, 1989).

Nead, Lynda, *The Victorian Babylon: People, Streets and Images in Nineteenth-Century London* (New Haven, CT: Yale University Press, 2000).
Nead, Lynda, 'The layering of pleasure: fashionable dress and visual culture in the mid-nineteenth century', *Nineteenth-Century Contexts: An Interdisciplinary Journal*, 35:5 (2013).
Nelson, Brian, *Zola and the Bourgeoisie: A Study of Themes and Techniques in* Les Rougon-Macquart (London: Macmillan, 1983).
Nesci, Catherine, *Le flâneur et les flâneuses. Les femmes et la ville à l'époque romantique* (Grenoble: Ellug, 2007).
Nogaret, Félix, *Réflexions d'un patriarche sur les voitures dites omnibus!* (Paris: Leclerc, 1828).
Les omnibus. Premier voyage de Cadet la Blague de la place de la Madeleine à la Bastille et retour (Paris: Chez Chassaignon, 1828).
O'Neil-Henry, Anne, *Mastering the Marketplace: Popular Literature in Nineteenth-Century France* (Lincoln, NE: University of Nebraska Press, 2017).
Papayanis, Nicholas, *Horse-Drawn Cabs and Omnibuses in Paris: The Idea of Circulation and the Business of Public Transit* (Baton Rouge, LA: Louisiana State University Press, 1996).
Papayanis, Nicholas, *Paris before Haussmann* (Baltimore, MD and London: Johns Hopkins University Press, 2004).
Paris en omnibus. Guide familier dans le Paris de 1869 (Paris Ancien et Paris Nouveau) par un simple voyageur en omnibus, en chemin de ceinture et en bateau mouche indiquant les rencontres et les correspondances de ces divers modes de locomotion dans Paris (Paris: Chez les principaux libraires et dans tous les bureaux d'omnibus, 1869).
Pinkney, David H., *Napoleon III and the Rebuilding of Paris* (Princeton, NJ: Princeton University Press, 1958).
Pinkney, David H., *Decisive Years in France 1840–1847* (Princeton, NJ: Princeton University Press, 1986).
Pollock, Griselda, *Vision and Difference: Femininity, Feminism and the Histories of Art* (London: Routledge, 1988).
Pollock, Griselda, *Mary Cassatt: Painter of Modern Women* (London: Thames and Hudson, 1998).
Preiss, Nathalie, *Les Physiologies en France au XIXe siècle* (Mont-de-Marsan: Editions Inter-Universitaires, 1999).
Prendergast, Christopher, *Paris and the Nineteenth-Century* (Oxford: Blackwell, 1995).
'Quelques remarques sur les omnibus', *Le Magasin pittoresque* (1843).
Raymond, Emmeline, 'L'Omnibus', *La Mode Illustrée* (27 October 1862), 351–2.
Renoy, Georges, *Paris au temps des omnibus* (Bruxelles: Rossel Edition, 1976).
Reverzy, Eléonore, *Portrait de l'artiste en fille de joie. La Littérature publique* (Paris: CNRS Édition, 2016).
Rice, Shelley, *Parisian Views* (Cambridge, MA: MIT Press, 1997).
Rich, Rachel, *Bourgeois Consumption: Food, Space and Identity in London and Paris, 1850–1914* (Manchester: Manchester University Press, 2011).
Riffaterre, Michael, 'Flaubert's presuppositions', in Naomi Schor and Henry F. Majewski (eds), *Flaubert and Postmodernism* (Lincoln, NE: University of Nebraska Press, 1984).

Roubaud, Jacques, *Ode à la ligne 29 des autobus parisiens* (Paris: Attila, 2013).
Sand, George and Sandeau, Jules, 'Le Commissionnaire', *George Sand: Œuvres complètes 1829–1831: George Sand avant 'Indiana'*, 2 vols, Yves Chastagnaret (ed.) (Paris: Honoré Champion, 2008).
Schivelbusch, Wolfgang, *The Railway Journey: The Industrialization of Time and Space in the Nineteenth Century* (Berkeley, CA: University of California Press, 1986).
Schwartz, Vanessa, *Spectacular Realities: Early Mass Culture in Fin-de-siècle Paris* (Berkeley, CA: University of California Press, 1998).
Sennett, Richard, *Flesh and Stone: The Body and the City in Western Civilization* (New York: Norton, 1994).
Sieburth, Richard, 'Same difference: the French *Physiologies*, 1840–1842', in Norman F. Cantor (ed.), *Notebooks in Cultural Analysis: An Annual Review* (Durham, NC: Duke University Press, 1984).
Siegel, François, *Les Archives inédites de la RATP* (Neuilly-sur-Seine: Lafon, 2011).
Silverman, Willa, *The New Bibliopolis, French Book Collectors and the Culture of Print, 1880–1914* (Toronto: University of Toronto Press, 2008).
Simmel, Georg, 'The metropolis and mental life', in Gary Bridge and Sophie Watson (eds), *The Blackwell City Reader* (Malden: Blackwell, 2002).
Soppelsa, Peter, 'The instrumentalisation of horses in nineteenth-century Paris', in Rob Boddice (ed.), *Anthropocentrism: Humans, Animals, Environments* (Leiden and Boston: Brill, 2011).
Soppelsa, Peter, 'The end of horse transportation in Belle-Époque Paris', *Interdisciplinary Studies in Literature and Environment*, 24:1 (2017), 113–29.
Soullier, Charles, *Les omnibus de Paris, pièce curieuse et utile à l'usage des voyageurs dans Paris, contenant une liste alphabétique des 31 omnibus, avec leurs parcours, etc., accompagnée de notes historiques et statistiques très intéressantes et d'un indicateur général des monuments, musées, etc.* (Paris: Cordier, 1863).
Spang, Rebecca L., *The Invention of the Restaurant: Paris and Modern Gastronomic Culture* (Cambridge, MA: Harvard University Press, 2001).
Stiénon, Valérie, 'La vie littéraire par le kaléidoscope des Physiologies', in *La Vie littéraire et artistique aux XIXe siècle* (2011).
Stiénon, Valérie, 'Le canon littéraire au crible des physiologies', *Revue d'Histoire Littéraire de la France*, 114:1 (2014), 131–41.
Stierle, Karlheinz, *La Capitale des signes: Paris et son discours* (Paris: La Maison des Sciences des Hommes, 2001).
Studeny, Christophe, *L'Invention de la vitesse* (Paris: Gallimard, 1995).
Sussman, George D., 'The wet nurse in Daumier's *Third-Class Carriage*', *Metropolitan Museum Journal*, 53 (2018), 83–95.
Tanner, Jessica, 'Speculative Paris: Zola's repossession of Paris', *L'Esprit Créateur*, 55:3 (2015), 114–26.
Terdiman, Richard, *Discourse/Counter-Discourse. The Theory and Practice of Symbolic Resistance in Nineteenth-Century France* (Ithaca, NY: Cornell University Press, 1985).
Terni, Jennifer, 'A genre for early mass culture: French vaudeville and the city, 1830–48', *Theater Journal*, 58:2 (2006), 221–8.
Terni, Jennifer, 'The omnibus and the shaping of the urban quotidian', *Cultural and Social History*, 11:2 (2015), 217–42.

Tester, Keith (ed.), *The Flâneur* (London: Routledge, 1994).
Texier, Edmond, 'Les voitures à Paris', *Tableau de Paris*, vol. 2 (Paris: Paulin et le Chevalier, 1852–53).
Thérenty, Marie-Eve, *Mosaïque: être écrivain entre presse et roman (1829–1836)* (Paris: Éditions Honoré Champion, 2003).
Thérenty, Marie-Eve and Vaillant, Alain (eds), *La Presse au XIXe siècle: les modes de diffusions d'une industrie culturelle* (Paris: Nouveau Monde, 2004).
Thomas, Greg, 'Women in public in the parks of Paris', in Aruna D'Souza and Tom McDonough (eds), *The Invisible Flâneuse? Gender, Public Space, and Visual Culture in Nineteenth-Century Paris* (Manchester: Manchester University Press, 2006).
Thompson, Victoria, *The Virtuous Marketplace: Women and Men, Money and Politics in Paris, 1830–1870* (Baltimore, MD: Johns Hopkins University Press, 2000).
Thompson, Victoria, 'Telling "spatial stories": urban space and bourgeois identities in early nineteenth-century Paris', *Journal of Modern History*, 75:3 (2003), 523–56.
Uzanne, Octave, *La Locomotion à travers le temps, les mœurs et l'espace. Résumé pittoresque et anecdotique de l'histoire générale des moyens de transports terrestres et aériens* (Paris: Librairies Paul Ollendorf, 1900).
Uzanne, Octave, 'Omnibus de Paris', *Le Monde Moderne*, 1.28 (1900), 481–94.
Vadillo, Ana Pareja, 'Phenomena in flux: the aesthetics and politics of travelling in modernity', in Ann L. Ardis and Leslie W. Lewis (eds), *Women's Experience of Modernity 1875–1945* (Baltimore: Johns Hopkins University Press, 2003).
Van Zanten, David, *Building Paris: Architectural Institutions and the Transformation of the French Capital, 1830–1870* (Cambridge: Cambridge University Press, 1994).
Walkowitz, Judith, *City of Dreadful Delight: Narratives of Sexual Danger in Late Victorian London* (Chicago, IL: University of Chicago Press, 1992).
Wechsler, Judith, *A Human Comedy: Physiognomy and Caricature in Nineteenth-Century Paris* (Chicago, IL: University of Chicago Press, 1982).
Wilson, Elizabeth, *The Sphinx in the City: Urban Life, the Control of Disorder, and Women* (Berkeley, CA: University of California Press, 1991).
Wilson, Elizabeth, 'The invisible flâneur', *New Left Review*, I.191 (1994), 90–110.
Wolff, Janet, 'The invisible flâneuse: women and the literature of modernity', *Theory, Culture, and Society*, 2:3 (1985), 37–46.
Zola, Emile, *La Curée* (Paris: Gallimard, 1981).
Zola, Emile, *Au Bonheur des Dames* (Paris: Flammarion, 1999).
Zola, Emile, *The Kill*, trans. Brian Nelson (Oxford: Oxford Univercity Press, 2004).
Zuber, Henri, Hallsted-Baumert, Sheila and Berton, Claude, *Guide des sources de l'histoire des transports publics urbains à Paris et en Ile-de-France, XIXe–XXe siècles* (Paris: Publications de la Sorbonne, 1998).

Index

Page numbers in italics indicate illustrations.

adultery
    fiacre as setting for 135, 159–60n5, 160n6
    omnibus as setting for 27, 80, 89, 119, 137, 140, 148–9
alienation 26, 28, 51–2, 55, 56, 84–92, 126, 127, 141, 165, 166, 168
Alkan, Charles-Valentin 31n44
    'Les Omnibus' 15, *16*
anonymity 55, 75, 85, 131n50, 135, 140–1, 166
aristocracy 57n18, 76, 78, 86, 96n60, 114–15, 119–20, 147
    Faubourg Saint-Germain and 11, 81, 117
    private carriage and 12
    Théâtre de l'Opéra and 35, 45
attire 38, 157
    exclusion of passengers based on 102, 111, 113
    as social marker 76, 135, 151
    see also fashion
autobus 21, 32n54
automobile 21, 32n54, 95n32

Balzac, Honoré de 6, 111, 122
    Ferragus 7, 160n7
    'Histoire et physiologie des Boulevards de Paris' 66–7
    Le père Goriot 13, 57n18
barricade 26, 110, 129n24, 130n25, 130n28
Baudelaire, Charles
    'A une passante' 85–6

flâneur 64, 75
'Le cygne' 9
'Les Foules' 75
the transitory 3, 55–6
'Une Charogne' 55–6
Baudry, Stanislas 13–15, 31n48, 35, 102
Benjamin, Walter 29n7, 136
    Arcades Project 63–4
    flâneur 63–4, 94n16
    panoramic literature 36, 56n5
Berman, Marshall 136
Berry, Duchesse de 15
board game, *Jeu des Omnibus et Dames Blanches* 2, *plate 2*
Boisgobey, Fortuné du, *Le Crime de l'omnibus* 28, 166, 168
bourgeoisie 11, 46, 120, 141–2, 161n14
buraliste 52, 83, 97n66
Byle-Mouillard, Elisabeth Félicie, *Manuel complet de la bonne compagnie* 108

cabriolet 8, 12, 35, 44, 45, 53, 102, 113
    fare for 15, 31n41, 56n2
caricature 2, 35, 37, 39, 40, 41, *41*, 42, *42*, 57n6, 73, 76, 121, 143
    see also Cham, 'Les nouveaux omnibus du boulevard pendant l'hiver'; Daumier, Honoré
carrosse à cinq sols 12–13, 31n36, 102
Cassatt, Mary 164n75
    En omnibus 158–9, *plate 8*

177

Cham, 'Les nouveaux omnibus du
    boulevard pendant l'hiver' 18, *22*
chance encounter
    'A une passante' (Baudelaire) 85–6
    omnibus as setting for 47, 56, 62, 84–6,
        92, 97–8n85, 116
    park as setting for 141, 142
    in vaudeville 47, 116
city guide 25, 62, 128
    Les jeunes voyageurs dans Paris
        (Flesselles) 67, 112–13, *114*
    see also literary guidebook
Clarétie, Jules 36
    'Les omnibus parisiens' 130n32
class/es
    equality/inclusiveness 26, 52, 92, 104,
        106, 107, 110, 115
    heterogeneity/mixing 5, 11, 26, 38,
        101–2, 104, 105, 109, 116, 117,
        121, 125, 128, 165
    see also aristocracy; bourgeoisie; lower
        classes; middle class; omnibus, as
        democratic; upper class; working
        class
Cohen, Margaret 25, 39, 46–7, 52, 57n11
Colette, *Claudine à Paris* 133
collective authorship 24, 25, 47, 49, 50,
    59n42, 156
conduct manual 25, 95–6n42, 122, 133–4
    Manuel complet de la bonne compagnie
        (Byle-Mouillard) 108, 133–4
conductor 26, 51, 52, 53, 55, 64, 81, 83–4,
    86, 102, 111, 115, 122–3, 126, 154,
    156, 166
    'Le Conducteur d'omnibus' (Friès) 83, 106
    'Le Conducteur et la couturière' 89
    'Physionomies parisiennes: le conducteur
        de l'omnibus' (Coppée) 65–6, 84
congestion 4, 6, 8, 13, 18, 138
consumer culture 29n7, 41
Coppée, François 36, 63
    'Croquis parisiens' 70–1
    'Physionomies parisiennes: le
        conducteur de l'omnibus' 65–6, 84
coucou 12, 35, 44, 102
crinoline 27, *27*
    accessing the *impériale* while wearing 20,
        31n47

cage 149, 151, 163n50
    Madame Crinoliska 150–1, *150*, 153,
        154, 163–4n59, 163n50

dandy 87–9, 108, 122
Darjou, A., 'Actualités' 102, *103*
Dartès, Emile 36
    Contes en omnibus 6, 36, 48, 59n38, 65,
        92, 144–6, *145*, *146*
Daumier, Honoré 25, 121
    'Commençant à trouver que l'impériale
        ...' 18, *21*
    'Désolé, citoyenne, mais on ne reçoit pas
        de chien' *114*, 114–15
    En omnibus 76, 78, *78*
    'Intérieur d'un omnibus' 124, *125*
    'Le mauvais côté des nouveaux omnibus'
        18, *19*
    'Madeleine—Bastille' 123, *124*
    'N'est-il pas vrais, brave turco ...' 74, *74*
    'Quinze centimes un bain complet ...'
        18, *20*
    'Un rencontre désagréable' 87–9, *88*
Delaveau, Guy 102
Delondre, Maurice, *En omnibus* 156–7,
    plate 7
Delord, Taxile 50, 59n42
    see also *Paris-en-omnibus*
department store 5, 128, 135, 152
    in *Au Bonheur des dames* 28, 166–7
driver 15, 26, 35, 49, 51, 64, 81, 83,
    97n66
    'Les cochers de fiacres aux prises avec
        ceux des omnibus' 40, *41*
    'Les Dames Blanches et le fiacre' (Frey)
        40, *42*
Du Camp, Maxime
    'Les voitures publiques' 14–15, 110,
        129n24
    *Paris, ses organes, ses fonctions et sa vie
        dans la seconde moitié du XIXe siècle*
        102
Dutacq, Armand 37

episodic narrative 6, 25, 49

fashion 10, 38, 69, 76, 81, 95n32, 95–6n42,
    96n50, 122, 124, 135, 151, 157

see also attire; crinoline; dandy; *ombrelle; paletot; parapluie*
Ferguson, Priscilla Parkhurst 7, 32n59, 37, 63, 64, 65, 93n5, 93n10, 94n11, 136
fiacre 7, 12, 45, 102, 126
  drivers 35, 41, *41*, 42, *42*, 44
  as setting for adultery 135, 159–60n5, 160n6
flâneur 8, 52, 93n10, 93nn5–6, 94n11
  in Baudelaire 64, 75
  in Benjamin 63–4, 94n16
  omnibus/narrator-passenger 26, 62, 63–6, 71–2, 75, 76, 82
Flaubert, Gustave
  L'éducation sentimentale 130n28
  letter to Colet 120–1, 131n49
  Madame Bovary 135, 160n6
Flesselles, Madame de, *Les jeunes voyageurs dans Paris* 67, 112–13, 114
Fouinet, Ernest, 'Un voyage en omnibus de la barrière du Thrône à la barrière de l'Étoile' 49, 62, 65, 66, 69, 85–6, 87, 94n19, 115–16, 143
Fournel, Victor, *Ce qu'on voit dans les rues de Paris* 69, 97n66
Fournier, Edouard, *Paris Démoli* 8–9, 30n23
Frémy, Arnould 50
  see also Paris-en-omnibus
French Revolution *see* revolution, of 1789
Frey, Jean Georges, 'Les Dames Blanches et le fiacre' 40, *42*
Friès, Charles, 'Le Conducteur d'omnibus' 83, 106

Gautier, Théophile
  Paris Démoli, preface to 8–9, 30n23
  Paris et les Parisiens au XIXe siècle, introduction to 9–10
Gavarni, Paul, 'Une aventure d'omnibus' 86, 97n77
Girardin, Delphine de 8
Girardin, Emile de 37
Gobert, 'Intérieur d'un équipage de la petite propriété' 122, *123*
Gourdon, Edouard, *Physiologie de l'omnibus* 25, 28, 36, 52–5, 64–5, 72–3, 76–8, 80, 81, 97n66, 105–6, 110, 111, 126, 143, 151, 160n7

Gozlan, Léon, *Le Triomphe des Omnibus* 87
Grandville, J. J. 121
  Les Métamorphoses du jour 122–3, *plate 5*
grisette 49, 50, 52, 108, 113, 122
Griveau, Lucien, 'En omnibus' 61–2, 78–9

Haussmannisation 3, 4, 6, 8–9, 10, 13, 64, 67, 137
  in *La Curée* 137–8, 140
heterogeneity 25, 38, 39, 49, 50, 52, 109, 117
horse, treatment of 3, 8, 15, 19, 20–1, 29n5, 29n20, 42, *42*, 50, 129n24
Huart, Louis, 'Les voitures publiques' 7–8, 25, 49–50, 113–14
  Physiologie du flaneur 63, 93n5
Hugo, Victor 22, 31n44, 36
  Les Misérables 26, 110–11, 164n63
  Notre-Dame de Paris 70

impériale 16–18, 20, 31n46, 126
  fare for 16, 102, *103*
  inconveniences of 18, *19*, *20*, *21*, *22*
  view from 70–2, 139
  women's access to 16–18, 20, 31n47

Janin, Jules 39–40, 97n65
July Monarchy 4, 41, 47, 93n6, 110, 152
July Revolution *see* revolution, of 1830

Kock, Paul de 25, 108

La Compagnie générale des omnibus (CGO) 18–20, 32n54
La Curée (Zola) 25, 28, 136, 137–40, 142, 160n13, 161n17, 161n21
La Mode Illustrée 73–4, 81, 95–6n42, 134
landau 7–8, 43, 57n18
La Presse 8, 21–2, *24*, 37
Lasserre, *Paris en omnibus, itinéraire pittoresque, historique et industrielle* 68–9
Le Charivari 18, *19*, *20*, *21*, 50, 57n6, 59n42, 74, *74*, 97n77, 132n53
Le Diable à Paris 46, 59n42
  'Histoire et physiologie des Boulevards de Paris' (Balzac) 66–7
Le Magasin pittoresque 106–7

L'Entreprise générale d'omnibus 13, 15–16, 18, 102
Les Français peints par eux-mêmes 25, 35–6, 37, 46–7, 59n42, 80
 'La femme adultère' (Lucas) 80, 160n5
 'Le Conducteur d'omnibus' (Friès) 83, 106
Le Siècle 37
Les omnibus. Premier voyage de Cadet la Blague de la place de la Madeleine à la Bastille et retour 47–8, 58–9n36, 148–9
Levy, Amy, 'Ballad of an omnibus' 158
L'Illustration 50, 76, 77
literary guidebook 2, 8–9, 24–5, 35–6, 37
 see also *Les Français peints par eux-mêmes*; *Paris, ou le livre des cent-et-un*
lithography 25, 27, 57n6, 105, 132n53, 135, 152, 160n12
 class mixing in 121–5
lorette 76, 80, 96n50, 151
Lorrain, Jean 36
Louis XIV 12, 40, 76
Louis XV 76
lower classes 43, 128
 anxieties concerning 12, 102, 105, 122, 162n36
 exclusion of, from *carrosse à cinq sols* 12–13, 102
Lucas, Hippolyte 160n5

Maison Aubert 37, 57n6
Marcus, Sharon 4, 32n59, 46, 136
mass transit 35, 38, 40, 47, 61, 63
 omnibus as first vehicle of 1, 2, 42, 103
Maupassant, Guy de 28, 63, 64
 'La Dot' 121, 125–8
 'Le père' 137, 140–2
 'Le père Mongilet' 71–2
metro 6, 21, 95n32, 168
micronarrative 25, 46–7
middle class 111, 123, 152
 exposure to lower classes 104–5, 123, 124–5
 physiologies' popularity among 37, 57n7
 restaurant and 161n14
 vaudeville's identification with 40, 120

women 95–6n42, 136–7, 158–9, 160n12
modernity 3, 55, 78, 84, 121, 136, 167
 cultural 4–5, 40, 46, 57n12
 omnibus as 3, 9, 25, 26, 28, 40, 46, 54, 56, 67, 69, 84, 156, 165–6, 168
 Parisian 2, 3–7, 11, 29n7, 63
 urban 1, 3, 26, 52, 62–4, 110, 115, 156, 165
 see also alienation; anonymity
Monet, Claude 162n32
Morlon, after 'Une poule mouillée' 152–4, *153*
multiple authorship *see* collective authorship

Napoléon III 4, 6, 18, 141
Nisard, Désiré 39–40
Nogaret, Félix, *Réflexions d'un patriarche sur les voitures dites omnibus!* 111–12, 130n32
Nouveau Tableau de Paris au XIXe siècle 35–6
'Les voitures publiques' (Huart) 7–8, 25, 35–6, 49–50, 113–14

ombrelle 45, 58n29
omnibus
 companies 13, 15–16, 18–20, 32n54, 53, 102, 111 18–20
 decommissioning/final journey/funeral of (1913) 2, *2*, 21–2, *23*, 24
 as democratic/'for all'/'for everybody' 1, 14, 26, 39, 40, 73, 101–2, 105–14
 fare for 1, 15, 35, 44, 101, 102–3, 119
 launching of (1828) 1–2, 7, 13, *14*, 35, 39, 102, 109, 130n35, 133, 140, *plate 1*
 lines 12, 15–16, 18–19, 52, 67, 68, 81, 102, 103–4, 116
  Batignolles–Clichy–Odéon 48, 81
  La Villette–Saint–Sulpice 21
  Madeleine–Bastille 11, 48, 123, *124*, 144
  Montmartre–St Germain 32n54
  Montrouge–Gare de l'Est 48
  Panthéon–Courcelles 89, 133, 159n1
 maps 16, *17*
 as microcosm of society 105–6, 126–7

as modernity 3, 9, 25, 26, 28, 40, 46, 54, 56, 67, 69, 84, 156, 165–6, 168
as a neologism 13–14, 26, 29n10, 38, 101
as outmoded/obsolete 11, 22, 28, 63, 70, 168
as 'vehicle of vice' 134, 137–42, 157–8
'Omnibus de Paris' (Uzanne) 62, 63, 70, 95n32, 101
  nostalgia 166, 167–8
  omnibus flâneur 75
  typology 81–3

paletot 120, 131n50
panoramic literature 25, 36–7, 46–7, 48, 56n4, 57n11, 62, 63, 67, 92, 105, 111
  Benjamin and 36, 56n5
  flâneur in 64, 75
  multiple authorship 25, 47
parapluie 45, 58n29
Parent-Duchâtelet, Alexandre, *De la prostitution dans la ville de Paris* 152
Paris
  Bastille 11, 70, 123
  Batignolles 18, 117, 139
  Bois de Boulogne 138
  Champs-Elysées 68
  Chaussée d'Antin 11, 30n30, 76, 113
  Faubourg Saint-Germain 11, 76, 81, 117
  Faubourg Saint-Honoré 30n30
  Left Bank 18
  le Marais 30n30, 76
  Madeleine 11, 70, 123
  Montmartre 18, 81
  mud covering the streets of 13, 43, 57n18, 107
  Notre-Dame de Lorette 27, *27*, 148
  Parc Monceau 140, 141–2, 162n32
  Place de la Bastille 69, 110
  Place de la Concorde 68
  Place de la Nation 95n28
  Place de l'Etoile 95n28
  Place Pigalle 166
  population growth of 7, 13, 18, 37, 86
  Right Bank 18, 1034
  Théâtre de l'Opéra 35, 40, 44–5, 58n26
  Théâtre des Italiens 58n26

universal expositions
  1855 18
  1867 68
  1900 95n32
  see also Haussmannisation
Paris-en-omnibus (Delord, Frémy, and Texier) 6, 25, 50–2, 59n43, 70, 106
  conductor 51, 83–4
  prostitute 154–6
  woman who gives birth on 51, 146–8
Paris, ou le livre des cent-et-un 25, 35–6, 46–7, 49, 97n65
park 105, 128, 159
  bourgeois and 135, 137, 141–2, 152, 162n29, 162n32
  chance encounters in 141, 142
Pascal, Blaise 12
Penne, M. de, 'Le public des omnibus dans les bureaux de correspondence' 76, *77*
Philipon, Charles 57n5
physiologie 2, 36–7, 46, 50, 56n5, 57n6, 80, 106
  Physiologie du flaneur (Huart) 63, 93n5
  as satire 37, 52
  see also Paris-en-omnibus; *Physiologie de l'omnibus*
Physiologie de l'omnibus (Gourdon) 25, 28, 36, 52–5, 64–5, 72–3, 80, 81, 151, 160n7
  buraliste 52, 97n66
  flâneur-narrator 53, 54, 65, 76–8
  omnibus as embodiment of revolution 110–11
  omnibus as microcosm of society 105–6, 126
  poet 52–3, 80
  wet nurse 143
Pissarro, Camille, *Boulevard des Italiens, soleil du matin* plate 1
popular song 2, 25, 36, 89–92, 141
  'Le Conducteur et la couturière' 89
  'Mon voisin d'omnibus' *91*, 91–2
  'Un mariage en omnibus' 89–91, *90*
popular theatre 35, 36, 37, 40, 44–6, 115
  see also vaudeville
private carriage *see* vehicle for hire
prostitute/prostitution 138, 152

181

Notre-Dame de Lorette's association with 27, 117, 148
omnibus as setting for 27, 28, 50, 89, 135, 137, 142, 148–9, 151–2, 154–6, 157, 163n48
proper ladies' exposure to 139, 151–2

Rachilde, *Monsieur Venus* 160n6, 161n21
Ratier, Victor
  'Échantillons de moeurs Parisiennes' 135, *plate 6*
  'Un banc d'Omnibus' 121–2, *plate 4*
Raymond, Emmeline 95–6n42
  'L'Omnibus' 73–4, 80–1, 107–8, 134
restaurant 50, 73, 135, 137, 161n14
  cabinet particulier 137, 138–9, 161n14
  Foyot 81, 96n60
  Père Lathuille 81, 96n60
revolution 11
  of 1789 11, 37, 55, 62, 78, 93n10, 101, 104, 111, 115, 122
  of 1830 104
  of 1848 110, 114, 130n28
  omnibus as embodiment of 26, 106, 110–11, 130n25, 130n28
Roannez, Duc de 12, 31n36
Roubaud, Jacques, *Ode à la ligne 29 des autobus parisiens* 1

Sahib, M., 'L'intérieur d'un omnibus' 38, *39*
Second Empire 4, 19–20, 59n42, 105, 137, 138, 140, 152, 163n51, 166
short story 2, 35
  Contes en omnibus (Dartés) 6, 36, 48, 59n38, 65, 92
    'Madeleine–Bastille' 144–6, *145*, *146*
  'La Dot' (Maupassant) 121, 125–8
  'Le père' (Maupassant) 137, 140–2
  'Le père Mongilet' (Maupassant) 71–2
  'Une aventure d'omnibus' (Gavarni) 86, 97n77
Simmel, Georg 4–5, 129n11, 136
Soullier, Charles, *Les Omnibus de Paris* 6, 52, 109
spectacle 3, 4, 28, 72, 115–16, 139, 159, 161n14
speed 4, 6–9, 11, 49, 85, 141

Texier, Edmond 50, 111
  'Les voitures de Paris' 110, 130n25
  Tableau de Paris 106
  see also Paris-en-omnibus
tram 5, 6, 20, 31n40

Un coup de foudre en omnibus 97–8n85
'Un voyage en omnibus de la barrière du Thrône à la barrière de l'Étoile' (Fouinet) 49, 62, 69, 115–16
  chance encounter 85–6, 87
  omnibus flâneur 65, 66, 94n19
  wet nurse 142–3
upper classes 12, 42, 43
Uzanne, Octave 28, 36, 62, 63, 69–70, 95n32, 166
  La Locomotion à travers le temps 10–11, 59n37, 95n32
  'Omnibus de Paris' 70, 75, 81–3, 95n32, 101, 128n1, 167–8
  'Perspective d'avenir: la locomotion future' 95n32

vaudeville 2, 41–2, 47, 62, 105, 115–16, 120
J'attends un omnibus 116–19
Les omnibus, ou la revue en voiture 25, 35, 40, 42–6, 58n21
Mon voisin d'omnibus 97n80, 119–20
popularity of 40–1
vehicle for hire 12, 15, 102, 113
  fare for 15
  turf war with omnibus 35, 40, 41, *41*, 42, *42*, 44–5
  see also cabriolet; coucou; fiacre
Vernier, Charles, 'Entrée dans un omnibus, rue Notre-Dame de Lorette' 27, *27*

wet nurse 27, 48, 135, 142–6, *145*, 157, 158, 162nn35–6
women
  exclusion of, from *impériale* 16–18
  middle class 95–6n42, 136–7, 158–9, 160n12
  newfound freedom/visibility of 26, 27–8, 158–9

sexual transgression of 15, 27, 89, 134–42, 158, 161n14, 165
unaccompanied 133, 151, 157, 160n12, 163n49
working-class 79, 114–15, 122, 124, 136–7, 147, 152, 156
see also prostitute; wet nurse
working class 38, 81, 102, 111
aspirations of 105, 110, 115, 124
Bastille's association with 11, 123
fashion markers of 58n29, 122, 124
middle-class exposure to 104–5, 121, 127–8
women 79, 114–15, 122, 124, 136–7, 148, 152, 156

Zola, Emile
Au Bonheur des dames 28, 161n17, 166–7, 168
La Curée 25, 28, 136, 137–40, 142, 160n13, 161n17, 161n21

EU authorised representative for GPSR:
Easy Access System Europe, Mustamäe tee 50,
10621 Tallinn, Estonia
gpsr.requests@easproject.com

www.ingramcontent.com/pod-product-compliance
Lightning Source LLC
Chambersburg PA
CBHW040903250426
43673CB00064B/1952